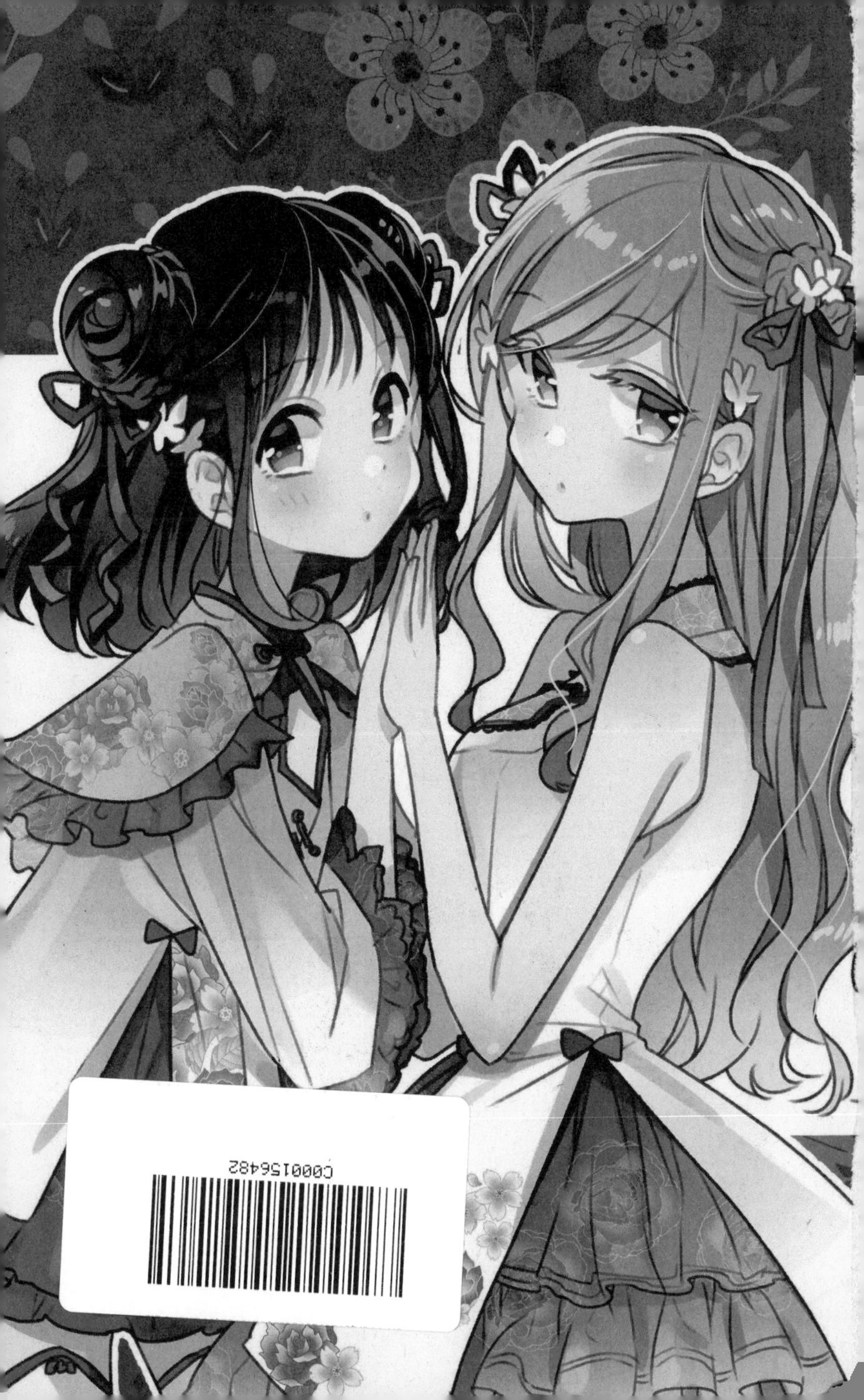

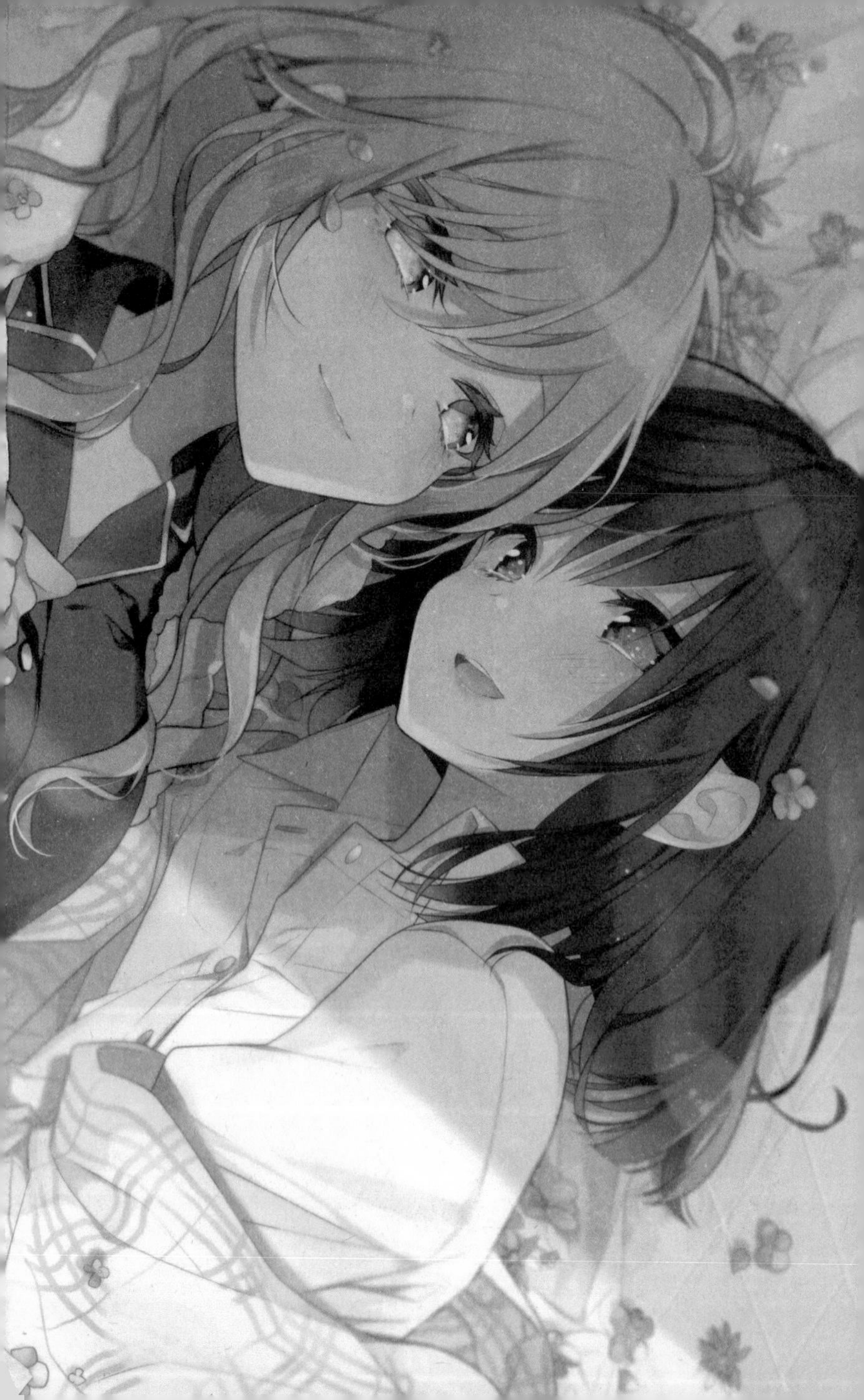

Futaribeya

A ROOM FOR TWO

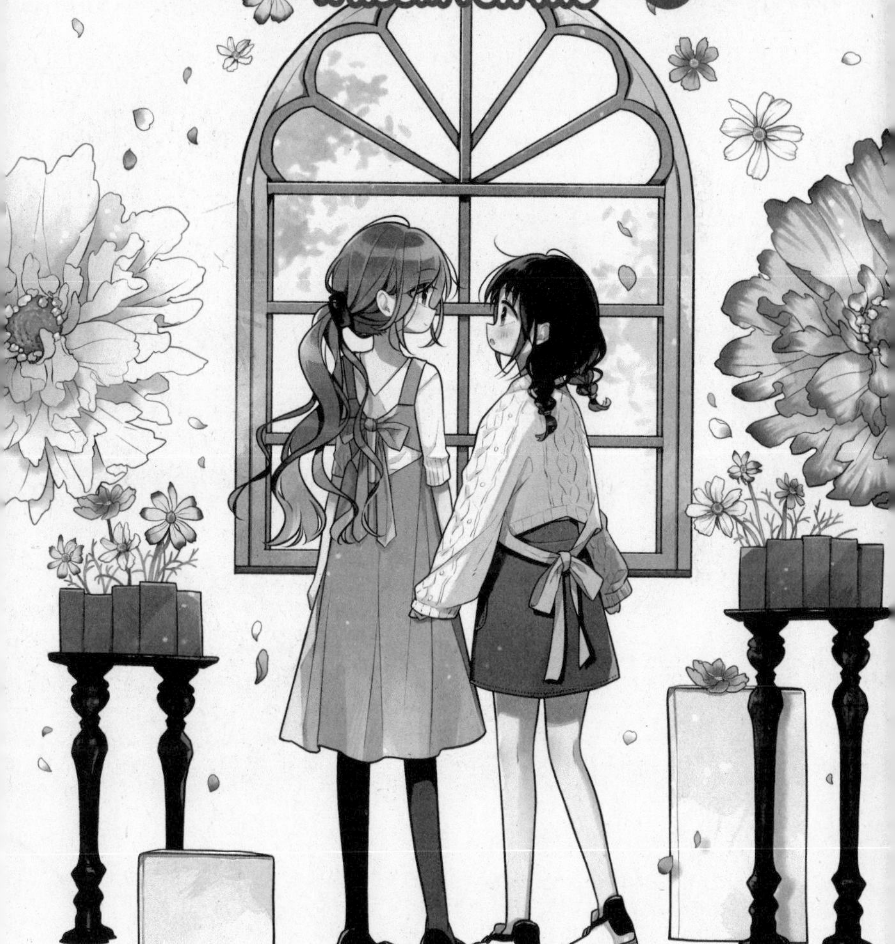

Yukiko

CHARACTER

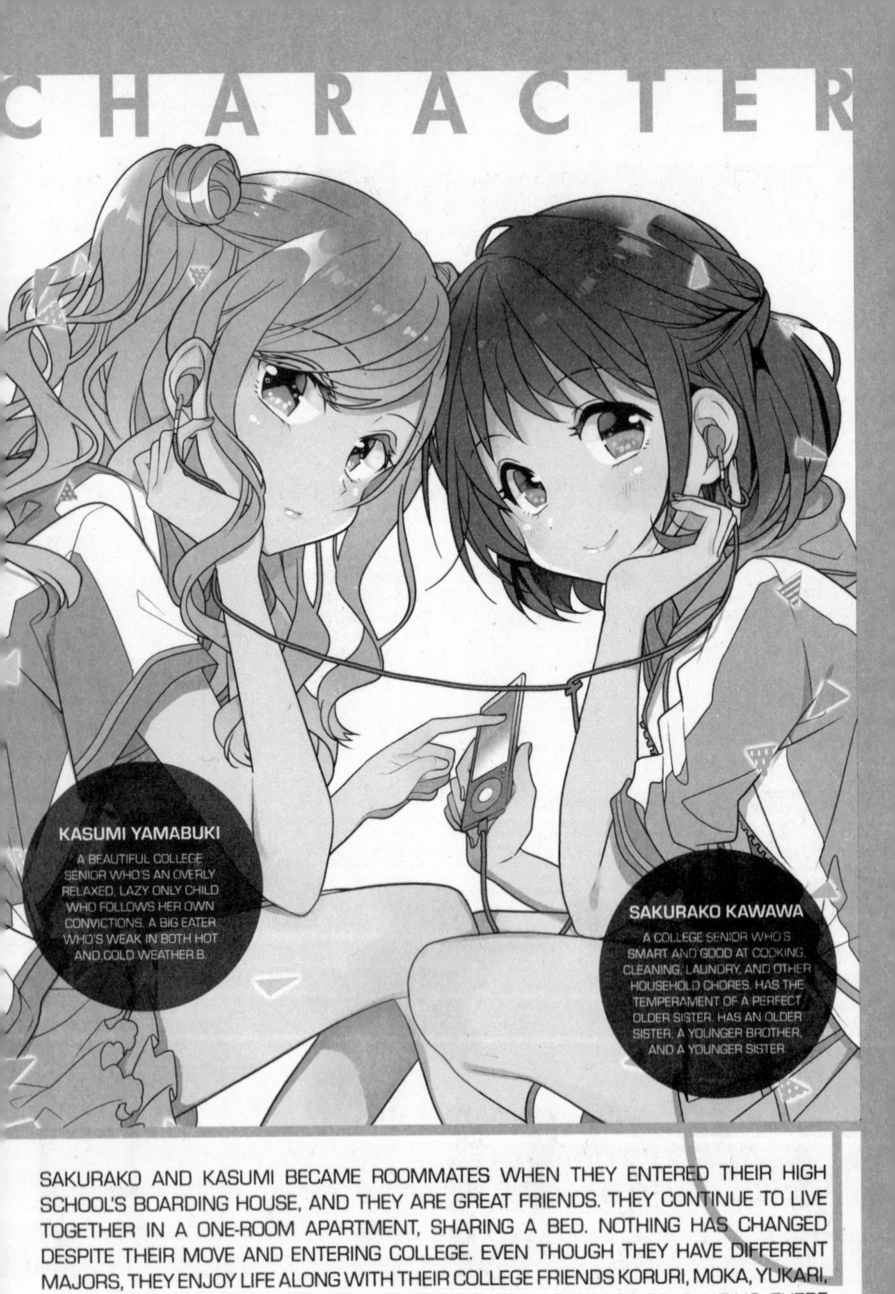
KASUMI YAMABUKI
A BEAUTIFUL COLLEGE SENIOR WHO'S AN OVERLY RELAXED, LAZY ONLY CHILD WHO FOLLOWS HER OWN CONVICTIONS. A BIG EATER WHO'S WEAK IN BOTH HOT AND COLD WEATHER.B.
SAKURAKO KAWAWA
A COLLEGE SENIOR WHO'S SMART AND GOOD AT COOKING, CLEANING, LAUNDRY, AND OTHER HOUSEHOLD CHORES. HAS THE TEMPERAMENT OF A PERFECT OLDER SISTER. HAS AN OLDER SISTER, A YOUNGER BROTHER, AND A YOUNGER SISTER.

SAKURAKO AND KASUMI BECAME ROOMMATES WHEN THEY ENTERED THEIR HIGH SCHOOL'S BOARDING HOUSE, AND THEY ARE GREAT FRIENDS. THEY CONTINUE TO LIVE TOGETHER IN A ONE-ROOM APARTMENT, SHARING A BED. NOTHING HAS CHANGED DESPITE THEIR MOVE AND ENTERING COLLEGE. EVEN THOUGH THEY HAVE DIFFERENT MAJORS, THEY ENJOY LIFE ALONG WITH THEIR COLLEGE FRIENDS KORURI, MOKA, YUKARI, AND THEIR UNDERCLASSMAN, SERI. NOW THAT THEY'RE CLOSE TO GRADUATING, THERE ARE LOTS OF CHANGES OCCURRING AROUND THEM.

S T O R Y and

MOKA NENASHI

A PSYCHOLOGY MAJOR LIKE SAKURAKO. SHE HAS A FREE VIEW ON LOVE AND OFTEN STAYS OVER AT KORURI'S HOUSE.

KORURI MASUI

STUDIES IN THE LIFE ENVIRONMENT STUDIES DEPARTMENT WITH KASUMI. SHE HAS A BAD SENSE OF DIRECTION AND IS UNABLE TO THROW THINGS AWAY.

SHOUKO AKASHI

SERI'S FORMER ROOMMATE WHO IS CURRENTLY WORKING. SHE HAS A FRANK PERSONALITY. EVERYONE CALLS HER SHOUKO.

SERI FURUYASHIKI

SAKURAKO AND KASUMI'S UNDERCLASSMAN FROM HIGH SCHOOL WHO GOES TO THEIR COLLEGE. SHE'S A SHELTERED RICH GIRL WHO USES POLITE SPEECH WITH EVERYONE SHE MEETS.

YUKARI

SAKURAKO AND KASUMI'S HIGH SCHOOL CLASSMATE WHO ATTENDS THE SAME COLLEGE AS THEM. SHE EVEN JOINED THE SAME CLUB AND WANTS TO BE A LIBRARIAN. THE NOVEL SHE WROTE WON AN AWARD AND WAS PUBLISHED.

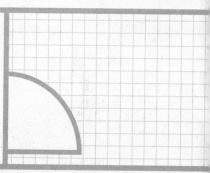

HINAKO

SHE'S SPOILED AND ABSOLUTELY LOVES SAKURAKO AND KASUMI. SHE HAS A TWIN BROTHER NAMED KAKERU. SHE CURRENTLY WORKS PART-TIME AT A CLOTHING STORE.

FUJIHO

HINAKO'S HIGH SCHOOL ROOMMATE. SHE'S ATTENDING A BEAUTY SCHOOL AND PLAYS IN A BAND.

Contents

Chapter 66.5: 005

Chapter 67: 007

Chapter 68: 019

Chapter 68.5: 031

Chapter 69: 033

Chapter 70: 045

Chapter 71 (Part 1): 057

Chapter 71.5: 063

Chapter 71 (Part 2): 066

Special Chapter #1 - "Time Sure Flies" : 071

Special Chapter #2 - "Let's Go See the Stars!" : 083

Side Story: 101

Special Chapter #3 - "Something I Wanted to Ask But Couldn't" : 103

Bonus Chapter - "Kodomobeya" : 121

Afterword: 126

Chapter 66.5

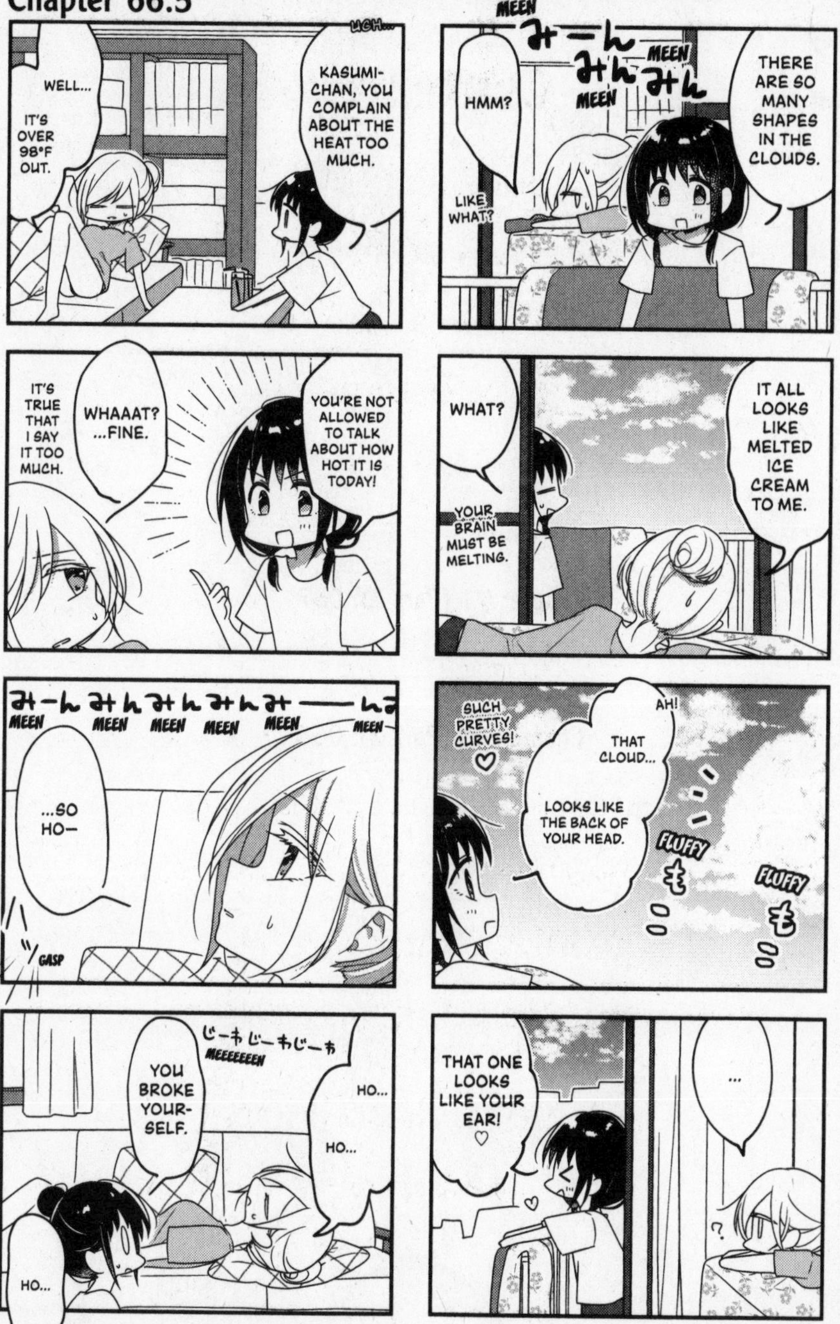
MEEN
みーん
MEEN
みんみん
MEEN
THERE ARE SO MANY SHAPES IN THE CLOUDS.
HMM?
LIKE WHAT?
IT ALL LOOKS LIKE MELTED ICE CREAM TO ME.
WHAT?
YOUR BRAIN MUST BE MELTING.
AH!
THAT CLOUD...
LOOKS LIKE THE BACK OF YOUR HEAD.
SUCH PRETTY CURVES! ♡
FLUFFY
FLUFFY
...
THAT ONE LOOKS LIKE YOUR EAR! ♡
UGH...
KASUMI-CHAN, YOU COMPLAIN ABOUT THE HEAT TOO MUCH.
WELL...
IT'S OVER 98°F OUT.
YOU'RE NOT ALLOWED TO TALK ABOUT HOW HOT IT IS TODAY!
WHAAAT? ...FINE.
IT'S TRUE THAT I SAY IT TOO MUCH.
MEEN MEEN MEEN MEEN MEEN MEEN
...SO HO—
GASP
MEEEEEEEN
HO...
HO...
YOU BROKE YOURSELF.
HO...

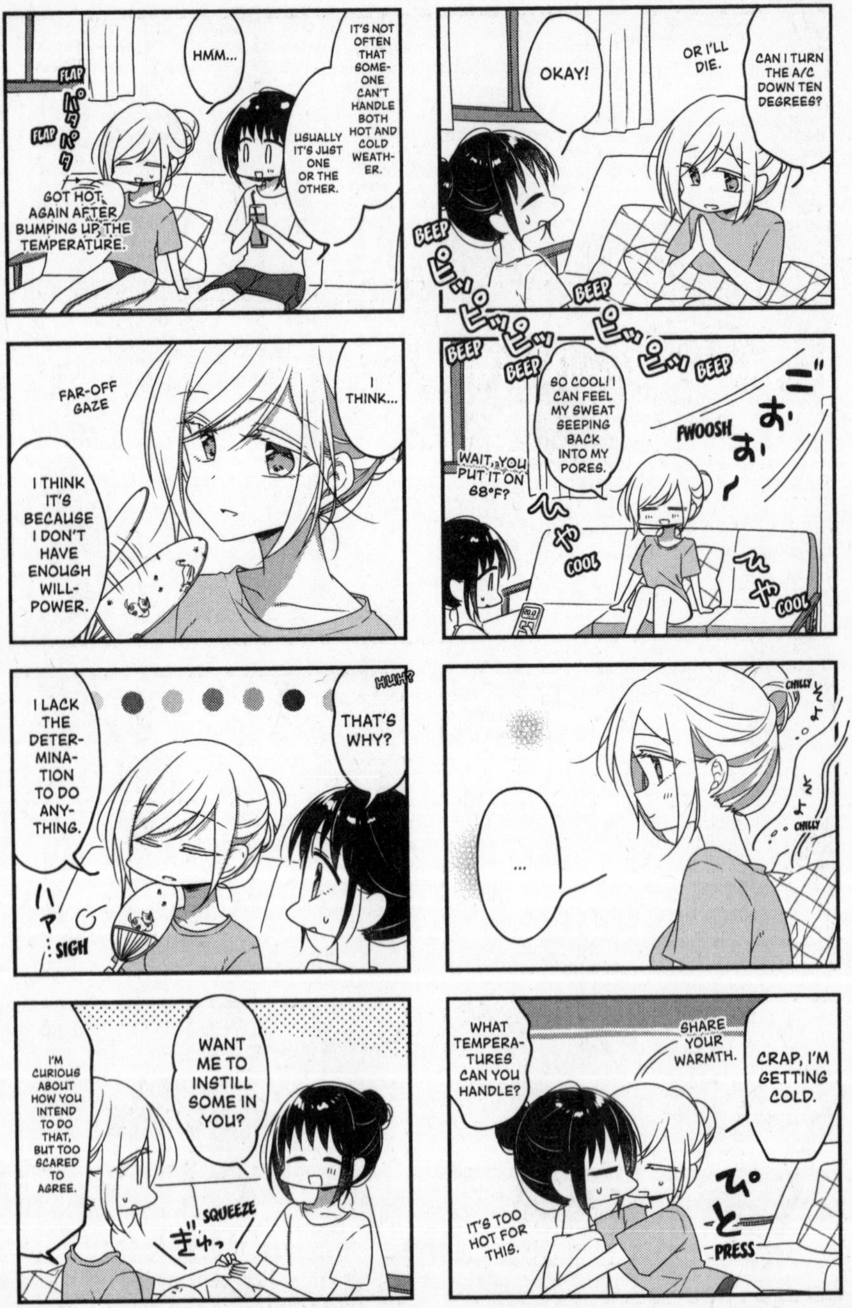
CAN I TURN THE A/C DOWN TEN DEGREES?
OR I'LL DIE.
OKAY!
ピッ BEEP
ピッ BEEP
ピッ BEEP
ピッ BEEP
ごおお〜 FWOOSH
SO COOL! I CAN FEEL MY SWEAT SEEPING BACK INTO MY PORES.
WAIT, YOU PUT IT ON 68°F?
ひや COOL
ひや COOL
そよ CHILLY
そよ CHILLY
...
CRAP, I'M GETTING COLD.
SHARE YOUR WARMTH.
WHAT TEMPERATURES CAN YOU HANDLE?
ぴと PRESS
IT'S TOO HOT FOR THIS.
IT'S NOT OFTEN THAT SOMEONE CAN'T HANDLE BOTH HOT AND COLD WEATHER.
USUALLY IT'S JUST ONE OR THE OTHER.
HMM...
パタパタ FLAP FLAP
GOT HOT AGAIN AFTER BUMPING UP THE TEMPERATURE.
I THINK...
FAR-OFF GAZE
I THINK IT'S BECAUSE I DON'T HAVE ENOUGH WILLPOWER.
HUH?
THAT'S WHY?
I LACK THE DETERMINATION TO DO ANYTHING.
ハァ… SIGH
WANT ME TO INSTILL SOME IN YOU?
I'M CURIOUS ABOUT HOW YOU INTEND TO DO THAT, BUT TOO SCARED TO AGREE.
ぎゅっ SQUEEZE

Chapter 67

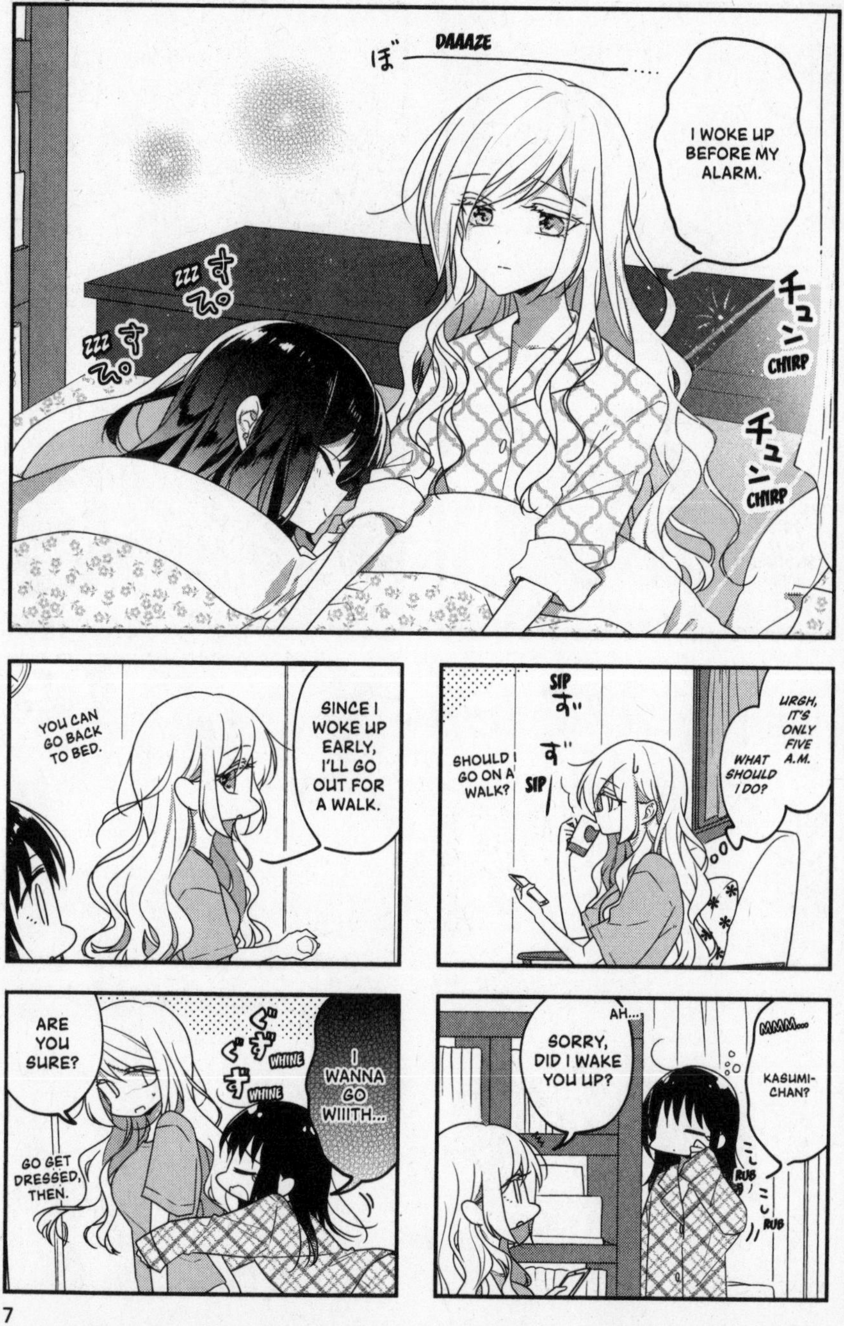
I WOKE UP BEFORE MY ALARM.
ぼ— DAAAZE ....
チュン CHIRP
チュン CHIRP
すぴ ZZZ
すぴ ZZZ
URGH, IT'S ONLY FIVE A.M.
WHAT SHOULD I DO?
SIP ず
ず SIP
SHOULD I GO ON A WALK?
SINCE I WOKE UP EARLY, I'LL GO OUT FOR A WALK.
YOU CAN GO BACK TO BED.
MMM...
KASUMI-CHAN?
AH...
SORRY, DID I WAKE YOU UP?
こし RUB
こし RUB
I WANNA GO WIIITH...
ぐず WHINE
ぐず WHINE
ARE YOU SURE?
GO GET DRESSED, THEN.

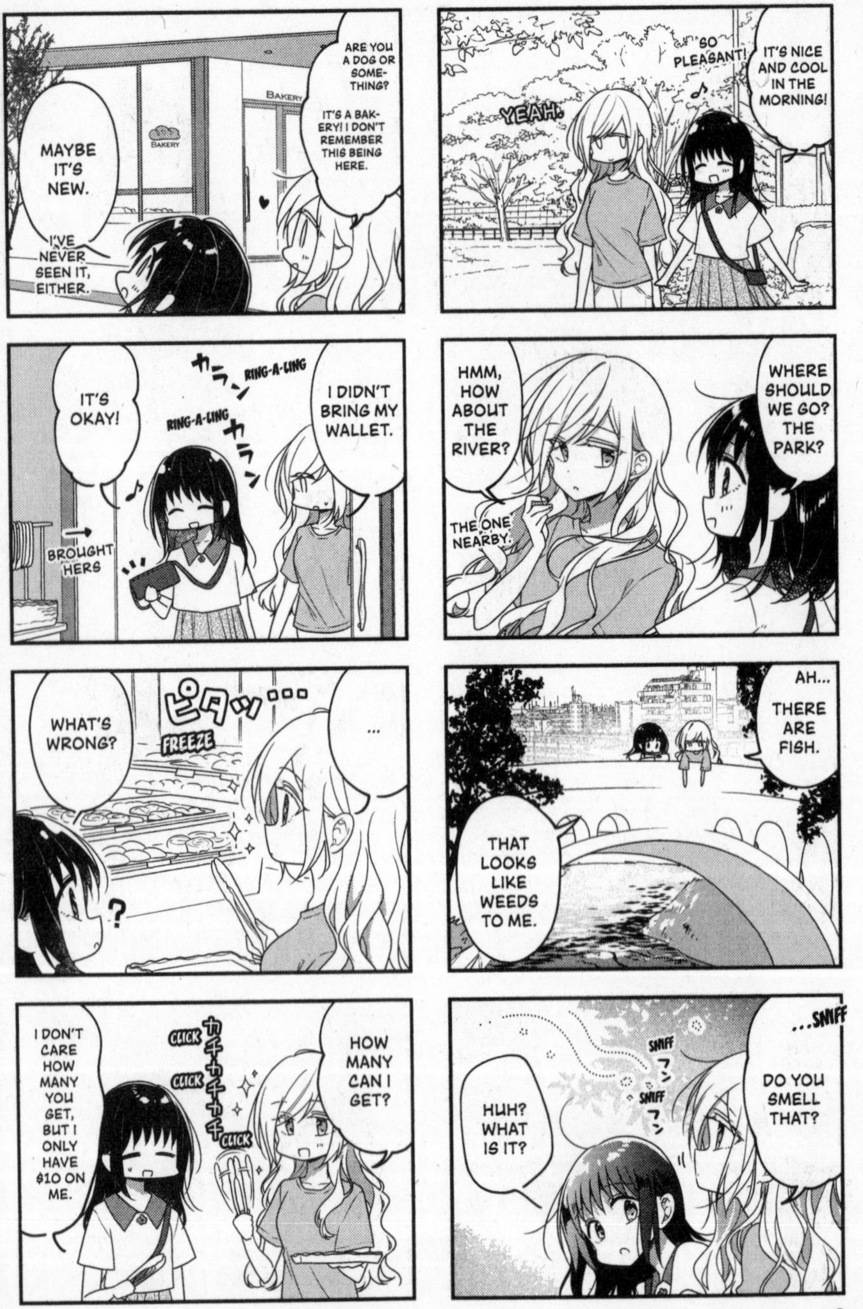
IT'S NICE AND COOL IN THE MORNING!
SO PLEASANT!
YEAH.
WHERE SHOULD WE GO? THE PARK?
HMM, HOW ABOUT THE RIVER?
THE ONE NEARBY.
AH... THERE ARE FISH.
THAT LOOKS LIKE WEEDS TO ME.
...SNIFF
DO YOU SMELL THAT?
フン SNIFF
フン SNIFF
HUH? WHAT IS IT?
ARE YOU A DOG OR SOME-THING?
IT'S A BAK-ERY! I DON'T REMEMBER THIS BEING HERE.
BAKERY
BAKERY
MAYBE IT'S NEW.
I'VE NEVER SEEN IT, EITHER.
I DIDN'T BRING MY WALLET.
カラン RING-A-LING
カラン RING-A-LING
IT'S OKAY!
BROUGHT HERS
...
ピタッ FREEZE
WHAT'S WRONG?
?
HOW MANY CAN I GET?
カチカチカチ CLICK CLICK CLICK
I DON'T CARE HOW MANY YOU GET, BUT I ONLY HAVE $10 ON ME.

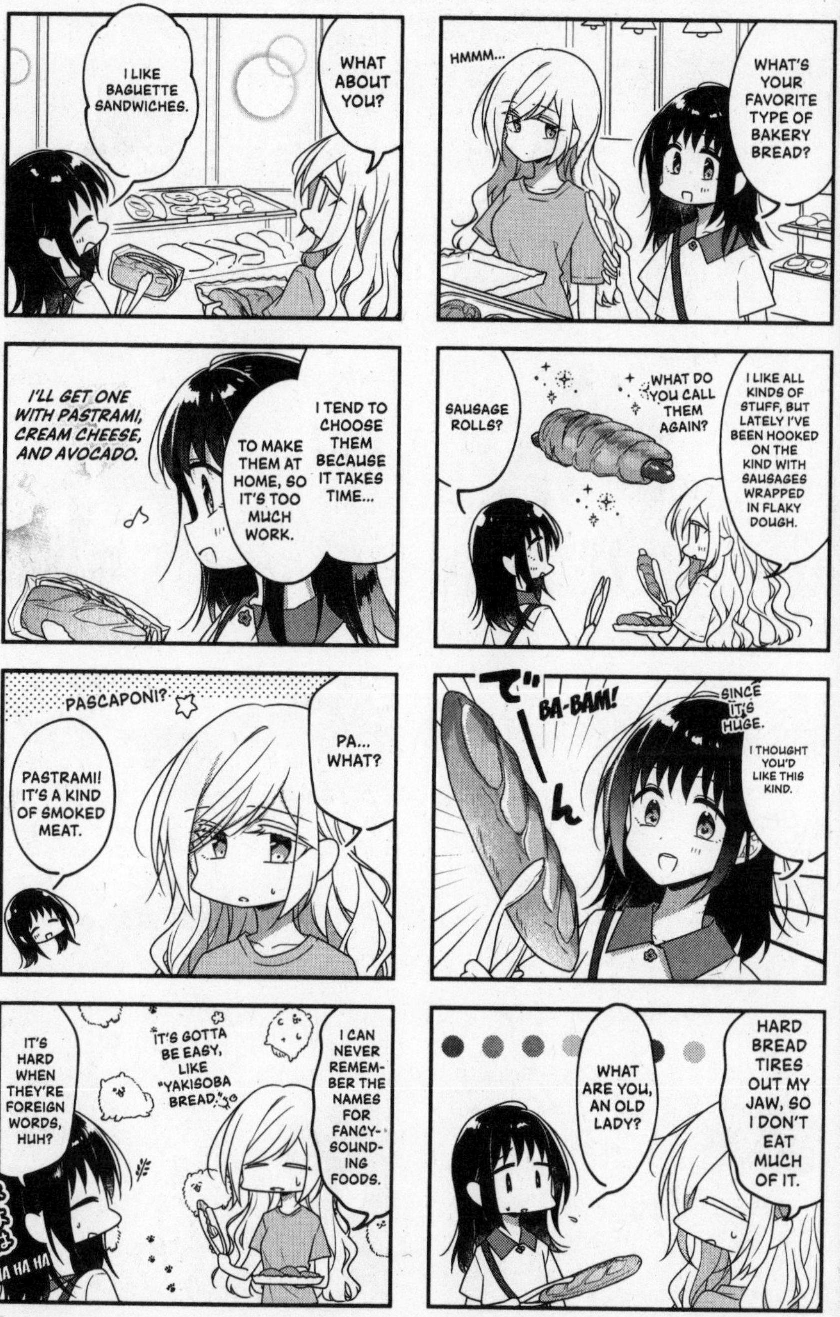
WHAT'S YOUR FAVORITE TYPE OF BAKERY BREAD?
HMMM...
I LIKE ALL KINDS OF STUFF, BUT LATELY I'VE BEEN HOOKED ON THE KIND WITH SAUSAGES WRAPPED IN FLAKY DOUGH.
WHAT DO YOU CALL THEM AGAIN?
SAUSAGE ROLLS?
SINCE IT'S HUGE.
I THOUGHT YOU'D LIKE THIS KIND.
で
ん
BA-BAM!
HARD BREAD TIRES OUT MY JAW, SO I DON'T EAT MUCH OF IT.
WHAT ARE YOU, AN OLD LADY?
WHAT ABOUT YOU?
I LIKE BAGUETTE SANDWICHES.
I TEND TO CHOOSE THEM BECAUSE IT TAKES TIME...
TO MAKE THEM AT HOME, SO IT'S TOO MUCH WORK.
I'LL GET ONE WITH PASTRAMI, CREAM CHEESE, AND AVOCADO.
PA... WHAT?
PASCAPONI?
PASTRAMI! IT'S A KIND OF SMOKED MEAT.
I CAN NEVER REMEMBER THE NAMES FOR FANCY-SOUNDING FOODS.
IT'S GOTTA BE EASY, LIKE "YAKISOBA BREAD."
IT'S HARD WHEN THEY'RE FOREIGN WORDS, HUH?
ははは
HA HA HA

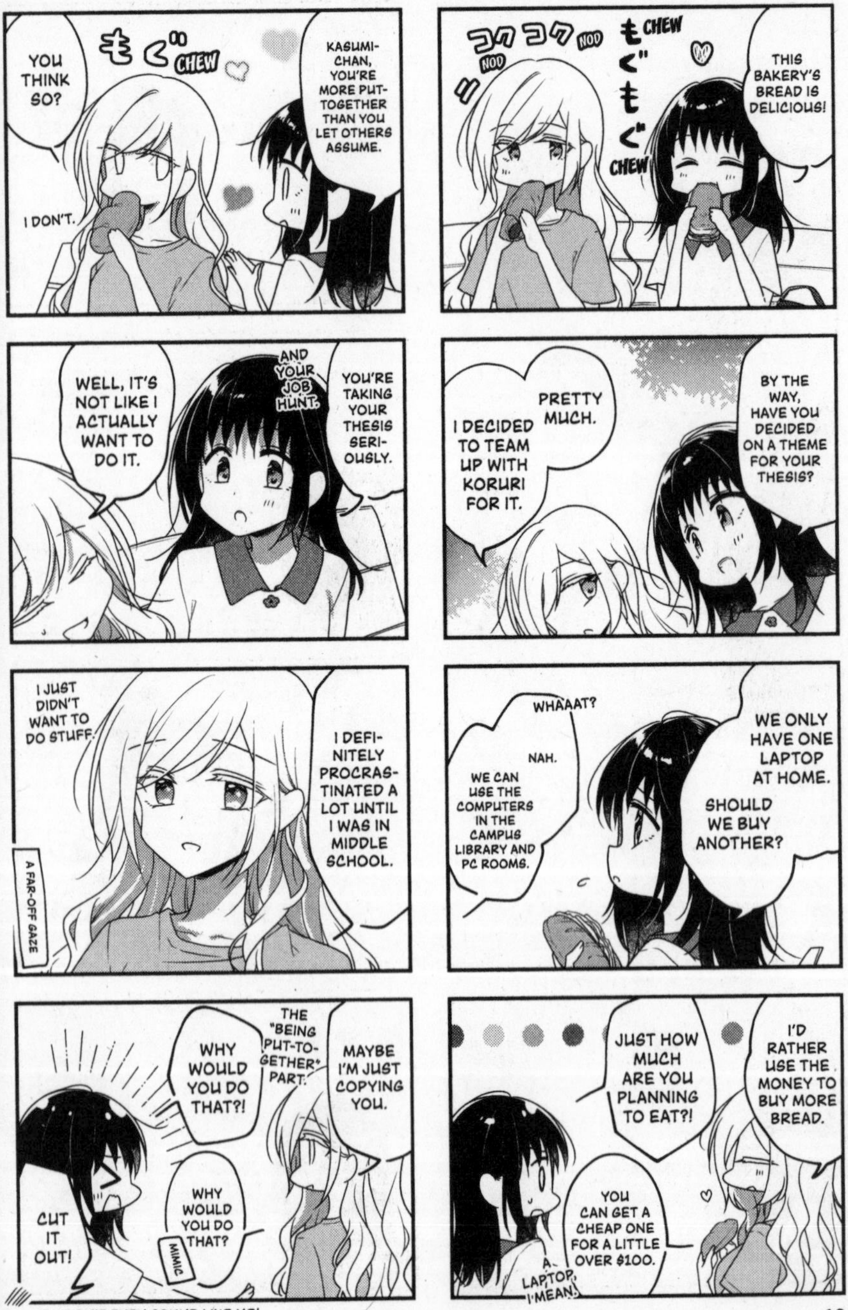
コクコク NOD NOD
もぐもぐ CHEW CHEW
THIS BAKERY'S BREAD IS DELICIOUS!
BY THE WAY, HAVE YOU DECIDED ON A THEME FOR YOUR THESIS?
PRETTY MUCH.
I DECIDED TO TEAM UP WITH KORURI FOR IT.
WE ONLY HAVE ONE LAPTOP AT HOME.
SHOULD WE BUY ANOTHER?
WHAAAT?
NAH.
WE CAN USE THE COMPUTERS IN THE CAMPUS LIBRARY AND PC ROOMS.
I'D RATHER USE THE MONEY TO BUY MORE BREAD.
JUST HOW MUCH ARE YOU PLANNING TO EAT?!
YOU CAN GET A CHEAP ONE FOR A LITTLE OVER $100.
A LAPTOP, I MEAN!
KASUMI-CHAN, YOU'RE MORE PUT-TOGETHER THAN YOU LET OTHERS ASSUME.
もぐ CHEW
YOU THINK SO?
I DON'T.
YOU'RE TAKING YOUR THESIS SERIOUSLY.
AND YOUR JOB HUNT.
WELL, IT'S NOT LIKE I ACTUALLY WANT TO DO IT.
I DEFINITELY PROCRASTINATED A LOT UNTIL I WAS IN MIDDLE SCHOOL.
I JUST DIDN'T WANT TO DO STUFF.
A FAR-OFF GAZE
MAYBE I'M JUST COPYING YOU.
THE "BEING PUT-TOGETHER" PART.
WHY WOULD YOU DO THAT?!
WHY WOULD YOU DO THAT?
MIMIC
CUT IT OUT!

YOU DON'T EVEN SOUND LIKE ME!

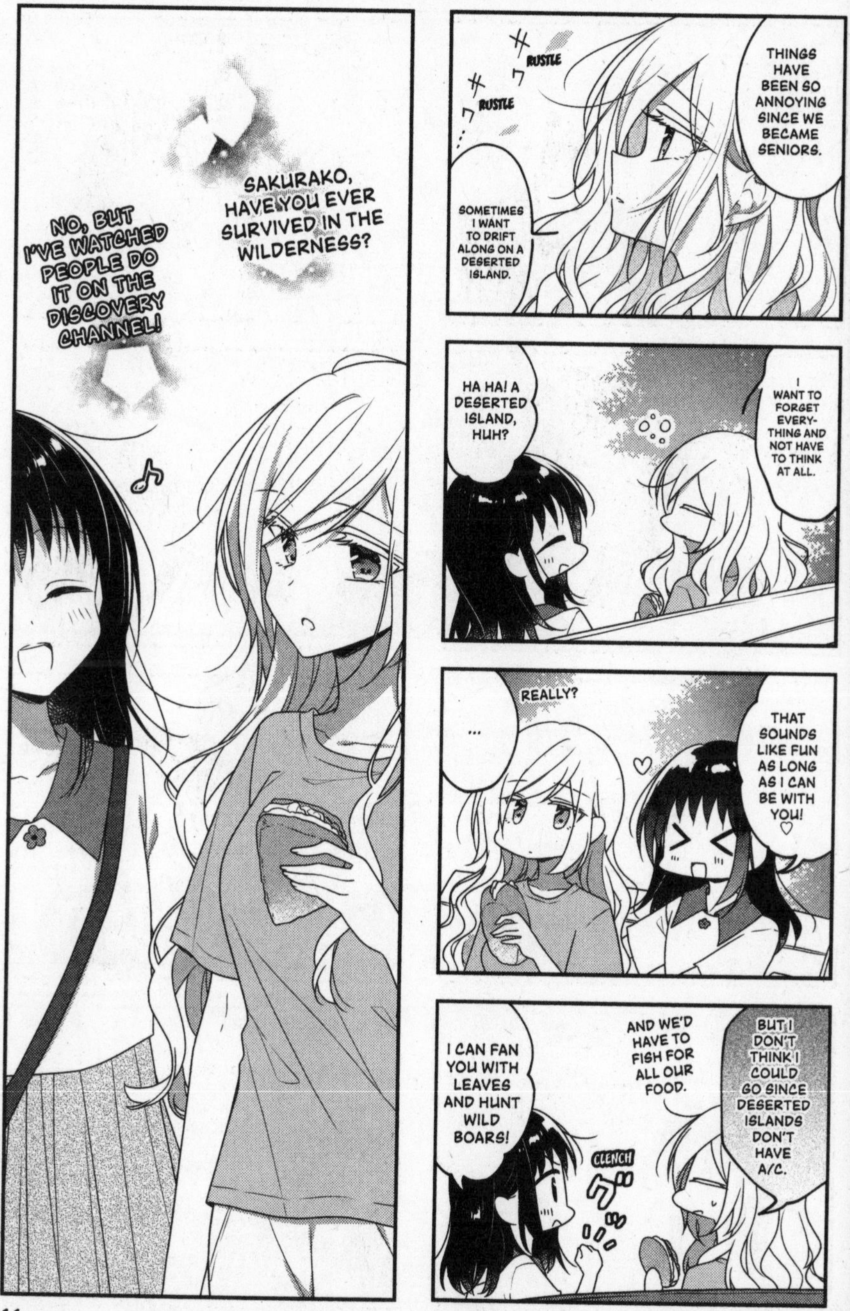
RUSTLE
RUSTLE
THINGS HAVE BEEN SO ANNOYING SINCE WE BECAME SENIORS.
SOMETIMES I WANT TO DRIFT ALONG ON A DESERTED ISLAND.
I WANT TO FORGET EVERYTHING AND NOT HAVE TO THINK AT ALL.
HA HA! A DESERTED ISLAND, HUH?
THAT SOUNDS LIKE FUN AS LONG AS I CAN BE WITH YOU! ♡
...
REALLY?
BUT I DON'T THINK I COULD GO SINCE DESERTED ISLANDS DON'T HAVE A/C.
AND WE'D HAVE TO FISH FOR ALL OUR FOOD.
I CAN FAN YOU WITH LEAVES AND HUNT WILD BOARS!
CLENCH
SAKURAKO, HAVE YOU EVER SURVIVED IN THE WILDERNESS?
NO, BUT I'VE WATCHED PEOPLE DO IT ON THE DISCOVERY CHANNEL!

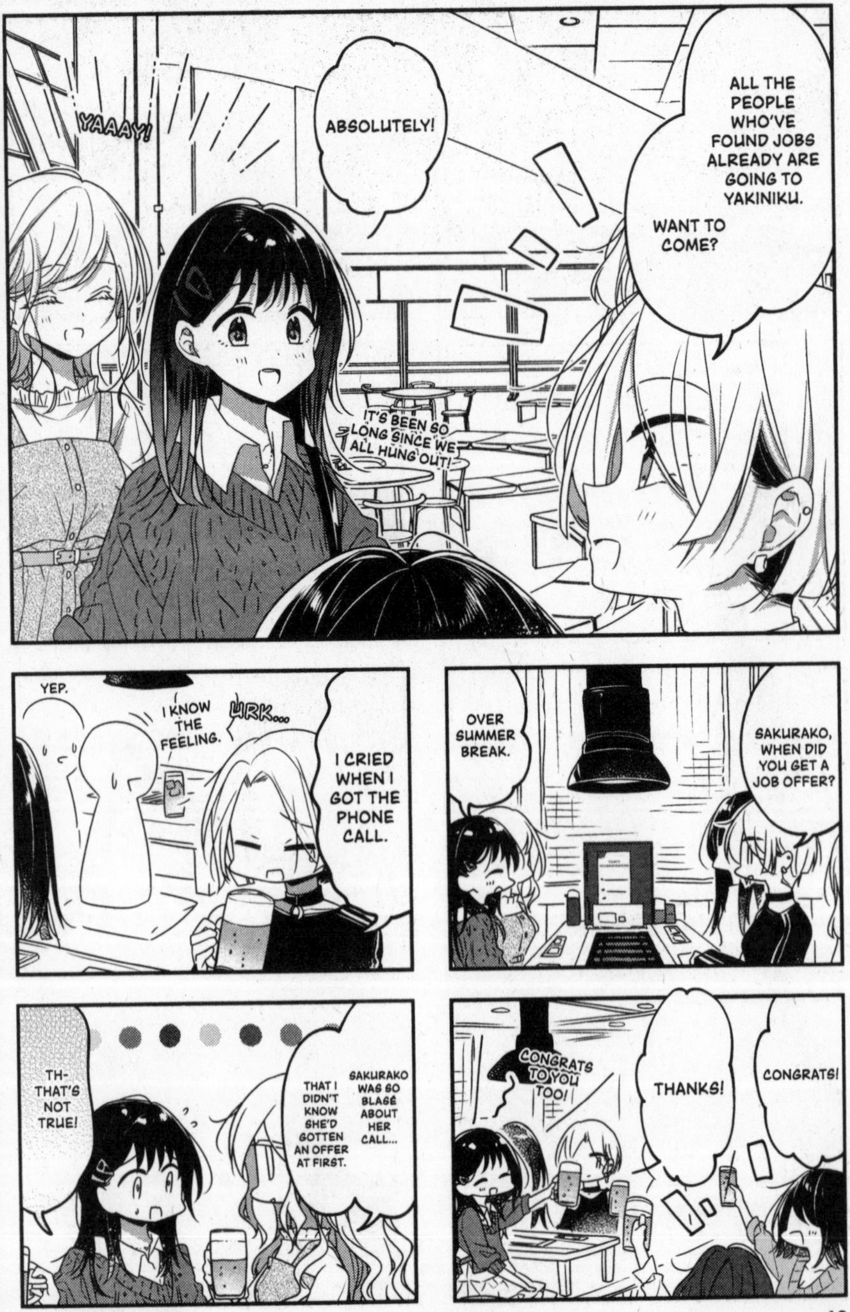
ALL THE PEOPLE WHO'VE FOUND JOBS ALREADY ARE GOING TO YAKINIKU.
WANT TO COME?
ABSOLUTELY!
YAAAY!
IT'S BEEN SO LONG SINCE WE ALL HUNG OUT!
SAKURAKO, WHEN DID YOU GET A JOB OFFER?
OVER SUMMER BREAK.
I CRIED WHEN I GOT THE PHONE CALL.
URK...
I KNOW THE FEELING.
YEP.
CONGRATS!
THANKS!
CONGRATS TO YOU TOO!
SAKURAKO WAS SO BLASÉ ABOUT HER CALL...
THAT I DIDN'T KNOW SHE'D GOTTEN AN OFFER AT FIRST.
TH-THAT'S NOT TRUE!

UGH, KASUMI-CHAN!

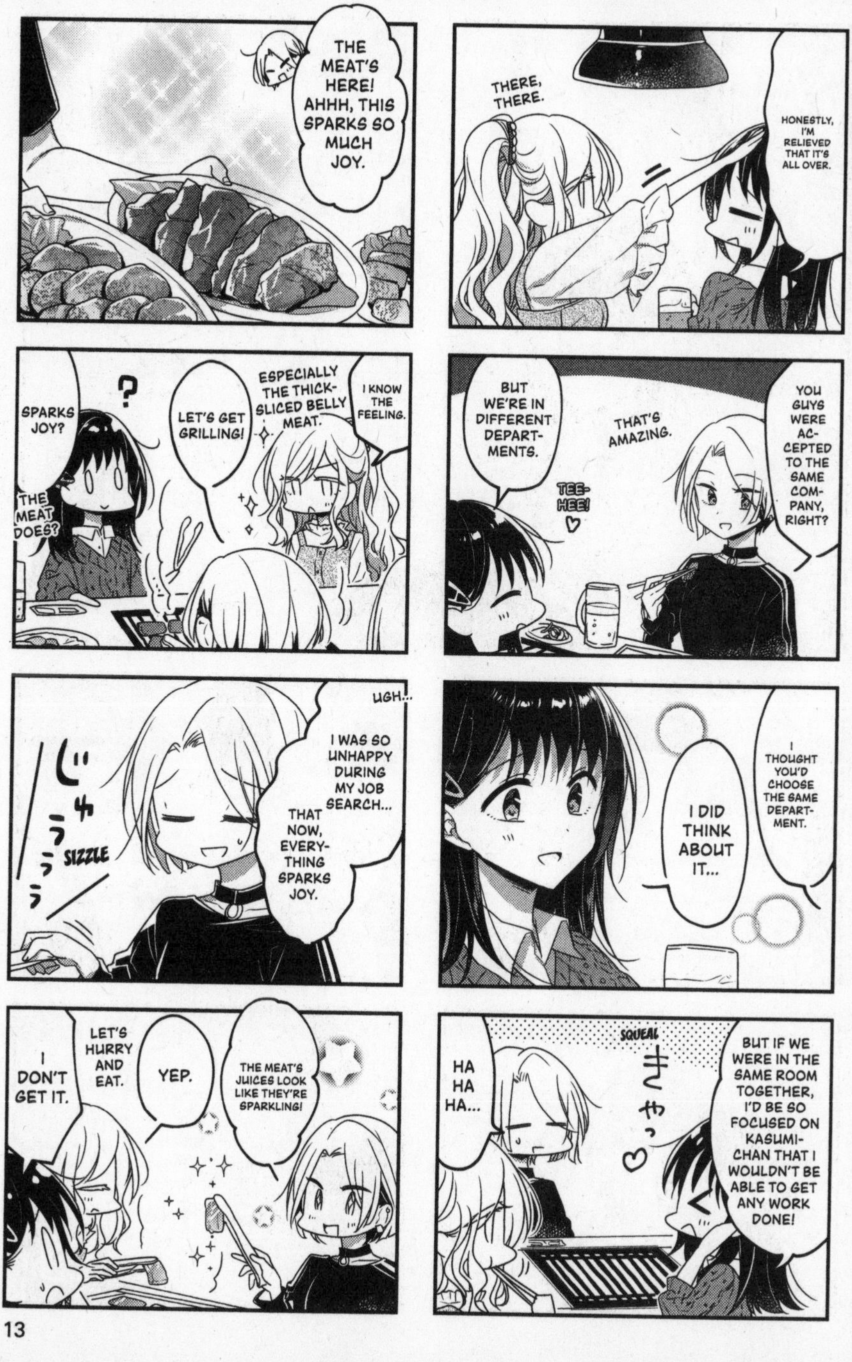
HONESTLY, I'M RELIEVED THAT IT'S ALL OVER.
THERE, THERE.
THE MEAT'S HERE! AHHH, THIS SPARKS SO MUCH JOY.
YOU GUYS WERE ACCEPTED TO THE SAME COMPANY, RIGHT?
THAT'S AMAZING.
BUT WE'RE IN DIFFERENT DEPARTMENTS.
TEE-HEE! ♥
I KNOW THE FEELING.
ESPECIALLY THE THICK-SLICED BELLY MEAT.
LET'S GET GRILLING!
?
SPARKS JOY?
THE MEAT DOES?
I THOUGHT YOU'D CHOOSE THE SAME DEPARTMENT.
I DID THINK ABOUT IT...
UGH...
I WAS SO UNHAPPY DURING MY JOB SEARCH...
THAT NOW, EVERYTHING SPARKS JOY.
じゅううう
SIZZLE
BUT IF WE WERE IN THE SAME ROOM TOGETHER, I'D BE SO FOCUSED ON KASUMI-CHAN THAT I WOULDN'T BE ABLE TO GET ANY WORK DONE!
SQUEAL
きゃっ ♥
HA HA HA...
THE MEAT'S JUICES LOOK LIKE THEY'RE SPARKLING!
YEP.
LET'S HURRY AND EAT.
I DON'T GET IT.

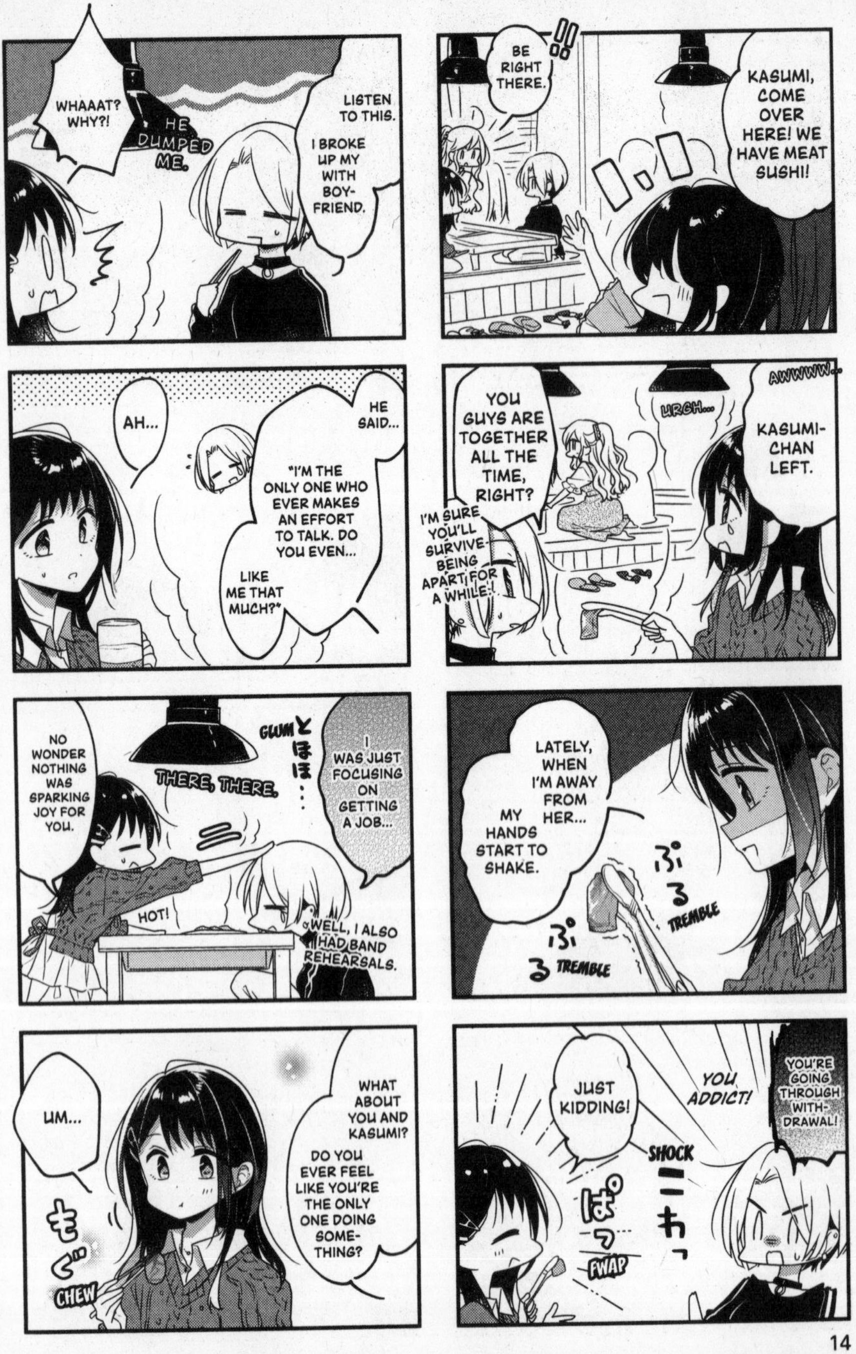
KASUMI, COME OVER HERE! WE HAVE MEAT SUSHI!
!!
BE RIGHT THERE.
LISTEN TO THIS.
I BROKE UP MY WITH BOY-FRIEND.
HE DUMPED ME.
WHAAAT? WHY?!
AWWWW...
KASUMI-CHAN LEFT.
URGH...
YOU GUYS ARE TOGETHER ALL THE TIME, RIGHT?
I'M SURE YOU'LL SURVIVE BEING APART FOR A WHILE.
HE SAID...
"I'M THE ONLY ONE WHO EVER MAKES AN EFFORT TO TALK. DO YOU EVEN...
LIKE ME THAT MUCH?"
AH...
LATELY, WHEN I'M AWAY FROM HER...
MY HANDS START TO SHAKE.
ぷる TREMBLE
ぷる TREMBLE
I WAS JUST FOCUSING ON GETTING A JOB...
GLUM とほほ...
THERE, THERE.
NO WONDER NOTHING WAS SPARKING JOY FOR YOU.
HOT!
WELL, I ALSO HAD BAND REHEARSALS.
YOU'RE GOING THROUGH WITH-DRAWAL!
YOU ADDICT!
JUST KIDDING!
SHOCK こわっ
ぱっ FWAP
WHAT ABOUT YOU AND KASUMI?
DO YOU EVER FEEL LIKE YOU'RE THE ONLY ONE DOING SOME-THING?
UM...
もぐ CHEW

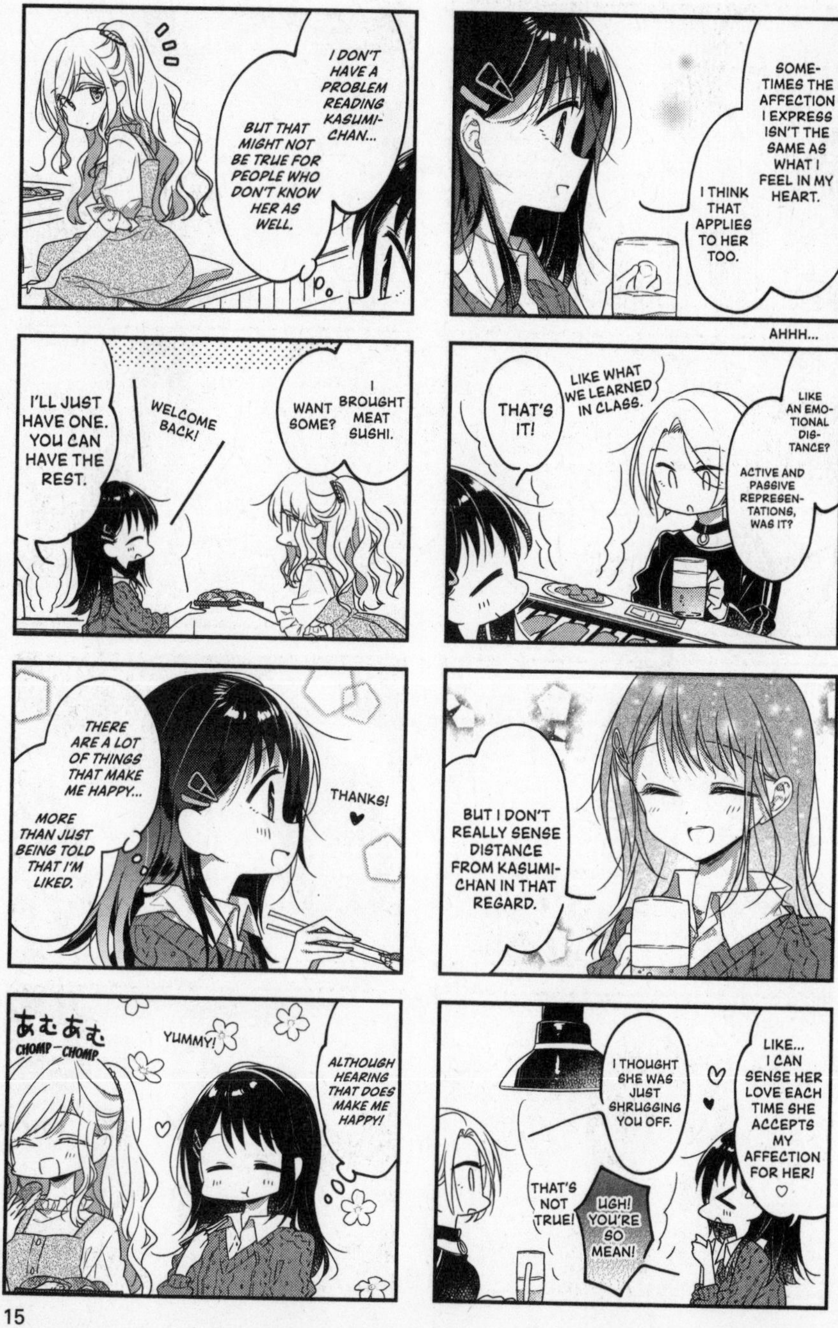
SOMETIMES THE AFFECTION I EXPRESS ISN'T THE SAME AS WHAT I FEEL IN MY HEART.
I THINK THAT APPLIES TO HER TOO.
I DON'T HAVE A PROBLEM READING KASUMI-CHAN...
BUT THAT MIGHT NOT BE TRUE FOR PEOPLE WHO DON'T KNOW HER AS WELL.
AHHH...
LIKE AN EMOTIONAL DISTANCE?
ACTIVE AND PASSIVE REPRESENTATIONS, WAS IT?
LIKE WHAT WE LEARNED IN CLASS.
THAT'S IT!
I BROUGHT MEAT SUSHI.
WANT SOME?
WELCOME BACK!
I'LL JUST HAVE ONE. YOU CAN HAVE THE REST.
BUT I DON'T REALLY SENSE DISTANCE FROM KASUMI-CHAN IN THAT REGARD.
THANKS!
THERE ARE A LOT OF THINGS THAT MAKE ME HAPPY...
MORE THAN JUST BEING TOLD THAT I'M LIKED.
LIKE... I CAN SENSE HER LOVE EACH TIME SHE ACCEPTS MY AFFECTION FOR HER!
I THOUGHT SHE WAS JUST SHRUGGING YOU OFF.
UGH! YOU'RE SO MEAN!
THAT'S NOT TRUE!
ALTHOUGH HEARING THAT DOES MAKE ME HAPPY!
YUMMY!
あむあむ
CHOMP-CHOMP

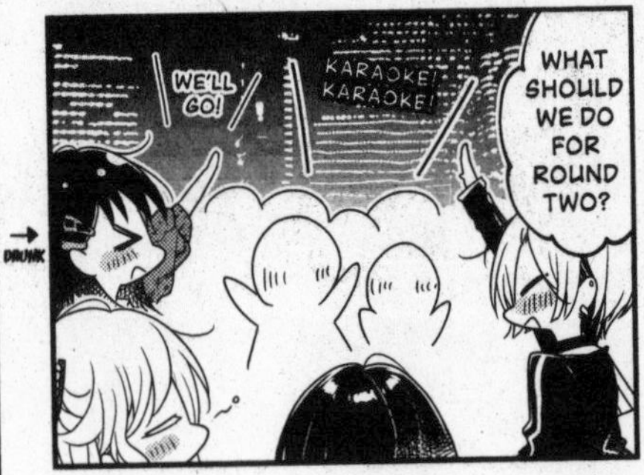
WHAT SHOULD WE DO FOR ROUND TWO?
KARAOKE! KARAOKE!
WE'LL GO!
DRUNK

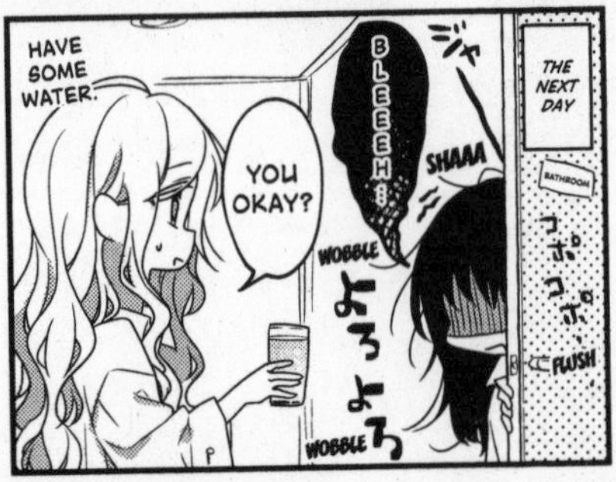
THE NEXT DAY
BATHROOM
コポコポ
FLUSH
ジャ
SHAAA
BLEEEEH...
YOU OKAY?
HAVE SOME WATER.
よろよろ
WOBBLE
WOBBLE

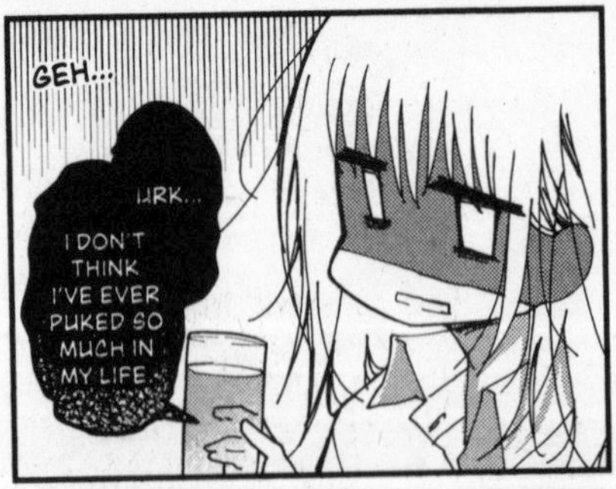
GEH...
URK...
I DON'T THINK I'VE EVER PUKED SO MUCH IN MY LIFE.

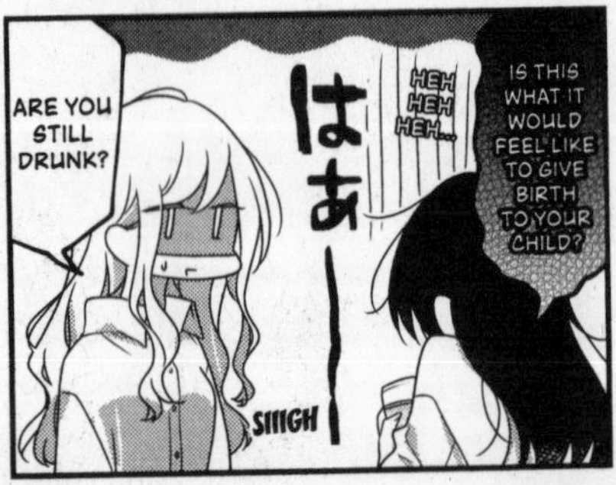
IS THIS WHAT IT WOULD FEEL LIKE TO GIVE BIRTH TO YOUR CHILD?
HEH HEH HEH...
はあー
SIIIGH
ARE YOU STILL DRUNK?

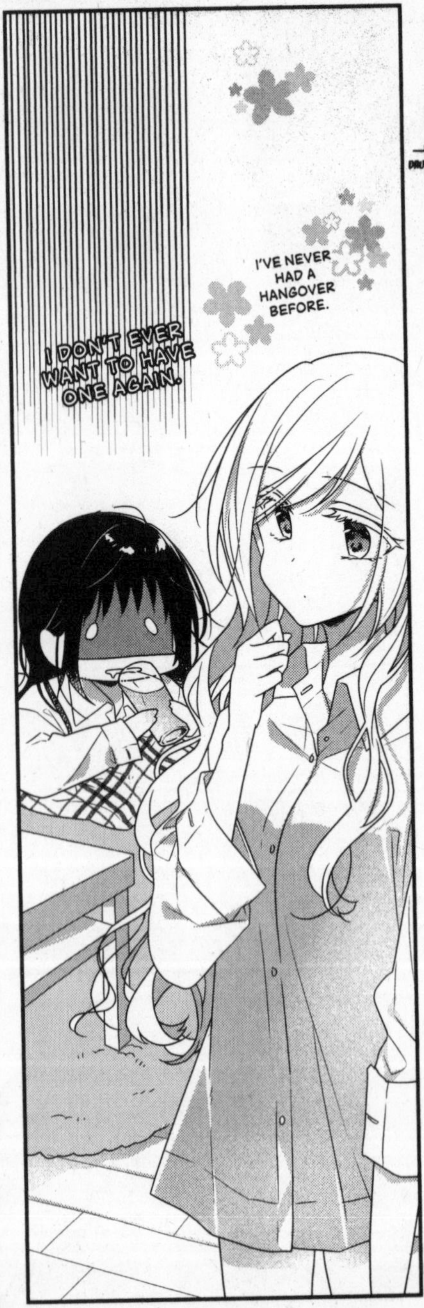
I'VE NEVER HAD A HANGOVER BEFORE.
I DON'T EVER WANT TO HAVE ONE AGAIN.

Illustration gallery of Yukiko

UNIFOOOORMS!

Futaribeya
A ROOM FOR TWO

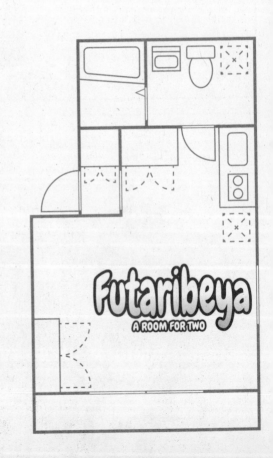

Chapter 68

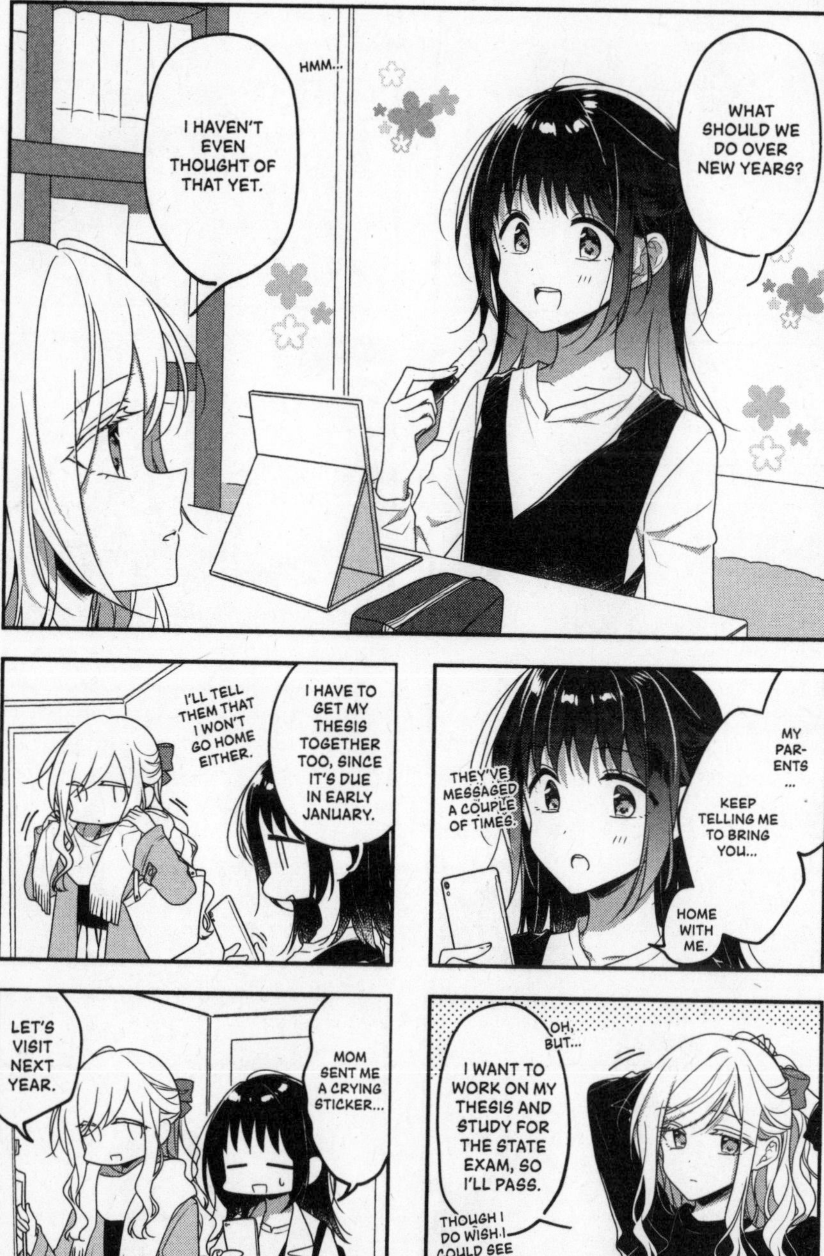
WHAT SHOULD WE DO OVER NEW YEARS?
HMM...
I HAVEN'T EVEN THOUGHT OF THAT YET.
MY PARENTS...
KEEP TELLING ME TO BRING YOU...
HOME WITH ME.
THEY'VE MESSAGED A COUPLE OF TIMES.
OH, BUT...
I WANT TO WORK ON MY THESIS AND STUDY FOR THE STATE EXAM, SO I'LL PASS.
THOUGH I DO WISH I COULD SEE THEM.
I HAVE TO GET MY THESIS TOGETHER TOO, SINCE IT'S DUE IN EARLY JANUARY.
I'LL TELL THEM THAT I WON'T GO HOME EITHER.
MOM SENT ME A CRYING STICKER...
LET'S VISIT NEXT YEAR.

HA HA HA

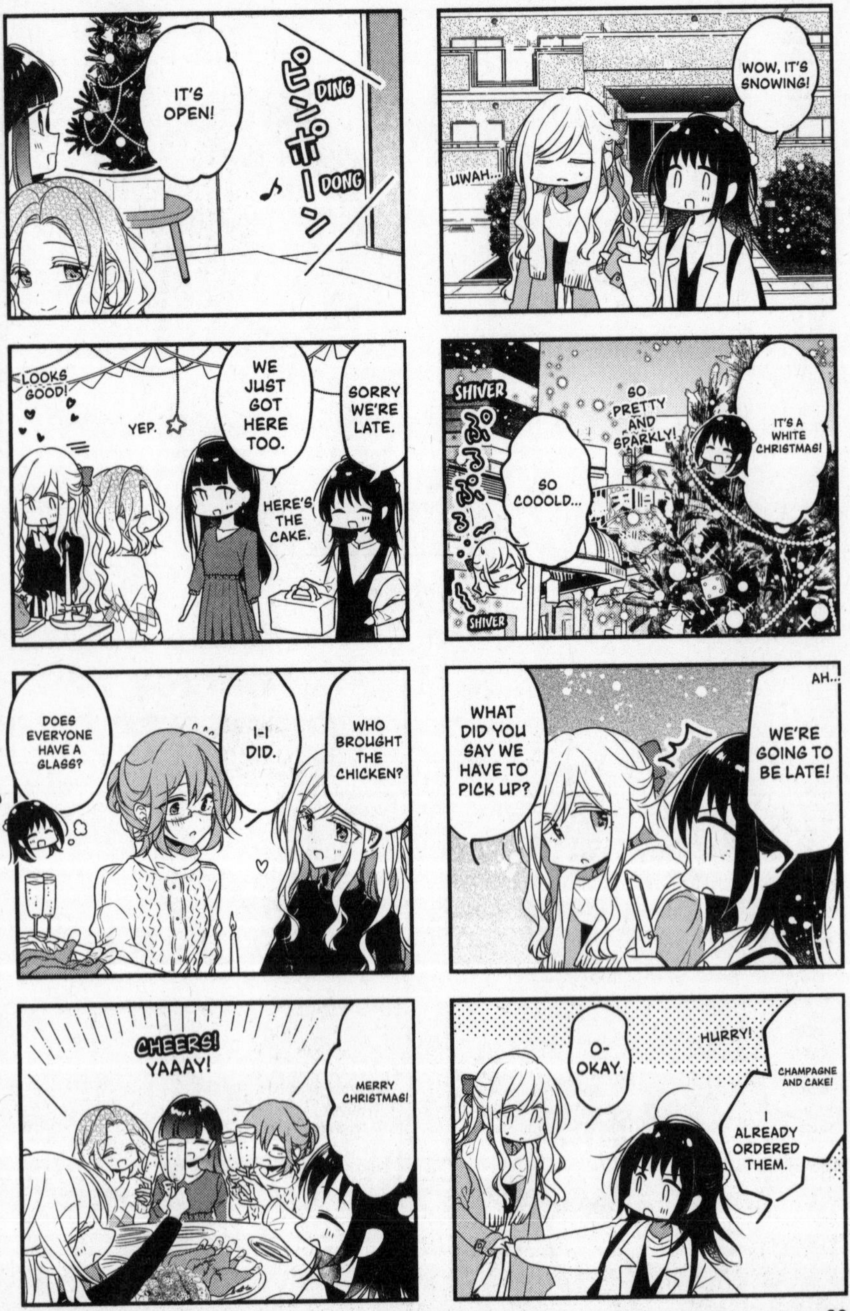
WOW, IT'S SNOWING!
UWAH...
IT'S A WHITE CHRISTMAS!
SO PRETTY AND SPARKLY!
SO COOOLD...
SHIVER
ぷるぷる
SHIVER
AH...
WE'RE GOING TO BE LATE!
WHAT DID YOU SAY WE HAVE TO PICK UP?
HURRY!
CHAMPAGNE AND CAKE!
I ALREADY ORDERED THEM.
O-OKAY.
ピンポーン
DING
DONG
IT'S OPEN!
SORRY WE'RE LATE.
HERE'S THE CAKE.
WE JUST GOT HERE TOO.
YEP.
LOOKS GOOD!
WHO BROUGHT THE CHICKEN?
I-I DID.
DOES EVERYONE HAVE A GLASS?
MERRY CHRISTMAS!
CHEERS!
YAAAY!

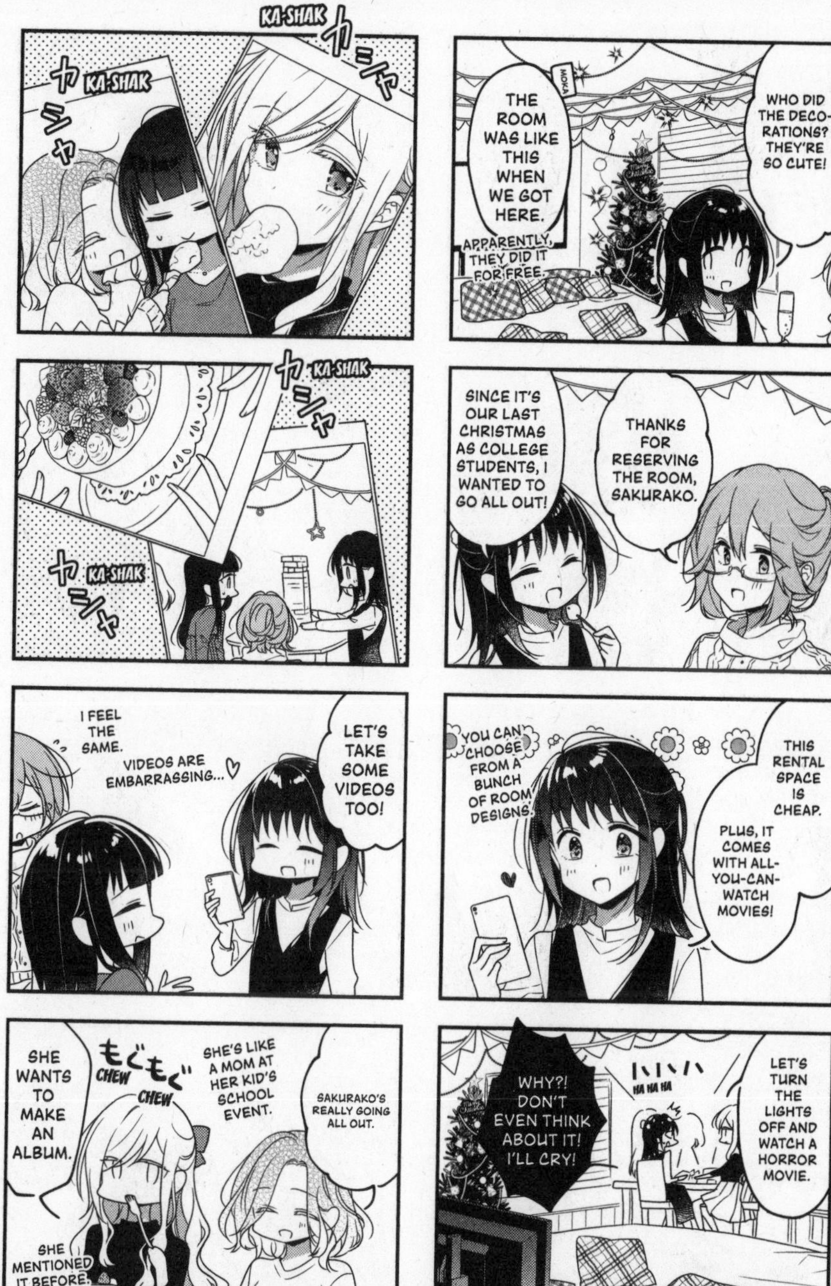
WHO DID THE DECORATIONS? THEY'RE SO CUTE!
MOKA
THE ROOM WAS LIKE THIS WHEN WE GOT HERE.
APPARENTLY, THEY DID IT FOR FREE.
KA-SHAK
KA-SHAK
THANKS FOR RESERVING THE ROOM, SAKURAKO.
SINCE IT'S OUR LAST CHRISTMAS AS COLLEGE STUDENTS, I WANTED TO GO ALL OUT!
KA-SHAK
KA-SHAK
THIS RENTAL SPACE IS CHEAP.
PLUS, IT COMES WITH ALL-YOU-CAN-WATCH MOVIES!
YOU CAN CHOOSE FROM A BUNCH OF ROOM DESIGNS.
LET'S TAKE SOME VIDEOS TOO!
I FEEL THE SAME.
VIDEOS ARE EMBARRASSING...
LET'S TURN THE LIGHTS OFF AND WATCH A HORROR MOVIE.
HA HA HA
WHY?! DON'T EVEN THINK ABOUT IT! I'LL CRY!
SAKURAKO'S REALLY GOING ALL OUT.
SHE'S LIKE A MOM AT HER KID'S SCHOOL EVENT.
CHEW CHEW
SHE WANTS TO MAKE AN ALBUM.
SHE MENTIONED IT BEFORE.

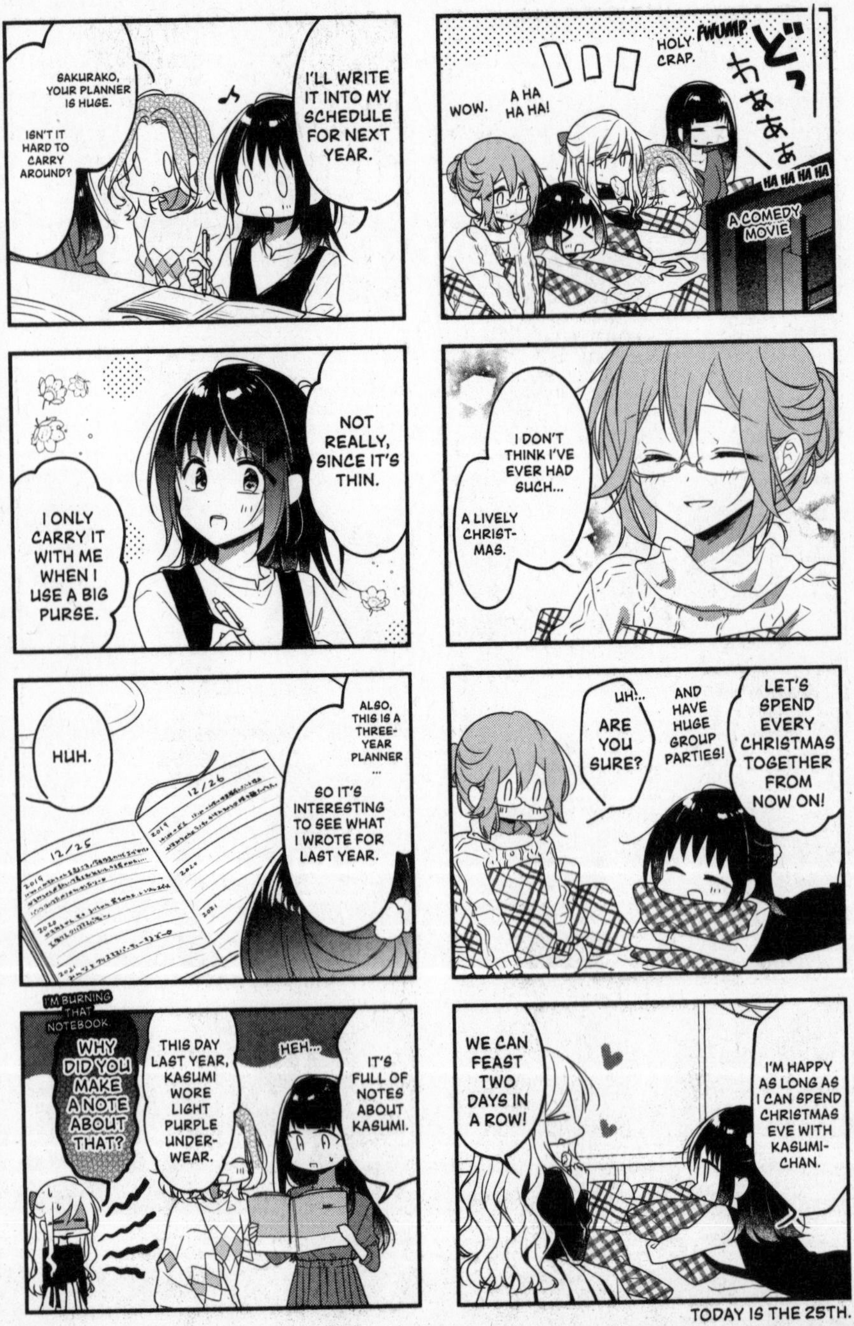
どっ
FWUMP
HOLY CRAP.
わぁぁぁ
A HA HA HA!
WOW.
HA HA HA HA
A COMEDY MOVIE
I DON'T THINK I'VE EVER HAD SUCH...
A LIVELY CHRISTMAS.
LET'S SPEND EVERY CHRISTMAS TOGETHER FROM NOW ON!
AND HAVE HUGE GROUP PARTIES!
UH...
ARE YOU SURE?
I'M HAPPY AS LONG AS I CAN SPEND CHRISTMAS EVE WITH KASUMI-CHAN.
WE CAN FEAST TWO DAYS IN A ROW!
I'LL WRITE IT INTO MY SCHEDULE FOR NEXT YEAR.
SAKURAKO, YOUR PLANNER IS HUGE.
ISN'T IT HARD TO CARRY AROUND?
NOT REALLY, SINCE IT'S THIN.
I ONLY CARRY IT WITH ME WHEN I USE A BIG PURSE.
ALSO, THIS IS A THREE-YEAR PLANNER...
SO IT'S INTERESTING TO SEE WHAT I WROTE FOR LAST YEAR.
HUH.
12/26
12/25
IT'S FULL OF NOTES ABOUT KASUMI.
HEH...
THIS DAY LAST YEAR, KASUMI WORE LIGHT PURPLE UNDERWEAR.
WHY DID YOU MAKE A NOTE ABOUT THAT?
I'M BURNING THAT NOTEBOOK.

TODAY IS THE 25TH.

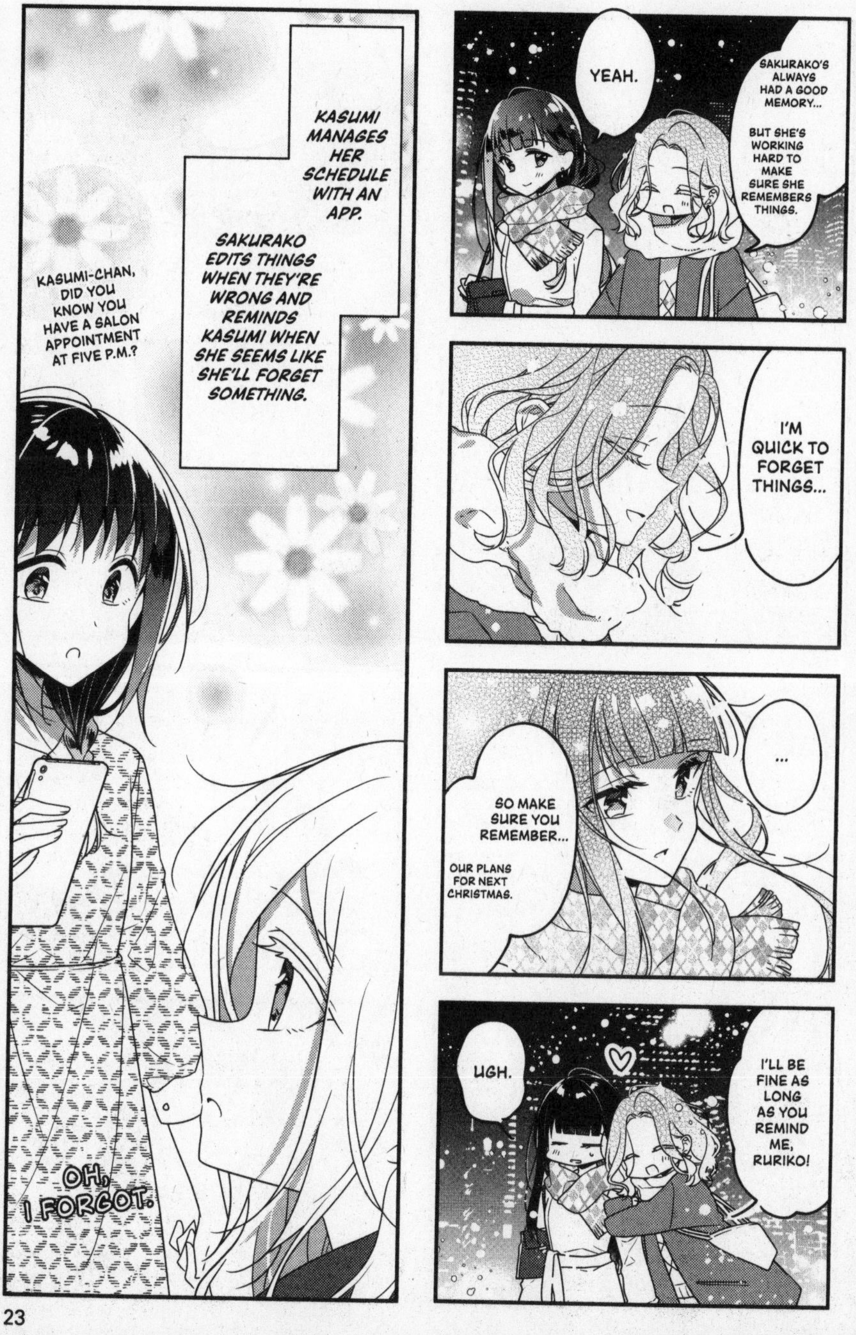
SAKURAKO'S ALWAYS HAD A GOOD MEMORY...
BUT SHE'S WORKING HARD TO MAKE SURE SHE REMEMBERS THINGS.
YEAH.
I'M QUICK TO FORGET THINGS...
...
SO MAKE SURE YOU REMEMBER...
OUR PLANS FOR NEXT CHRISTMAS.
I'LL BE FINE AS LONG AS YOU REMIND ME, RURIKO!
UGH.
KASUMI MANAGES HER SCHEDULE WITH AN APP.
SAKURAKO EDITS THINGS WHEN THEY'RE WRONG AND REMINDS KASUMI WHEN SHE SEEMS LIKE SHE'LL FORGET SOMETHING.
KASUMI-CHAN, DID YOU KNOW YOU HAVE A SALON APPOINTMENT AT FIVE P.M.?
OH, I FORGOT.

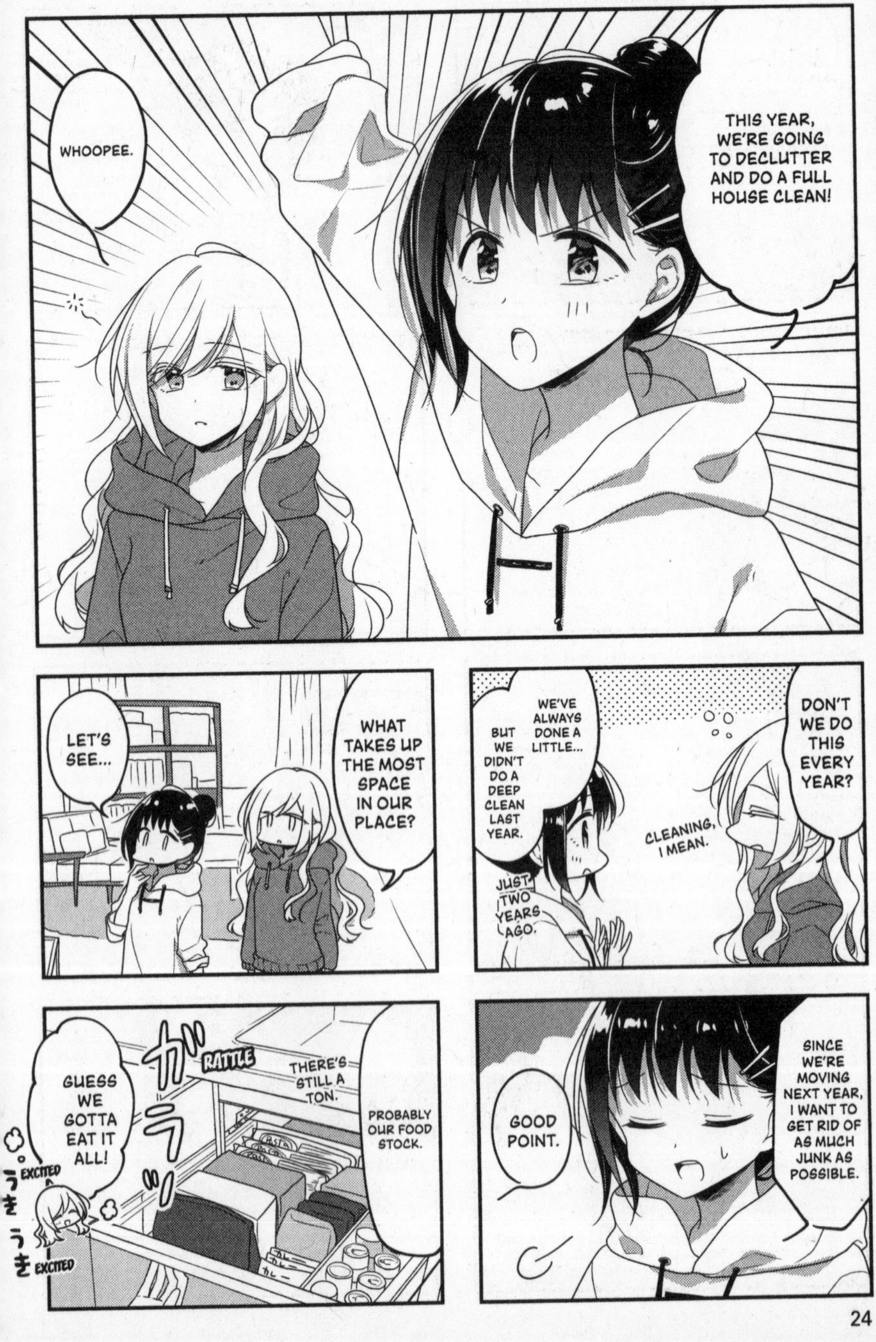
THIS YEAR, WE'RE GOING TO DECLUTTER AND DO A FULL HOUSE CLEAN!
WHOOPEE.
DON'T WE DO THIS EVERY YEAR?
CLEANING, I MEAN.
WE'VE ALWAYS DONE A LITTLE...
BUT WE DIDN'T DO A DEEP CLEAN LAST YEAR.
JUST TWO YEARS AGO.
WHAT TAKES UP THE MOST SPACE IN OUR PLACE?
LET'S SEE...
SINCE WE'RE MOVING NEXT YEAR, I WANT TO GET RID OF AS MUCH JUNK AS POSSIBLE.
GOOD POINT.
PROBABLY OUR FOOD STOCK.
THERE'S STILL A TON.
ガラッ
RATTLE
GUESS WE GOTTA EAT IT ALL!
うき
EXCITED
うき
EXCITED

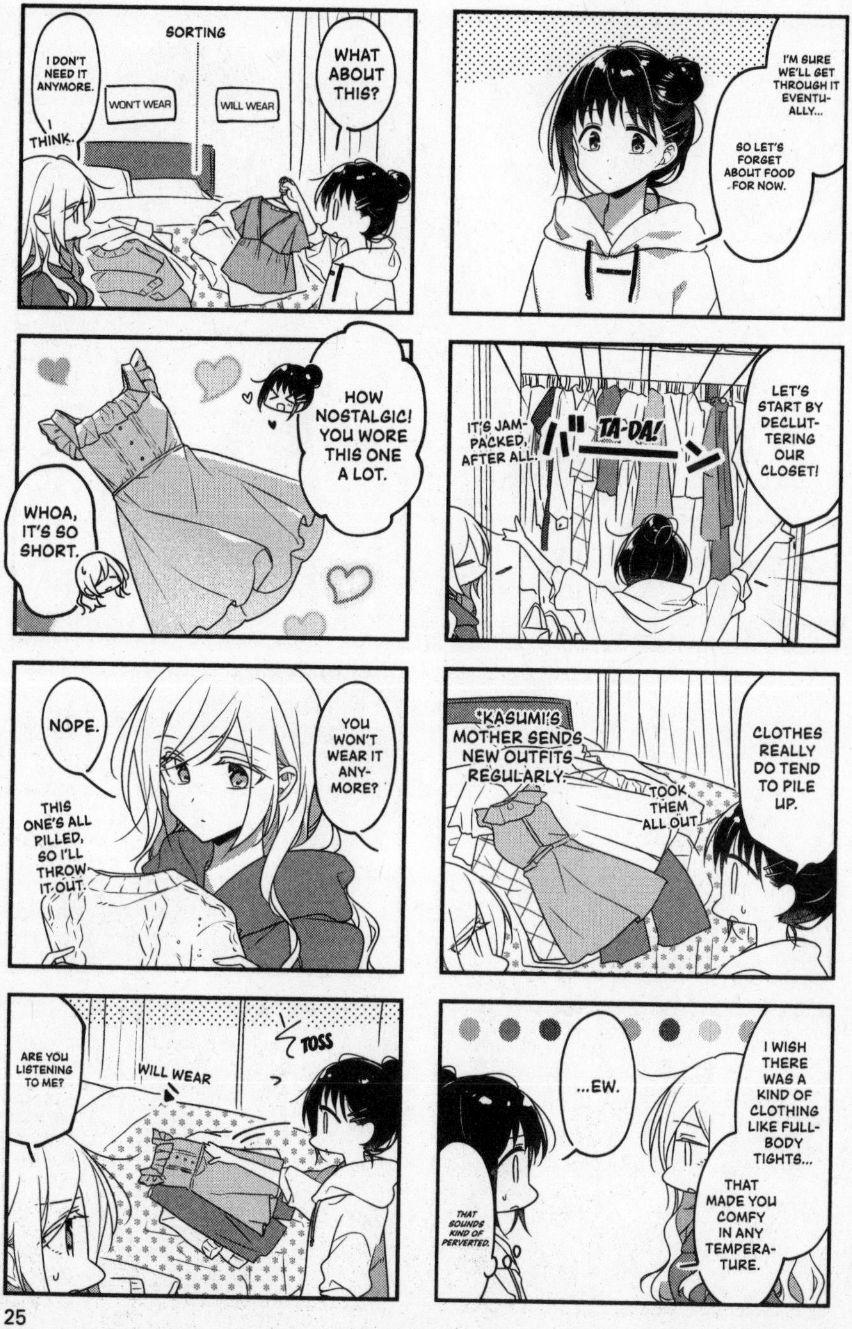

I'M SURE WE'LL GET THROUGH IT EVENTU-ALLY...
SO LET'S FORGET ABOUT FOOD FOR NOW.
LET'S START BY DECLUT-TERING OUR CLOSET!
TA-DA!
IT'S JAM-PACKED, AFTER ALL.
CLOTHES REALLY DO TEND TO PILE UP.
TOOK THEM ALL OUT
*KASUMI'S MOTHER SENDS NEW OUTFITS REGULARLY.
I WISH THERE WAS A KIND OF CLOTHING LIKE FULL-BODY TIGHTS...
THAT MADE YOU COMFY IN ANY TEMPERA-TURE.
...EW.
THAT SOUNDS KIND OF PERVERTED.
WHAT ABOUT THIS?
SORTING
WILL WEAR
WON'T WEAR
I DON'T NEED IT ANYMORE.
I THINK.
HOW NOSTALGIC! YOU WORE THIS ONE A LOT.
WHOA, IT'S SO SHORT.
YOU WON'T WEAR IT ANY-MORE?
NOPE.
THIS ONE'S ALL PILLED, SO I'LL THROW IT OUT.
TOSS
WILL WEAR
ARE YOU LISTENING TO ME?

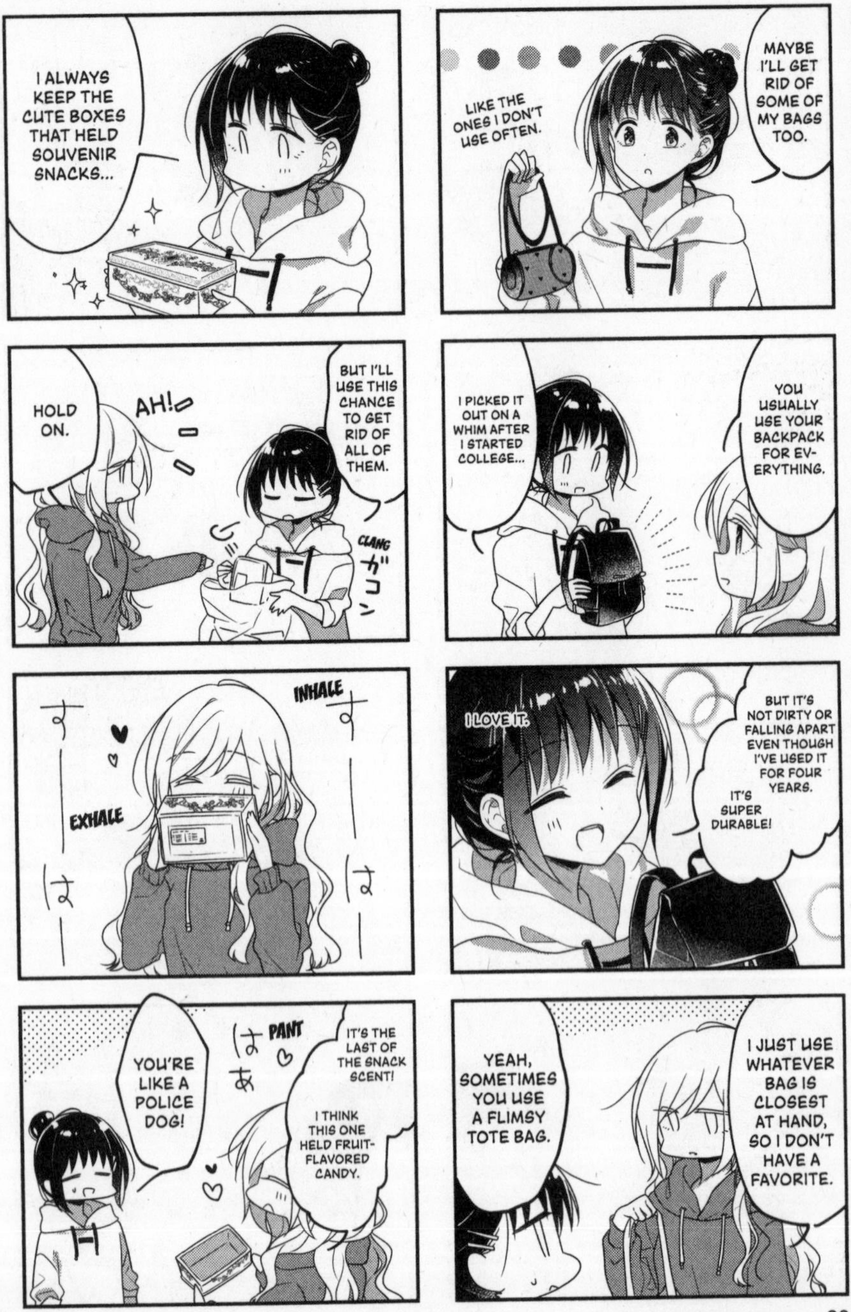
MAYBE I'LL GET RID OF SOME OF MY BAGS TOO.
LIKE THE ONES I DON'T USE OFTEN.
I ALWAYS KEEP THE CUTE BOXES THAT HELD SOUVENIR SNACKS...
YOU USUALLY USE YOUR BACKPACK FOR EV-ERYTHING.
I PICKED IT OUT ON A WHIM AFTER I STARTED COLLEGE...
BUT I'LL USE THIS CHANCE TO GET RID OF ALL OF THEM.
CLANG
ガコン
AH!
HOLD ON.
BUT IT'S NOT DIRTY OR FALLING APART EVEN THOUGH I'VE USED IT FOR FOUR YEARS.
IT'S SUPER DURABLE!
I LOVE IT.
INHALE
すー
はー
EXHALE
すー
はー
I JUST USE WHATEVER BAG IS CLOSEST AT HAND, SO I DON'T HAVE A FAVORITE.
YEAH, SOMETIMES YOU USE A FLIMSY TOTE BAG.
IT'S THE LAST OF THE SNACK SCENT!
I THINK THIS ONE HELD FRUIT-FLAVORED CANDY.
PANT
はあ
YOU'RE LIKE A POLICE DOG!

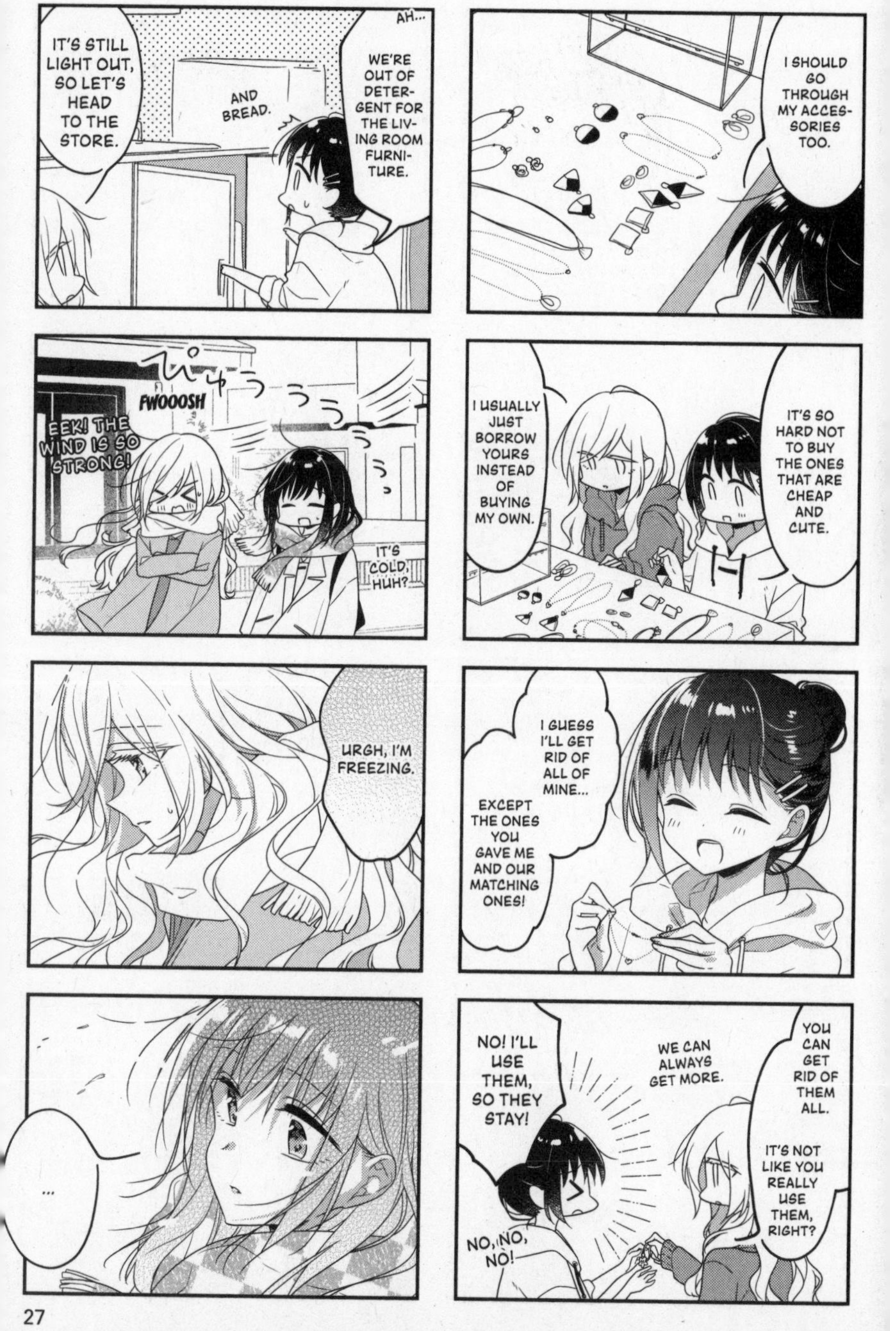
I SHOULD GO THROUGH MY ACCESSORIES TOO.
IT'S SO HARD NOT TO BUY THE ONES THAT ARE CHEAP AND CUTE.
I USUALLY JUST BORROW YOURS INSTEAD OF BUYING MY OWN.
I GUESS I'LL GET RID OF ALL OF MINE...
EXCEPT THE ONES YOU GAVE ME AND OUR MATCHING ONES!
YOU CAN GET RID OF THEM ALL.
IT'S NOT LIKE YOU REALLY USE THEM, RIGHT?
WE CAN ALWAYS GET MORE.
NO! I'LL USE THEM, SO THEY STAY!
NO, NO, NO!
AH...
WE'RE OUT OF DETERGENT FOR THE LIVING ROOM FURNITURE.
AND BREAD.
IT'S STILL LIGHT OUT, SO LET'S HEAD TO THE STORE.
ぴゅうううう
FWOOOSH
IT'S COLD, HUH?
EEK! THE WIND IS SO STRONG!
URGH, I'M FREEZING.
...

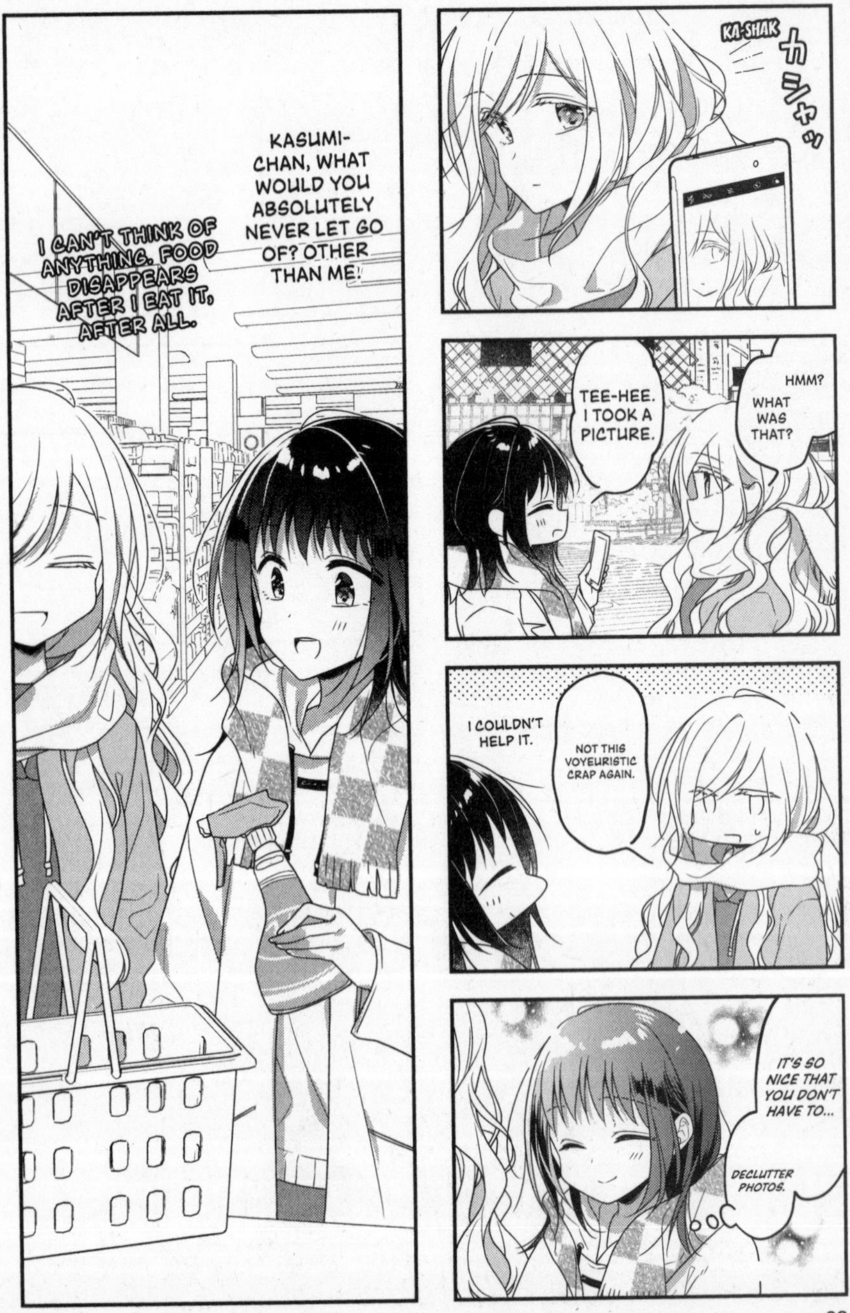
KA-SHAK
カシャッ
HMM? WHAT WAS THAT?
TEE-HEE. I TOOK A PICTURE.
NOT THIS VOYEURISTIC CRAP AGAIN.
I COULDN'T HELP IT.
IT'S SO NICE THAT YOU DON'T HAVE TO...
DECLUTTER PHOTOS.
KASUMI-CHAN, WHAT WOULD YOU ABSOLUTELY NEVER LET GO OF? OTHER THAN ME!
I CAN'T THINK OF ANYTHING. FOOD DISAPPEARS AFTER I EAT IT, AFTER ALL.

Illustration gallery of Yukiko

I DREW THIS OVER NEW YEAR'S.

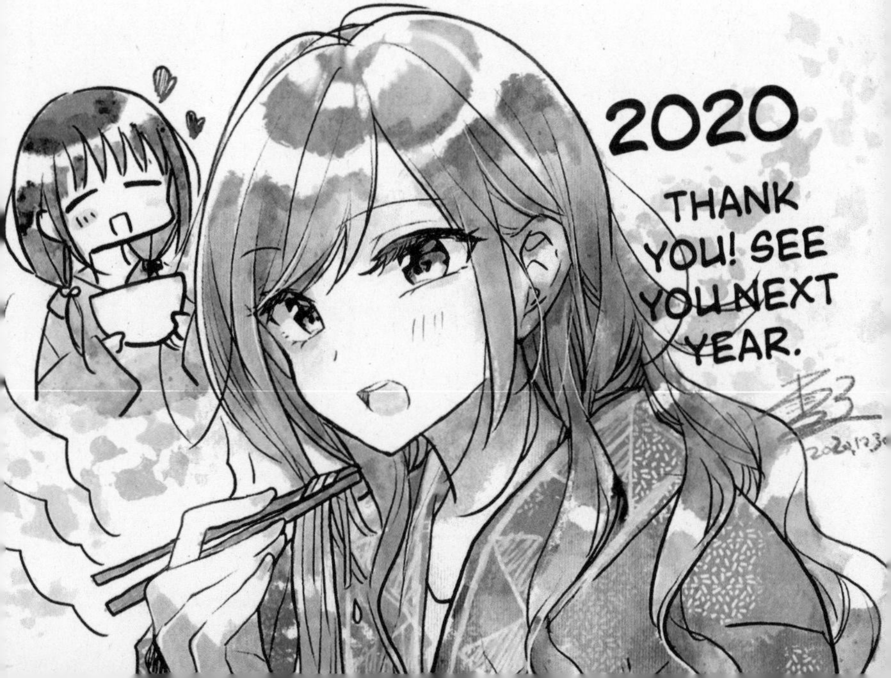
2020
THANK YOU! SEE YOU NEXT YEAR.

Futaribeya
A ROOM FOR TWO

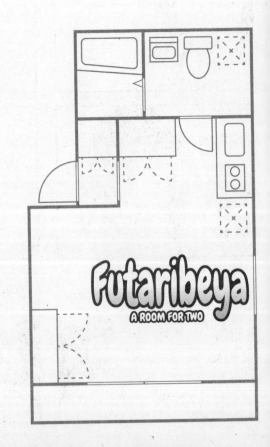

Chapter 68.5

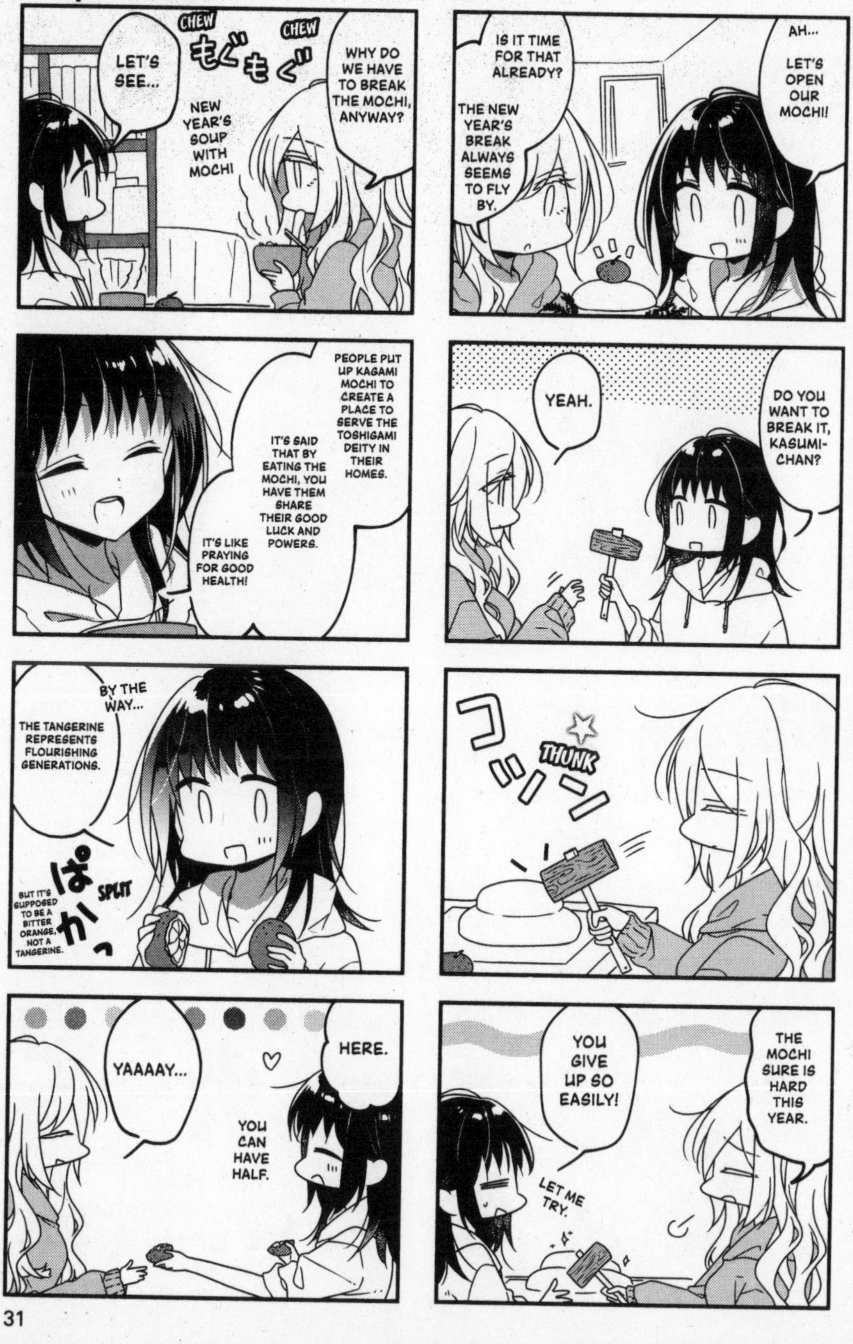

AH... LET'S OPEN OUR MOCHI!
IS IT TIME FOR THAT ALREADY?
THE NEW YEAR'S BREAK ALWAYS SEEMS TO FLY BY.
WHY DO WE HAVE TO BREAK THE MOCHI, ANYWAY?
CHEW
もぐもぐ
CHEW
LET'S SEE...
NEW YEAR'S SOUP WITH MOCHI
DO YOU WANT TO BREAK IT, KASUMI-CHAN?
YEAH.
PEOPLE PUT UP KAGAMI MOCHI TO CREATE A PLACE TO SERVE THE TOSHIGAMI DEITY IN THEIR HOMES.
IT'S SAID THAT BY EATING THE MOCHI, YOU HAVE THEM SHARE THEIR GOOD LUCK AND POWERS.
IT'S LIKE PRAYING FOR GOOD HEALTH!
THUNK
BY THE WAY...
THE TANGERINE REPRESENTS FLOURISHING GENERATIONS.
ぱかっ
SPLIT
BUT IT'S SUPPOSED TO BE A BITTER ORANGE, NOT A TANGERINE.
THE MOCHI SURE IS HARD THIS YEAR.
YOU GIVE UP SO EASILY!
LET ME TRY.
HERE.
YAAAAY...
YOU CAN HAVE HALF.

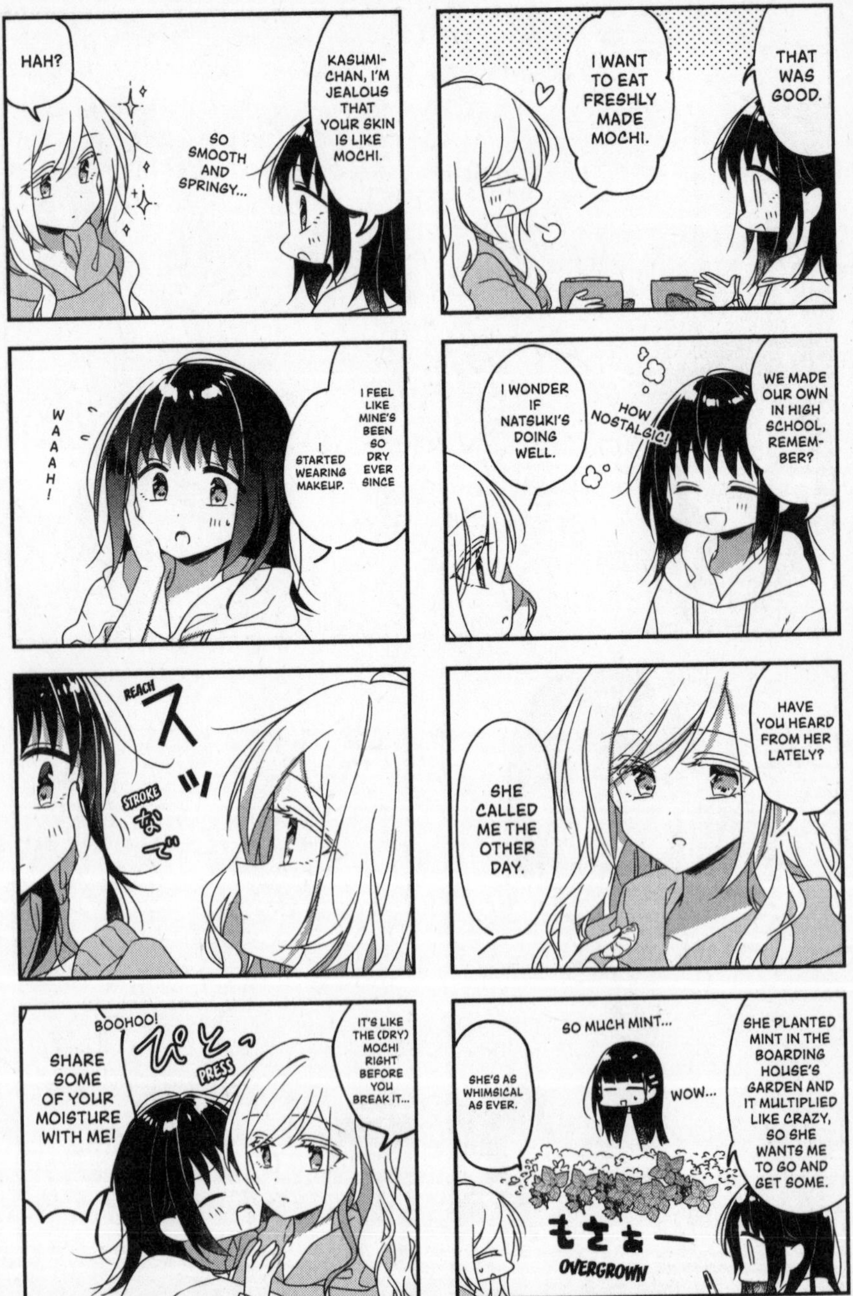
THAT WAS GOOD.
I WANT TO EAT FRESHLY MADE MOCHI.
WE MADE OUR OWN IN HIGH SCHOOL, REMEMBER?
HOW NOSTALGIC!
I WONDER IF NATSUKI'S DOING WELL.
HAVE YOU HEARD FROM HER LATELY?
SHE CALLED ME THE OTHER DAY.
SHE PLANTED MINT IN THE BOARDING HOUSE'S GARDEN AND IT MULTIPLIED LIKE CRAZY, SO SHE WANTS ME TO GO AND GET SOME.
SO MUCH MINT...
WOW...
SHE'S AS WHIMSICAL AS EVER.
もさぁー
OVERGROWN
KASUMI-CHAN, I'M JEALOUS THAT YOUR SKIN IS LIKE MOCHI.
SO SMOOTH AND SPRINGY...
HAH?
I FEEL LIKE MINE'S BEEN SO DRY EVER SINCE
I STARTED WEARING MAKEUP.
WAAAAH!
REACH
スッ
STROKE
なで
IT'S LIKE THE (DRY) MOCHI RIGHT BEFORE YOU BREAK IT...
ぴとっ
PRESS
BOOHOO!
SHARE SOME OF YOUR MOISTURE WITH ME!

Chapter 69

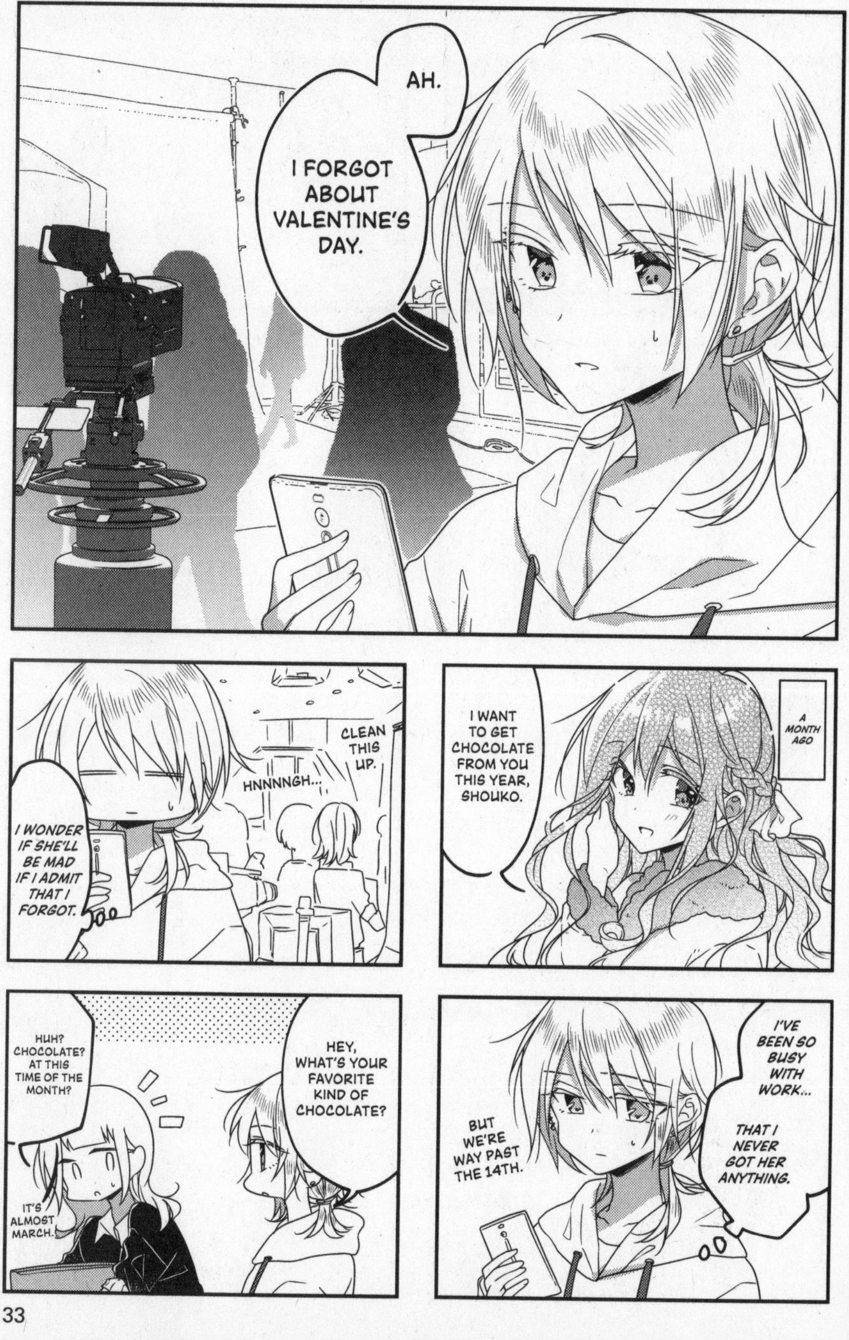
AH.
I FORGOT ABOUT VALENTINE'S DAY.
A MONTH AGO
I WANT TO GET CHOCOLATE FROM YOU THIS YEAR, SHOUKO.
CLEAN THIS UP.
HNNNNGH...
I WONDER IF SHE'LL BE MAD IF I ADMIT THAT I FORGOT.
I'VE BEEN SO BUSY WITH WORK...
THAT I NEVER GOT HER ANYTHING.
BUT WE'RE WAY PAST THE 14TH.
HEY, WHAT'S YOUR FAVORITE KIND OF CHOCOLATE?
HUH? CHOCOLATE? AT THIS TIME OF THE MONTH?
IT'S ALMOST MARCH.

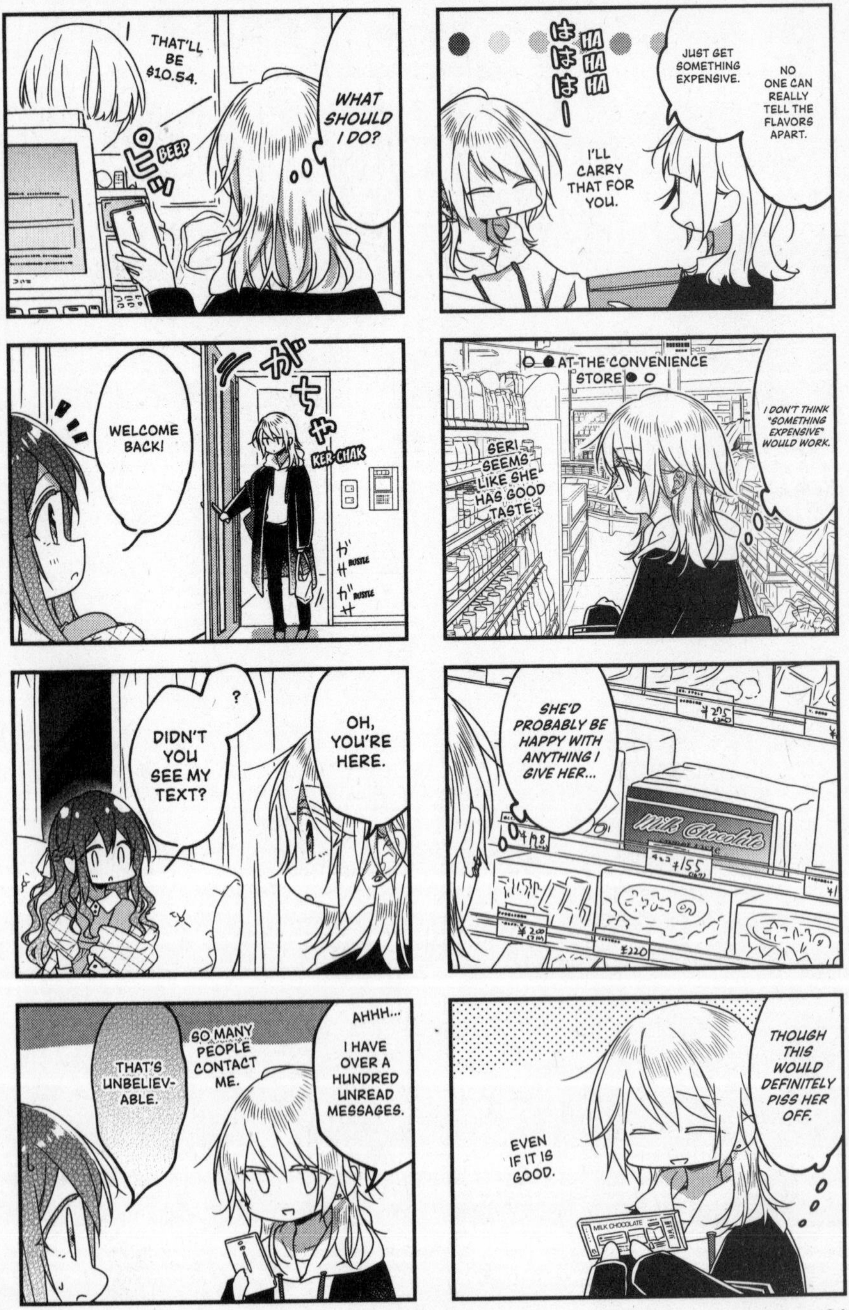
JUST GET SOMETHING EXPENSIVE.
NO ONE CAN REALLY TELL THE FLAVORS APART.
はははー
HA HA HA
I'LL CARRY THAT FOR YOU.
I DON'T THINK "SOMETHING EXPENSIVE" WOULD WORK.
AT THE CONVENIENCE STORE
SERI SEEMS LIKE SHE HAS GOOD TASTE.
SHE'D PROBABLY BE HAPPY WITH ANYTHING I GIVE HER...
Milk Chocolate
¥155
¥220
THOUGH THIS WOULD DEFINITELY PISS HER OFF.
EVEN IF IT IS GOOD.
MILK CHOCOLATE
WHAT SHOULD I DO?
THAT'LL BE $10.54.
ピッ
BEEP
WELCOME BACK!
ガチャ
KER-CHAK
ガサ
BUSTLE
ガサ
BUSTLE
OH, YOU'RE HERE.
DIDN'T YOU SEE MY TEXT?
?
AHHH...
I HAVE OVER A HUNDRED UNREAD MESSAGES.
SO MANY PEOPLE CONTACT ME.
THAT'S UNBELIEV-ABLE.

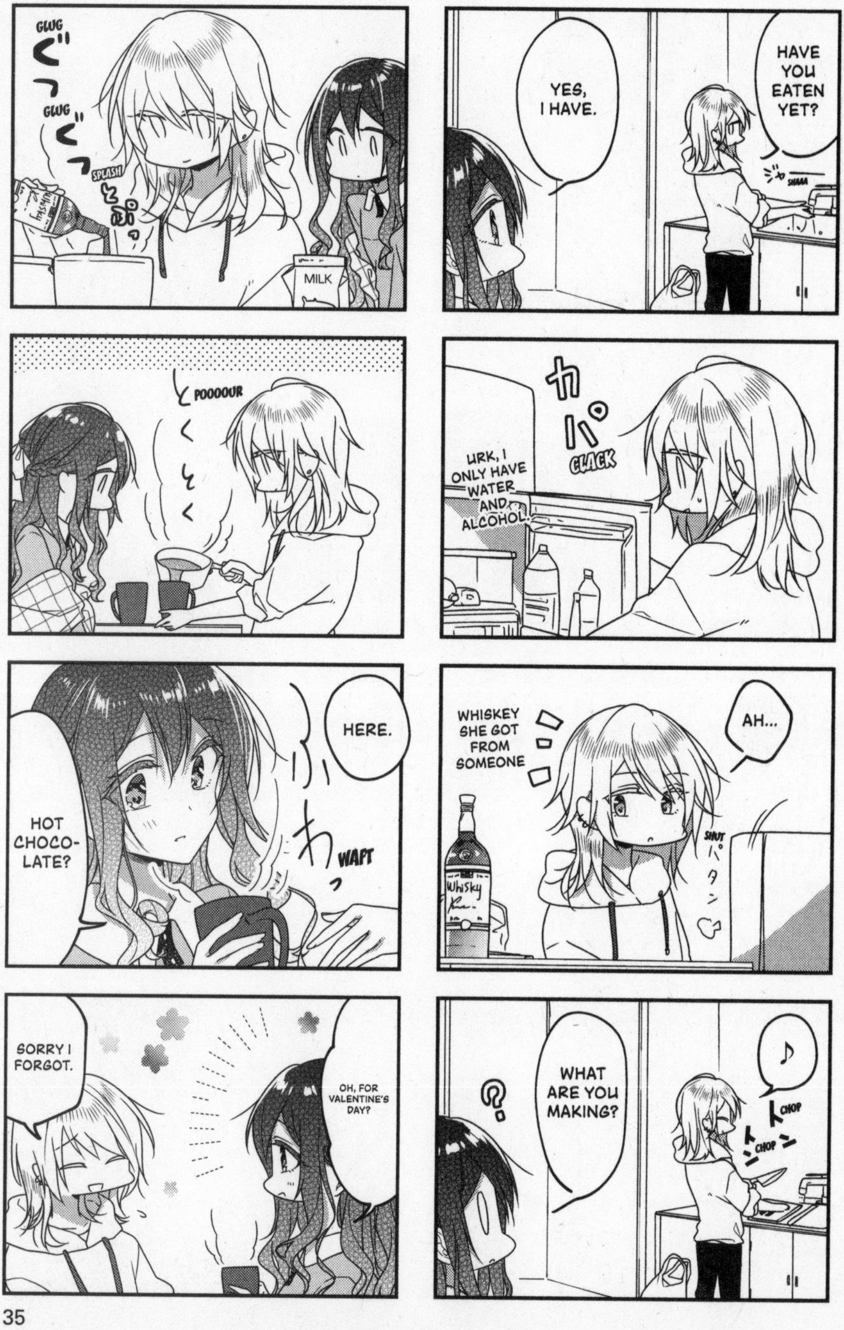
HAVE YOU EATEN YET?
SHAAA
YES, I HAVE.
GLUG
GLUG
SPLASH
Whisky
MILK
CLACK
URK, I ONLY HAVE WATER AND ALCOHOL.
POOOOUR
AH...
WHISKEY SHE GOT FROM SOMEONE
SHUT
Whisky
HERE.
WAFT
HOT CHOCO-LATE?
♪
CHOP
CHOP
WHAT ARE YOU MAKING?
?
OH, FOR VALENTINE'S DAY?
SORRY I FORGOT.

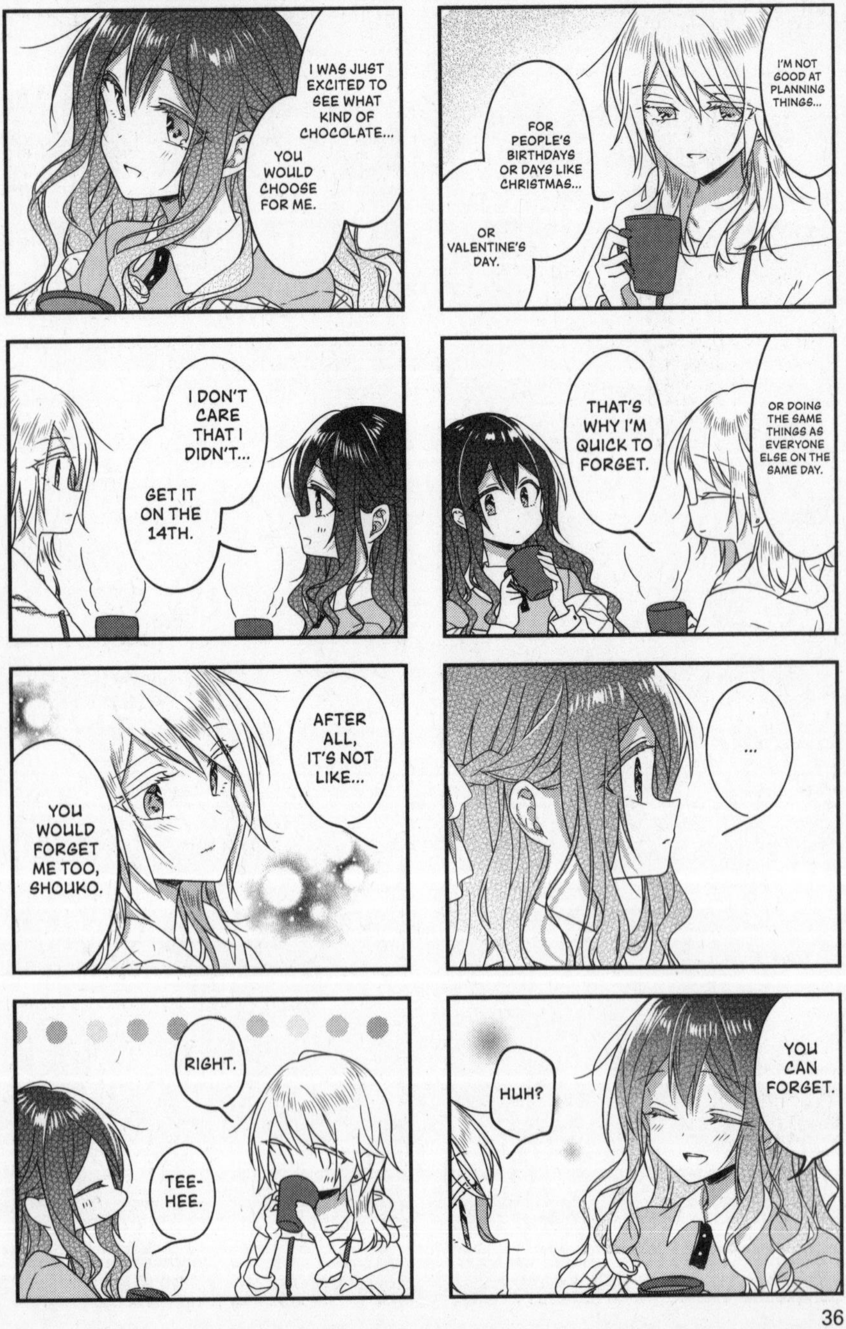
I'M NOT GOOD AT PLANNING THINGS...
FOR PEOPLE'S BIRTHDAYS OR DAYS LIKE CHRISTMAS...
OR VALENTINE'S DAY.
I WAS JUST EXCITED TO SEE WHAT KIND OF CHOCOLATE...
YOU WOULD CHOOSE FOR ME.
OR DOING THE SAME THINGS AS EVERYONE ELSE ON THE SAME DAY.
THAT'S WHY I'M QUICK TO FORGET.
I DON'T CARE THAT I DIDN'T...
GET IT ON THE 14TH.
...
AFTER ALL, IT'S NOT LIKE...
YOU WOULD FORGET ME TOO, SHOUKO.
YOU CAN FORGET.
HUH?
RIGHT.
TEE-HEE.

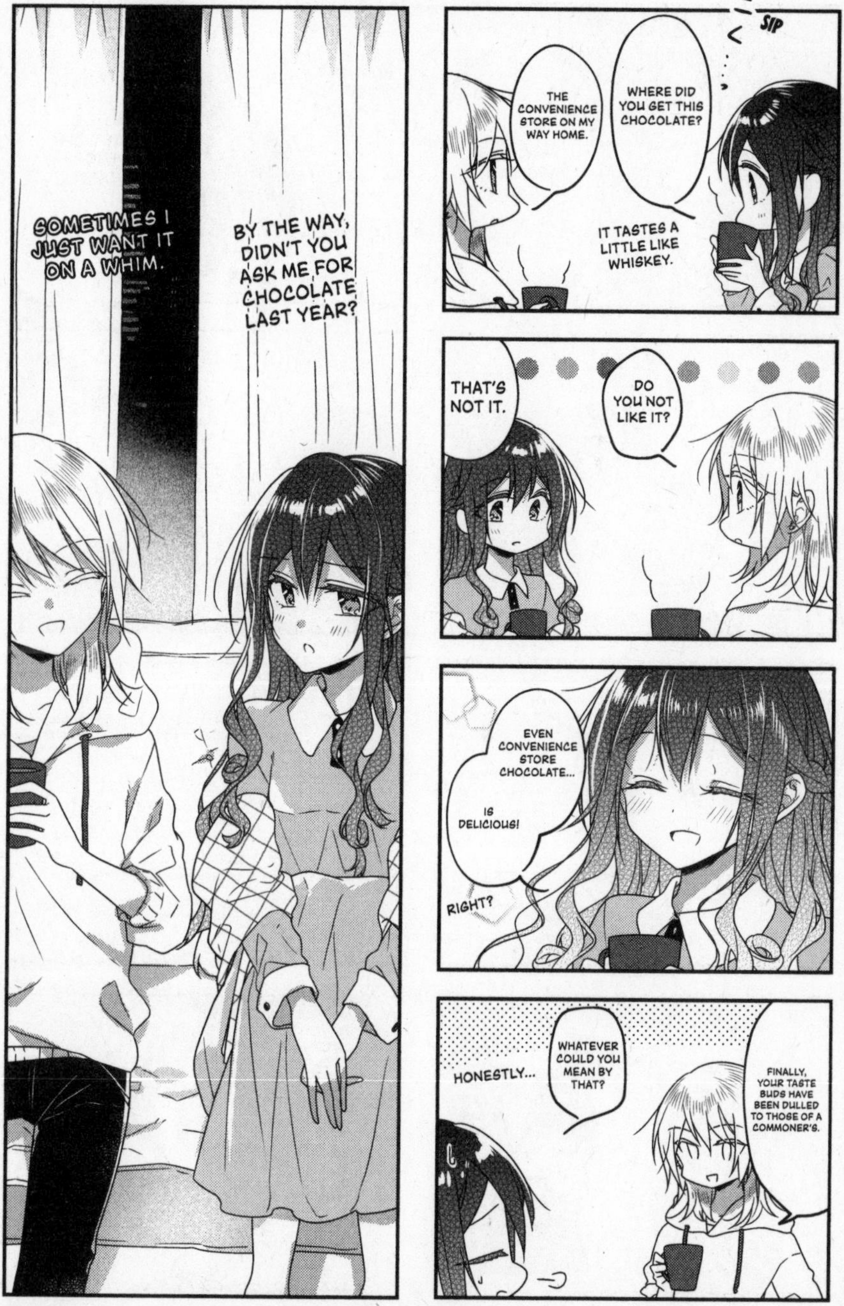
SIP
WHERE DID YOU GET THIS CHOCOLATE?
THE CONVENIENCE STORE ON MY WAY HOME.
IT TASTES A LITTLE LIKE WHISKEY.
DO YOU NOT LIKE IT?
THAT'S NOT IT.
EVEN CONVENIENCE STORE CHOCOLATE...
IS DELICIOUS!
RIGHT?
FINALLY, YOUR TASTE BUDS HAVE BEEN DULLED TO THOSE OF A COMMONER'S.
WHATEVER COULD YOU MEAN BY THAT?
HONESTLY...
BY THE WAY, DIDN'T YOU ASK ME FOR CHOCOLATE LAST YEAR?
SOMETIMES I JUST WANT IT ON A WHIM.

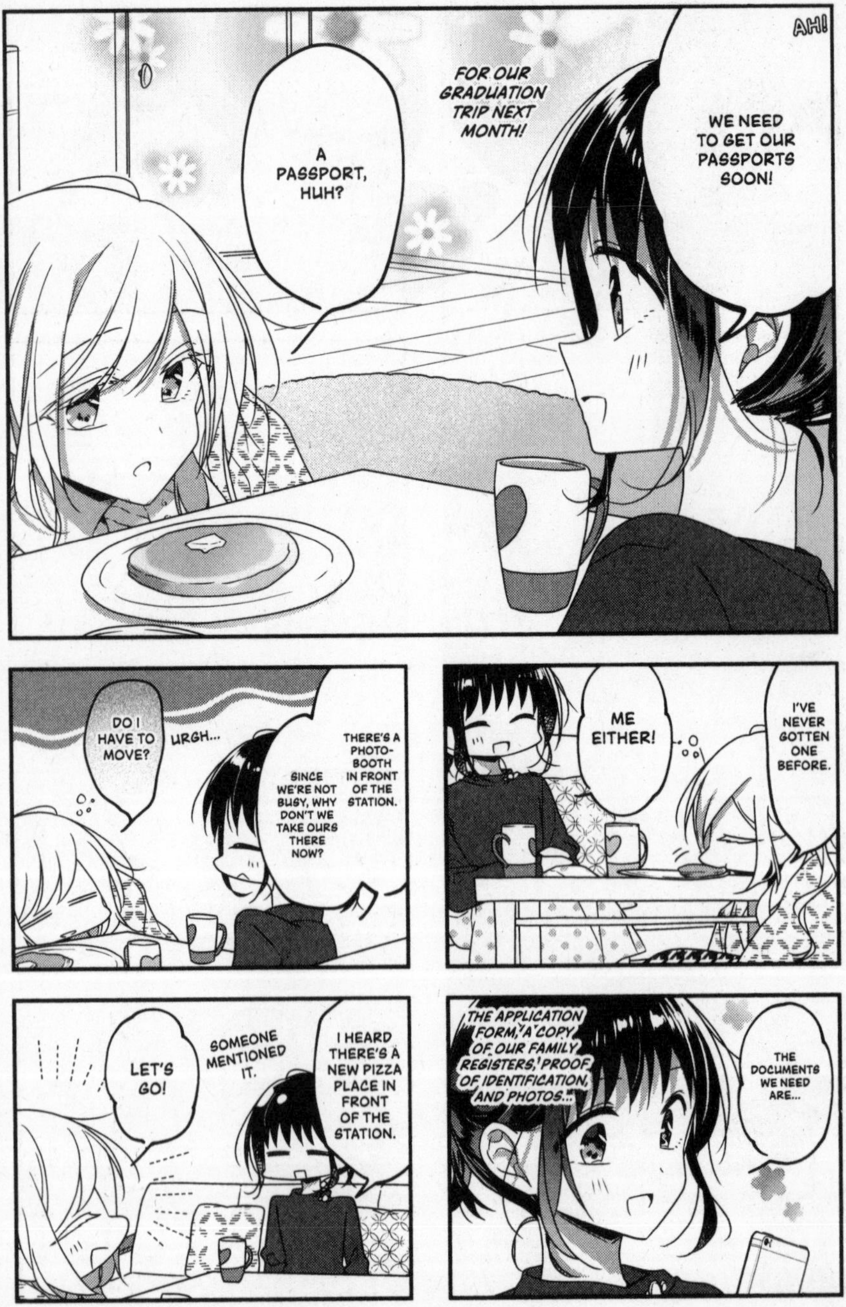
AH!
WE NEED TO GET OUR PASSPORTS SOON!
FOR OUR GRADUATION TRIP NEXT MONTH!
A PASSPORT, HUH?
I'VE NEVER GOTTEN ONE BEFORE.
ME EITHER!
THERE'S A PHOTO-BOOTH IN FRONT OF THE STATION.
SINCE WE'RE NOT BUSY, WHY DON'T WE TAKE OURS THERE NOW?
URGH...
DO I HAVE TO MOVE?
THE DOCUMENTS WE NEED ARE...
THE APPLICATION FORM, A COPY OF OUR FAMILY REGISTERS, PROOF OF IDENTIFICATION, AND PHOTOS...
I HEARD THERE'S A NEW PIZZA PLACE IN FRONT OF THE STATION.
SOMEONE MENTIONED IT.
LET'S GO!

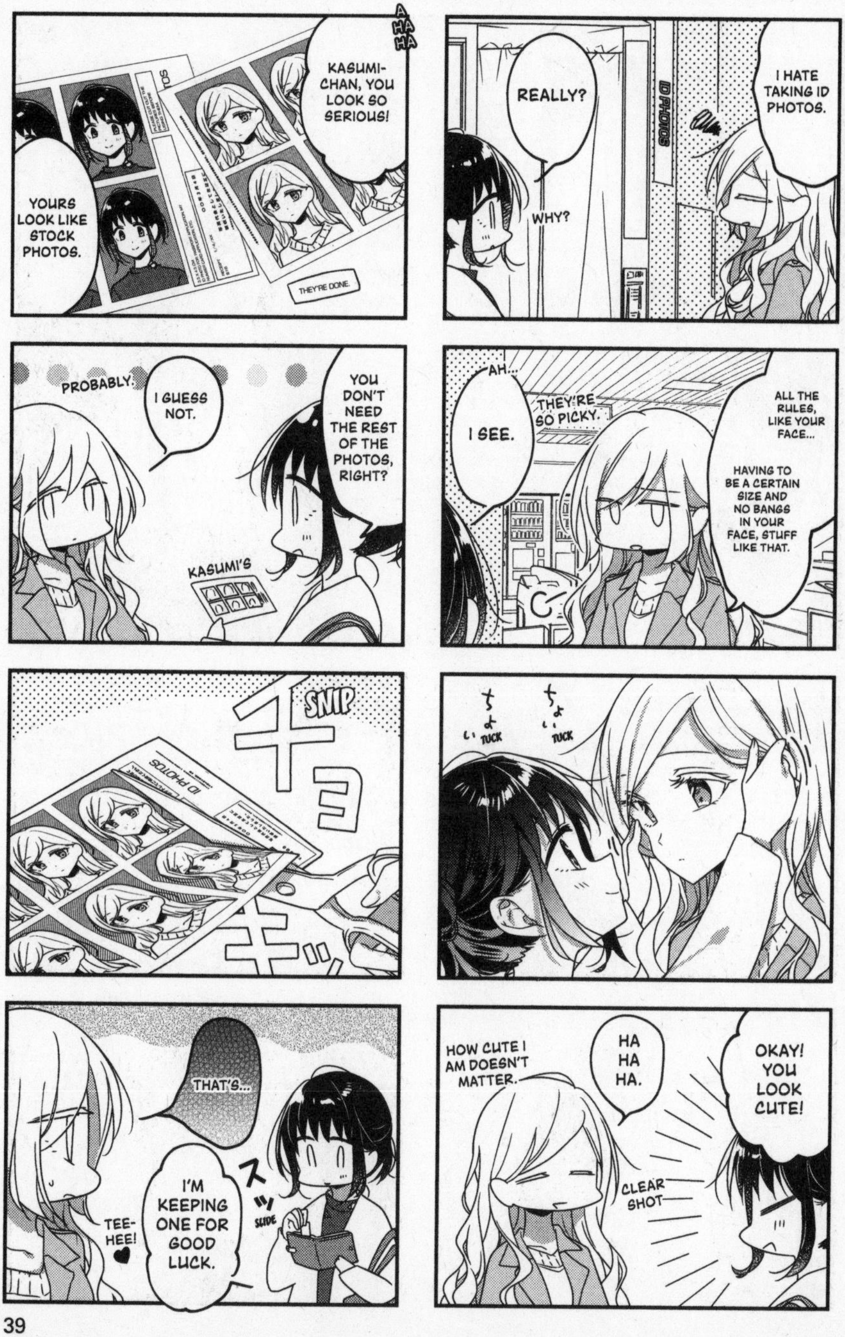
I HATE TAKING ID PHOTOS.
REALLY?
ID PHOTOS
WHY?
A HA HA
KASUMI-CHAN, YOU LOOK SO SERIOUS!
YOURS LOOK LIKE STOCK PHOTOS.
THEY'RE DONE.
ALL THE RULES, LIKE YOUR FACE...
HAVING TO BE A CERTAIN SIZE AND NO BANGS IN YOUR FACE, STUFF LIKE THAT.
THEY'RE SO PICKY.
AH...
I SEE.
YOU DON'T NEED THE REST OF THE PHOTOS, RIGHT?
I GUESS NOT.
PROBABLY.
KASUMI'S
ちょい TUCK
ちょい TUCK
SNIP
チョキッ
ID PHOTOS
OKAY! YOU LOOK CUTE!
HA HA HA.
HOW CUTE I AM DOESN'T MATTER.
CLEAR SHOT
THAT'S...
I'M KEEPING ONE FOR GOOD LUCK.
TEE-HEE!
スッ SLIDE

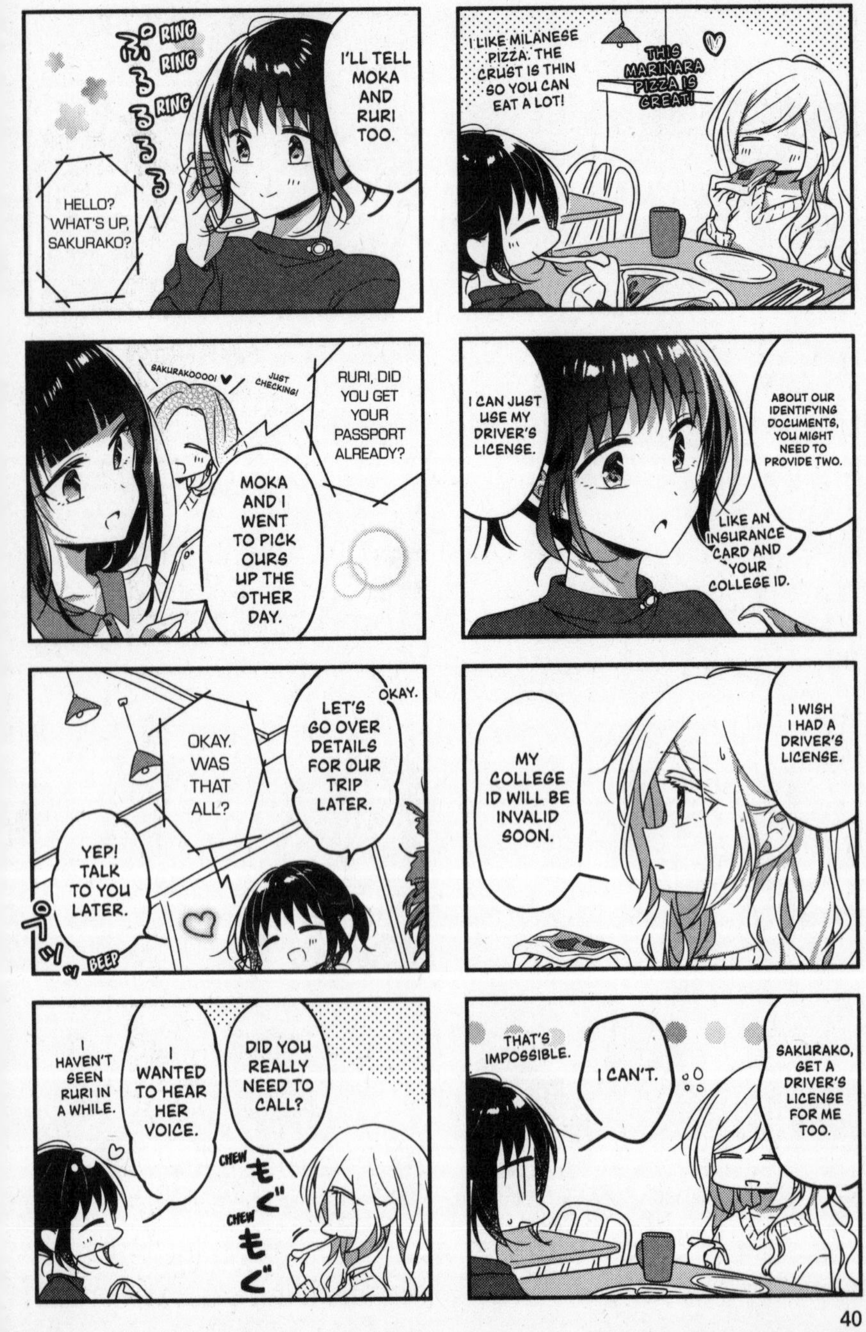
THIS MARINARA PIZZA IS GREAT!
I LIKE MILANESE PIZZA. THE CRUST IS THIN SO YOU CAN EAT A LOT!
ABOUT OUR IDENTIFYING DOCUMENTS, YOU MIGHT NEED TO PROVIDE TWO.
LIKE AN INSURANCE CARD AND YOUR COLLEGE ID.
I CAN JUST USE MY DRIVER'S LICENSE.
I WISH I HAD A DRIVER'S LICENSE.
MY COLLEGE ID WILL BE INVALID SOON.
SAKURAKO, GET A DRIVER'S LICENSE FOR ME TOO.
I CAN'T.
THAT'S IMPOSSIBLE.
I'LL TELL MOKA AND RURI TOO.
ぷるるる RING RING RING
HELLO? WHAT'S UP, SAKURAKO?
RURI, DID YOU GET YOUR PASSPORT ALREADY?
JUST CHECKING!
SAKURAKOOOO! ♥
MOKA AND I WENT TO PICK OURS UP THE OTHER DAY.
OKAY.
LET'S GO OVER DETAILS FOR OUR TRIP LATER.
OKAY. WAS THAT ALL?
YEP! TALK TO YOU LATER.
ピッ BEEP
DID YOU REALLY NEED TO CALL?
I WANTED TO HEAR HER VOICE.
I HAVEN'T SEEN RURI IN A WHILE.
もぐ CHEW もぐ CHEW

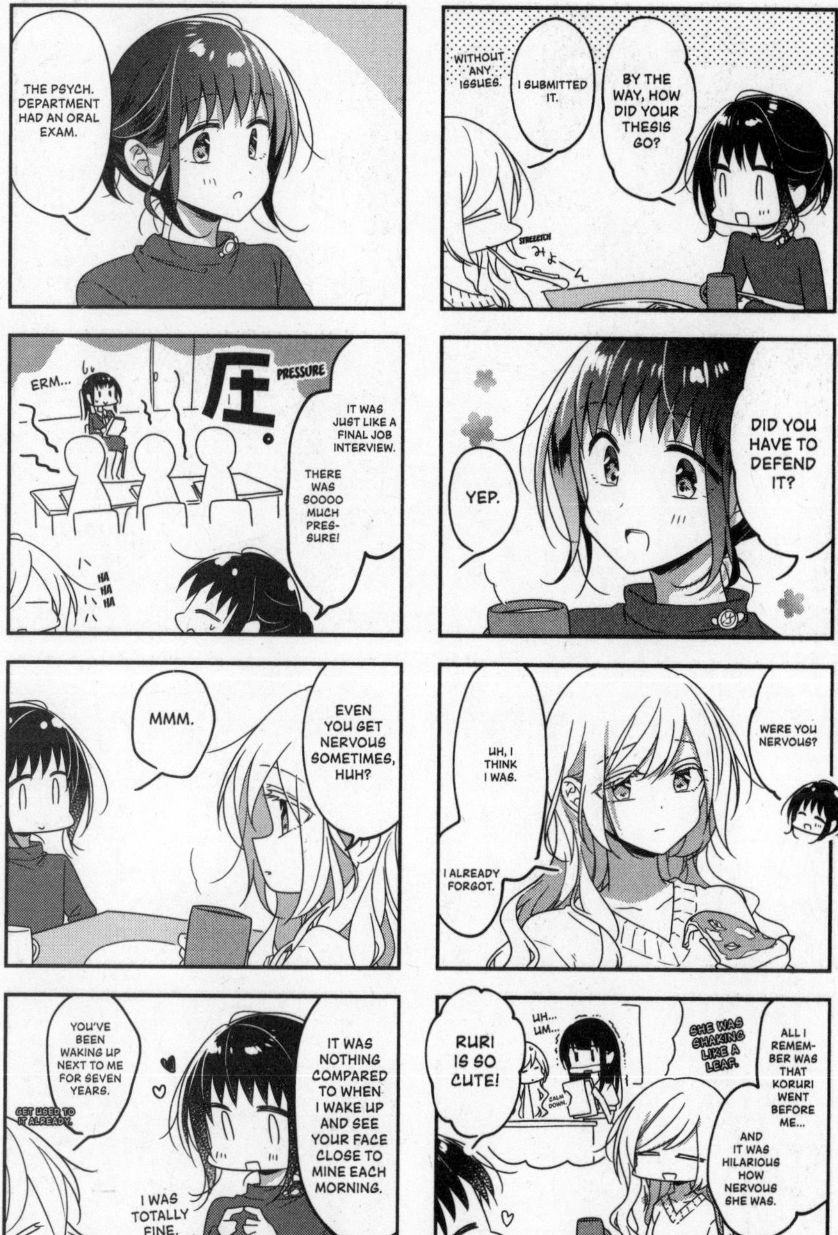
BY THE WAY, HOW DID YOUR THESIS GO?
I SUBMITTED IT.
WITHOUT ANY ISSUES.
STREEETCH
みよ〜ん
THE PSYCH. DEPARTMENT HAD AN ORAL EXAM.
DID YOU HAVE TO DEFEND IT?
YEP.
IT WAS JUST LIKE A FINAL JOB INTERVIEW.
THERE WAS SOOOO MUCH PRES-SURE!
PRESSURE
圧
ERM...
HA HA HA
WERE YOU NERVOUS?
UH, I THINK I WAS.
I ALREADY FORGOT.
EVEN YOU GET NERVOUS SOMETIMES, HUH?
MMM.
ALL I REMEM-BER WAS THAT KORURI WENT BEFORE ME...
SHE WAS SHAKING LIKE A LEAF.
AND IT WAS HILARIOUS HOW NERVOUS SHE WAS.
UH... UM...
CALM DOWN.
RURI IS SO CUTE!
IT WAS NOTHING COMPARED TO WHEN I WAKE UP AND SEE YOUR FACE CLOSE TO MINE EACH MORNING.
YOU'VE BEEN WAKING UP NEXT TO ME FOR SEVEN YEARS.
GET USED TO IT ALREADY.
I WAS TOTALLY FINE.

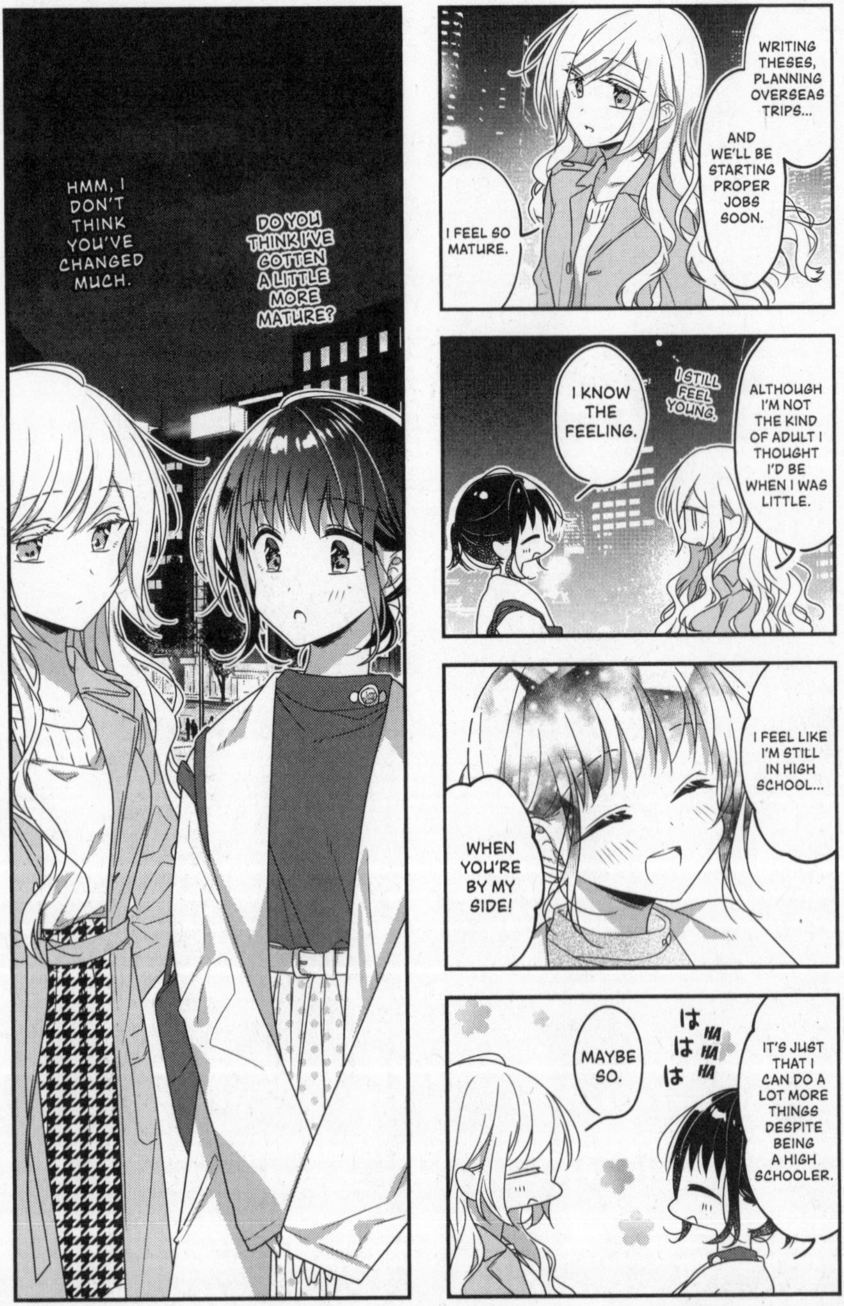
WRITING THESES, PLANNING OVERSEAS TRIPS...
AND WE'LL BE STARTING PROPER JOBS SOON.
I FEEL SO MATURE.
ALTHOUGH I'M NOT THE KIND OF ADULT I THOUGHT I'D BE WHEN I WAS LITTLE.
I STILL FEEL YOUNG.
I KNOW THE FEELING.
I FEEL LIKE I'M STILL IN HIGH SCHOOL...
WHEN YOU'RE BY MY SIDE!
IT'S JUST THAT I CAN DO A LOT MORE THINGS DESPITE BEING A HIGH SCHOOLER.
ははは HA HA HA
MAYBE SO.
DO YOU THINK I'VE GOTTEN A LITTLE MORE MATURE?
HMM, I DON'T THINK YOU'VE CHANGED MUCH.

Illustration gallery of Yukiko

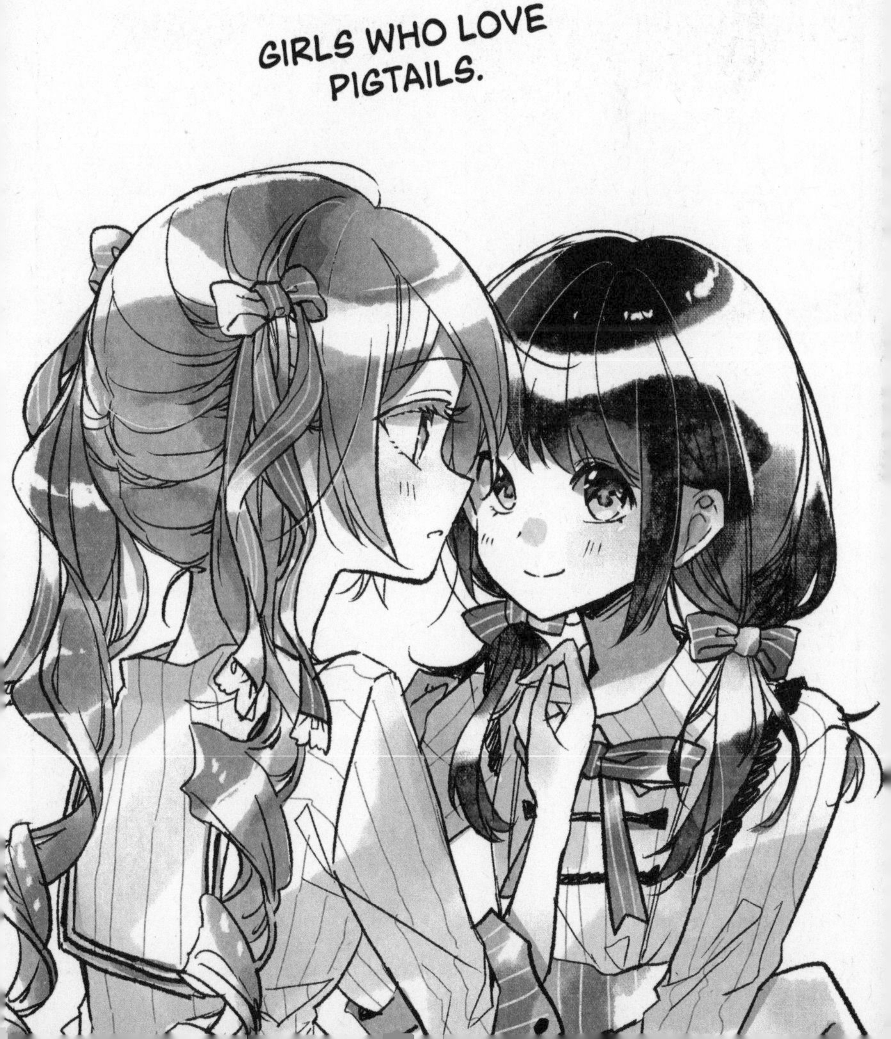
GIRLS WHO LOVE PIGTAILS.

Futaribeya
A ROOM FOR TWO

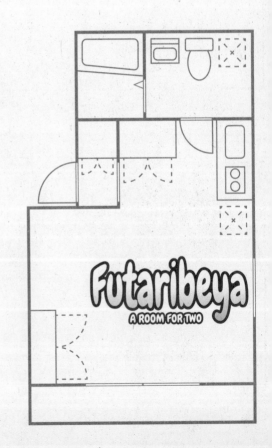

Chapter 70

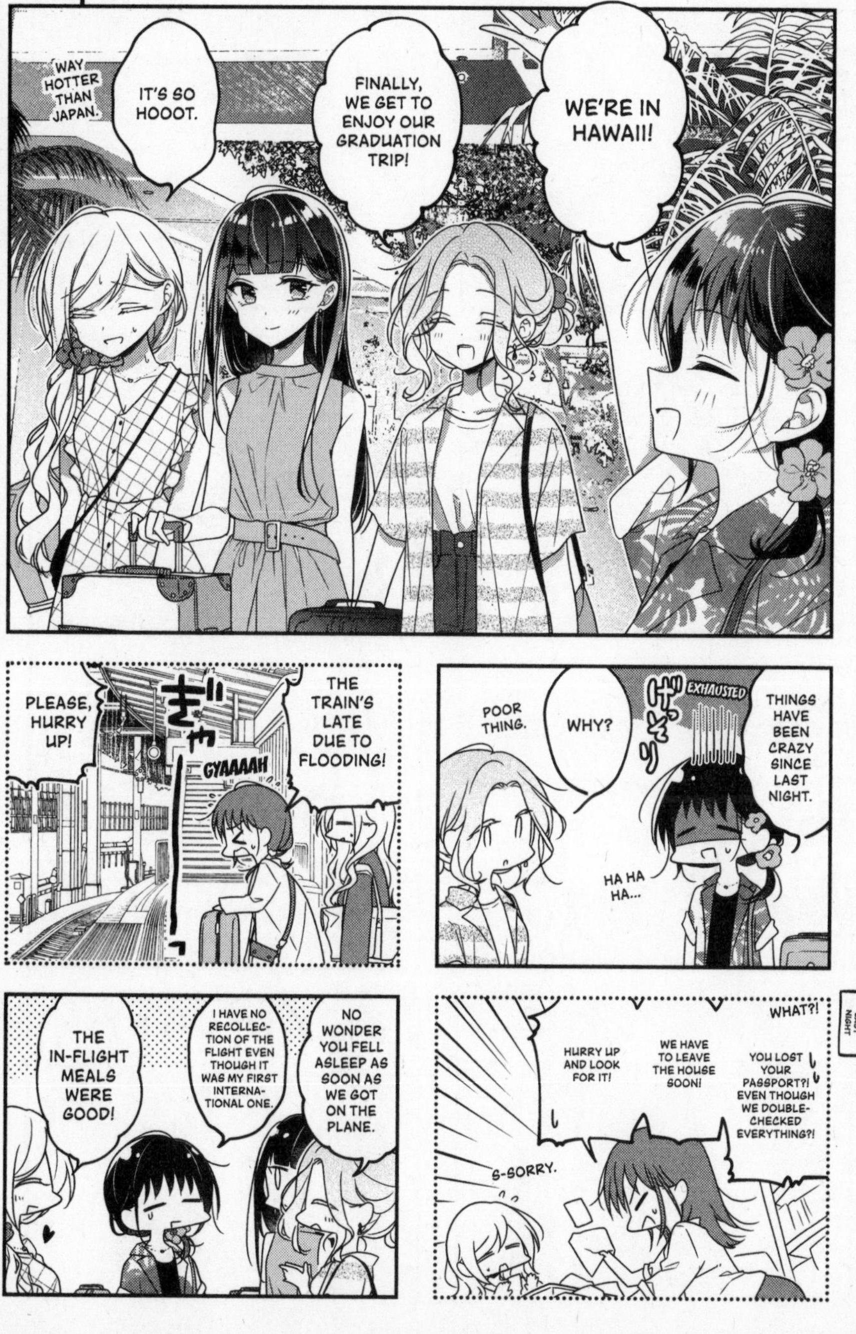
WE'RE IN HAWAII!
FINALLY, WE GET TO ENJOY OUR GRADUATION TRIP!
IT'S SO HOOOT.
WAY HOTTER THAN JAPAN.
THINGS HAVE BEEN CRAZY SINCE LAST NIGHT.
EXHAUSTED
WHY?
POOR THING.
HA HA HA...
THE TRAIN'S LATE DUE TO FLOODING!
GYAAAAH
PLEASE, HURRY UP!
LAST NIGHT
WHAT?!
YOU LOST YOUR PASSPORT?! EVEN THOUGH WE DOUBLE-CHECKED EVERYTHING?!
WE HAVE TO LEAVE THE HOUSE SOON!
HURRY UP AND LOOK FOR IT!
S-SORRY.
NO WONDER YOU FELL ASLEEP AS SOON AS WE GOT ON THE PLANE.
I HAVE NO RECOLLECTION OF THE FLIGHT EVEN THOUGH IT WAS MY FIRST INTERNATIONAL ONE.
THE IN-FLIGHT MEALS WERE GOOD!

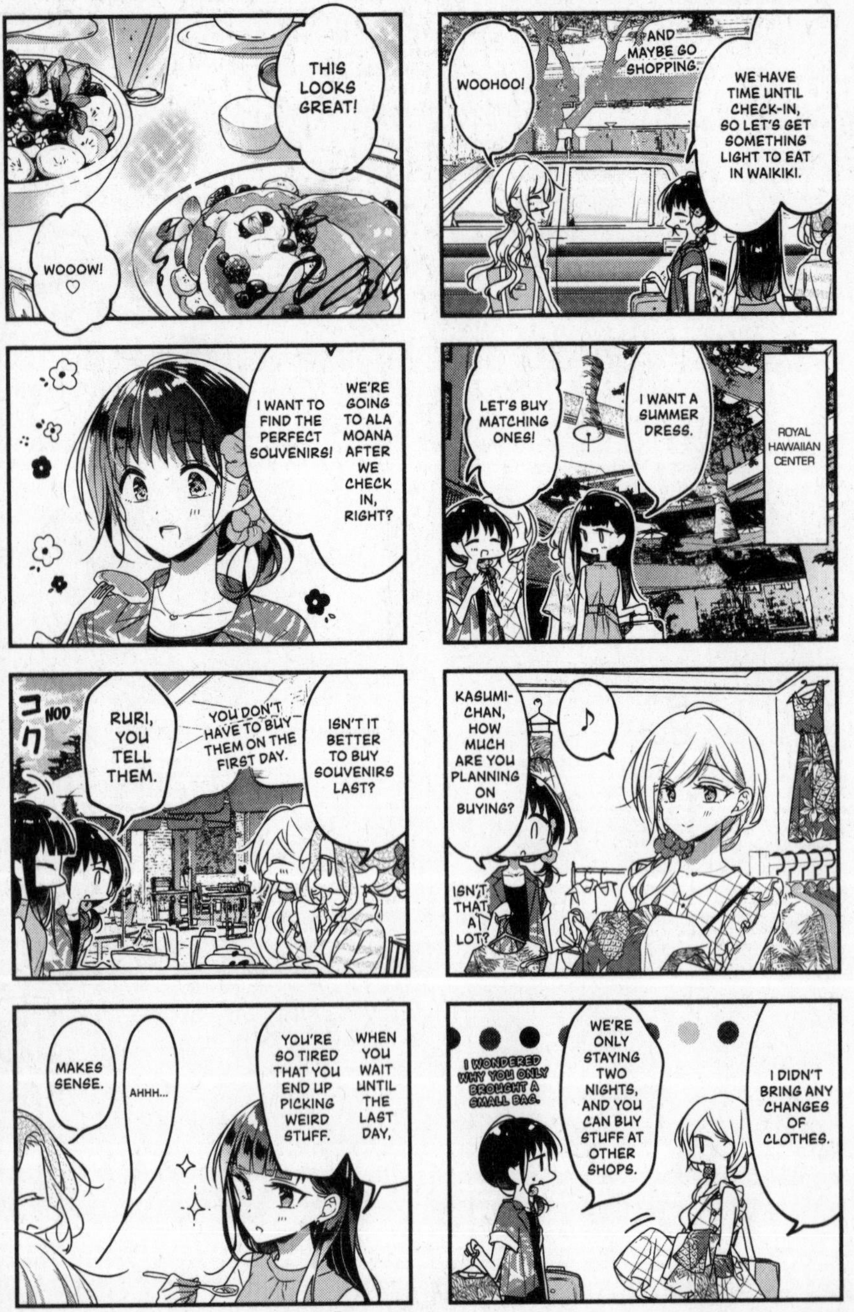
WE HAVE TIME UNTIL CHECK-IN, SO LET'S GET SOMETHING LIGHT TO EAT IN WAIKIKI.
AND MAYBE GO SHOPPING.
WOOHOO!
THIS LOOKS GREAT!
WOOOW! ♡
ROYAL HAWAIIAN CENTER
I WANT A SUMMER DRESS.
LET'S BUY MATCHING ONES!
WE'RE GOING TO ALA MOANA AFTER WE CHECK IN, RIGHT?
I WANT TO FIND THE PERFECT SOUVENIRS!
♪
KASUMI-CHAN, HOW MUCH ARE YOU PLANNING ON BUYING?
ISN'T THAT A LOT?
ISN'T IT BETTER TO BUY SOUVENIRS LAST?
YOU DON'T HAVE TO BUY THEM ON THE FIRST DAY.
RURI, YOU TELL THEM.
コク NOD
I DIDN'T BRING ANY CHANGES OF CLOTHES.
WE'RE ONLY STAYING TWO NIGHTS, AND YOU CAN BUY STUFF AT OTHER SHOPS.
I WONDERED WHY YOU ONLY BROUGHT A SMALL BAG.
WHEN YOU WAIT UNTIL THE LAST DAY,
YOU'RE SO TIRED THAT YOU END UP PICKING WEIRD STUFF.
AHHH...
MAKES SENSE.

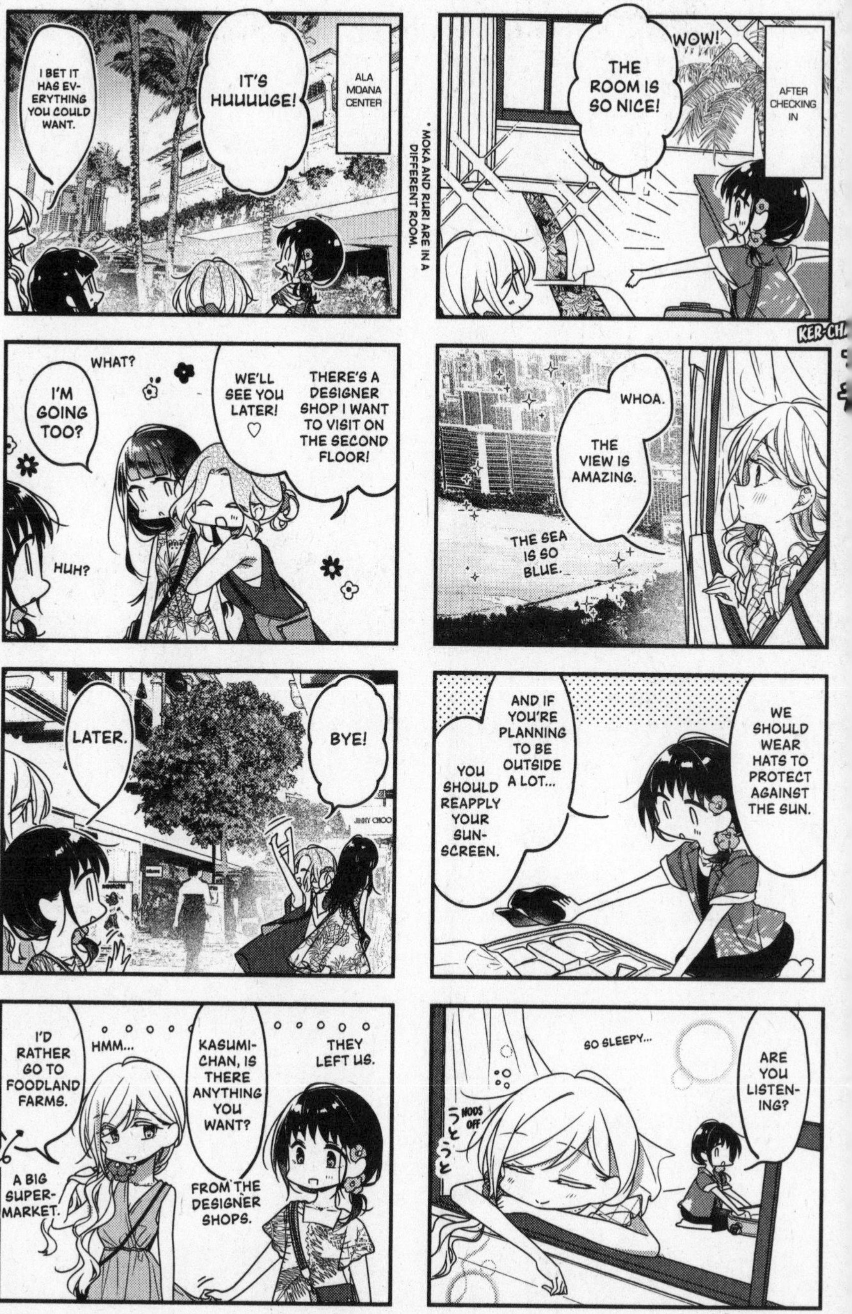
AFTER CHECKING IN
WOW!
THE ROOM IS SO NICE!
KER-CHA
* MOKA AND RURI ARE IN A DIFFERENT ROOM.
WHOA.
THE VIEW IS AMAZING.
THE SEA IS SO BLUE.
WE SHOULD WEAR HATS TO PROTECT AGAINST THE SUN.
AND IF YOU'RE PLANNING TO BE OUTSIDE A LOT...
YOU SHOULD REAPPLY YOUR SUN-SCREEN.
ARE YOU LISTEN-ING?
SO SLEEPY...
NODS OFF
うとうと
ALA MOANA CENTER
IT'S HUUUUGE!
I BET IT HAS EV-ERYTHING YOU COULD WANT.
THERE'S A DESIGNER SHOP I WANT TO VISIT ON THE SECOND FLOOR!
WE'LL SEE YOU LATER! ♡
WHAT?
I'M GOING TOO?
HUH?
BYE!
LATER.
THEY LEFT US.
KASUMI-CHAN, IS THERE ANYTHING YOU WANT?
FROM THE DESIGNER SHOPS.
HMM...
I'D RATHER GO TO FOODLAND FARMS.
A BIG SUPER-MARKET.

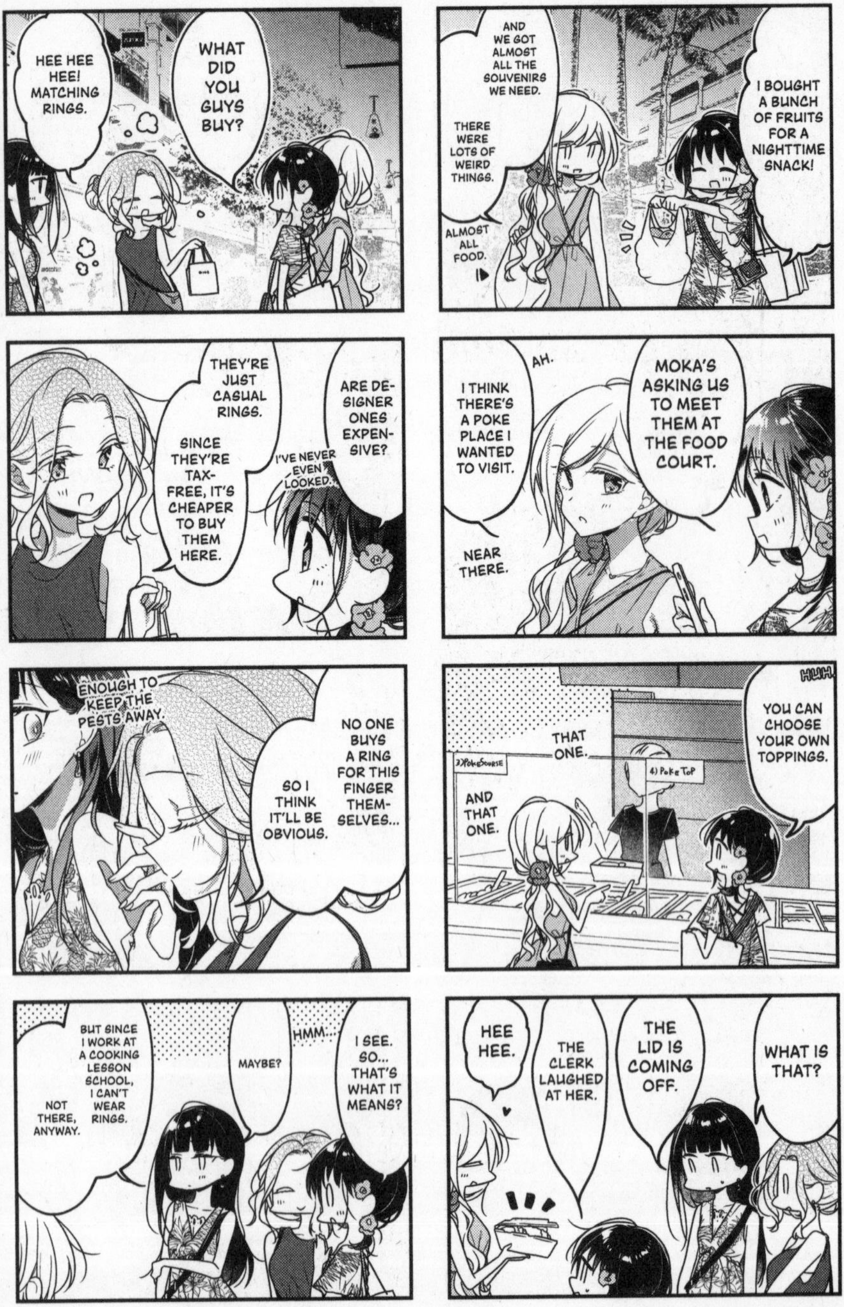
I BOUGHT A BUNCH OF FRUITS FOR A NIGHTTIME SNACK!
AND WE GOT ALMOST ALL THE SOUVENIRS WE NEED.
THERE WERE LOTS OF WEIRD THINGS.
ALMOST ALL FOOD.
WHAT DID YOU GUYS BUY?
HEE HEE HEE! MATCHING RINGS.
MOKA'S ASKING US TO MEET THEM AT THE FOOD COURT.
AH.
I THINK THERE'S A POKE PLACE I WANTED TO VISIT.
NEAR THERE.
ARE DESIGNER ONES EXPENSIVE?
I'VE NEVER EVEN LOOKED.
THEY'RE JUST CASUAL RINGS.
SINCE THEY'RE TAX-FREE, IT'S CHEAPER TO BUY THEM HERE.
HUH.
YOU CAN CHOOSE YOUR OWN TOPPINGS.
THAT ONE.
4) PokeTop
3) PokeSourse
AND THAT ONE.
NO ONE BUYS A RING FOR THIS FINGER THEMSELVES...
SO I THINK IT'LL BE OBVIOUS.
ENOUGH TO KEEP THE PESTS AWAY.
WHAT IS THAT?
THE LID IS COMING OFF.
THE CLERK LAUGHED AT HER.
HEE HEE.
I SEE. SO... THAT'S WHAT IT MEANS?
HMM...
MAYBE?
BUT SINCE I WORK AT A COOKING LESSON SCHOOL, I CAN'T WEAR RINGS.
NOT THERE, ANYWAY.

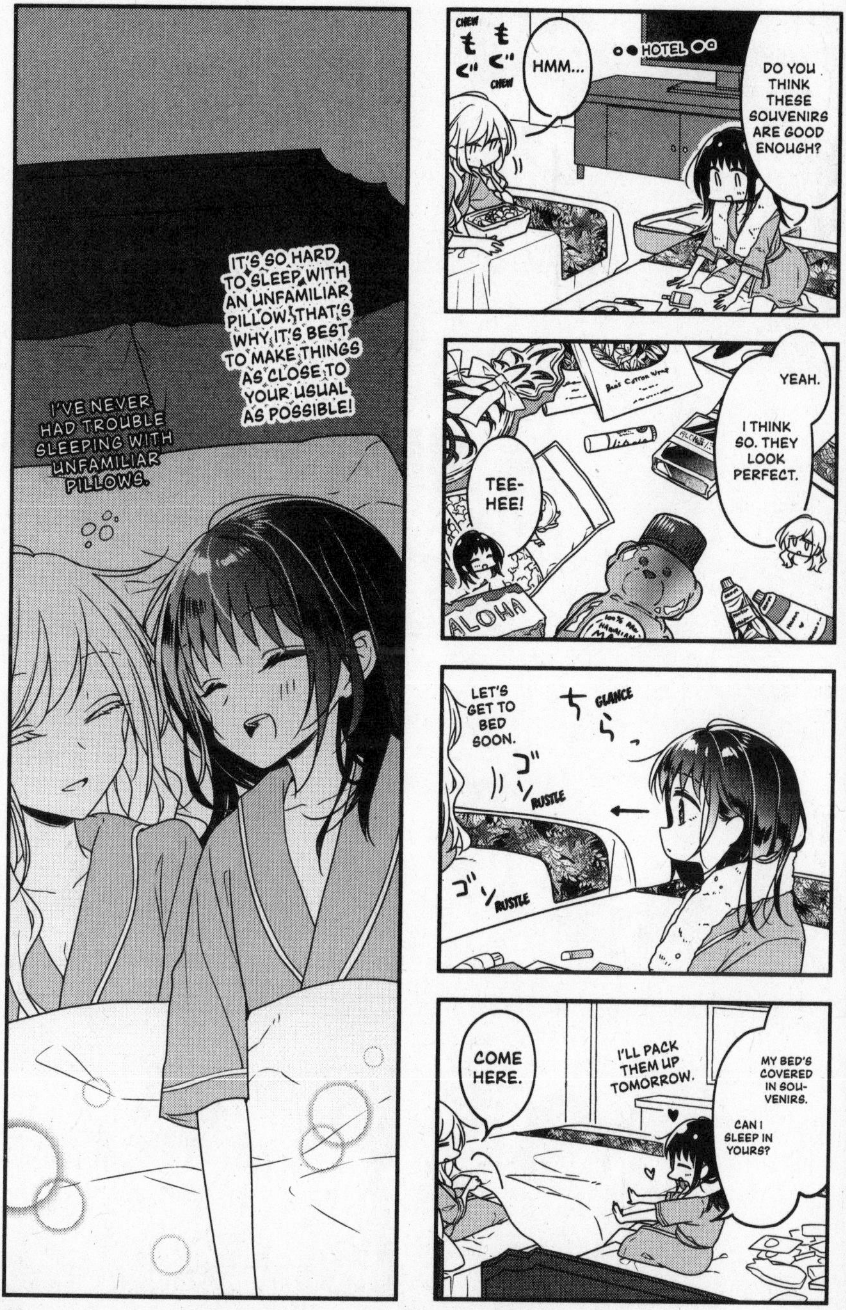
DO YOU THINK THESE SOUVENIRS ARE GOOD ENOUGH?
HOTEL
HMM...
CHEW もぐ
CHEW もぐ
YEAH.
I THINK SO. THEY LOOK PERFECT.
TEE-HEE!
ALOHA
ちらっ GLANCE
LET'S GET TO BED SOON.
ゴソ RUSTLE
ゴソ RUSTLE
MY BED'S COVERED IN SOU-VENIRS.
CAN I SLEEP IN YOURS?
I'LL PACK THEM UP TOMORROW.
COME HERE.
IT'S SO HARD TO SLEEP WITH AN UNFAMILIAR PILLOW. THAT'S WHY IT'S BEST TO MAKE THINGS AS CLOSE TO YOUR USUAL AS POSSIBLE!
I'VE NEVER HAD TROUBLE SLEEPING WITH UNFAMILIAR PILLOWS.

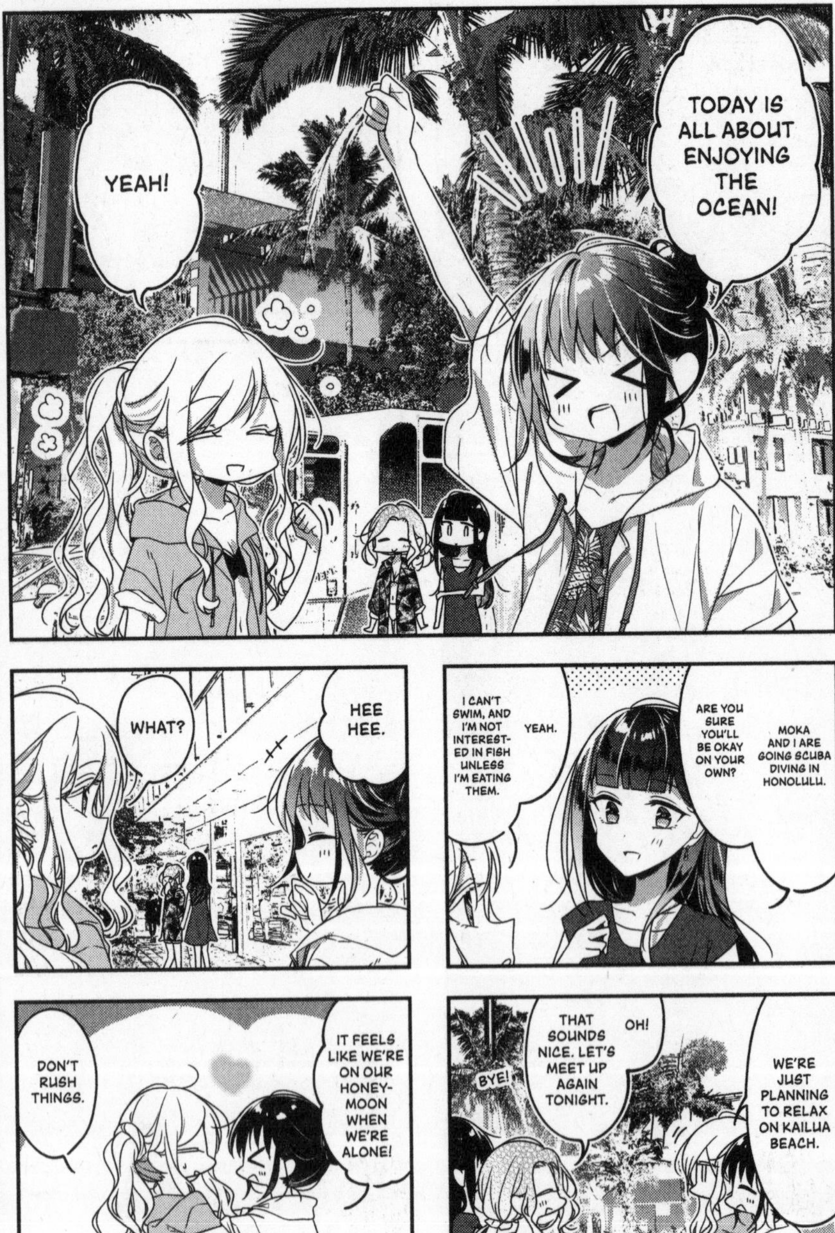
TODAY IS ALL ABOUT ENJOYING THE OCEAN!
YEAH!
MOKA AND I ARE GOING SCUBA DIVING IN HONOLULU.
ARE YOU SURE YOU'LL BE OKAY ON YOUR OWN?
YEAH.
I CAN'T SWIM, AND I'M NOT INTEREST-ED IN FISH UNLESS I'M EATING THEM.
HEE HEE.
WHAT?
WE'RE JUST PLANNING TO RELAX ON KAILUA BEACH.
OH!
THAT SOUNDS NICE. LET'S MEET UP AGAIN TONIGHT.
BYE!
IT FEELS LIKE WE'RE ON OUR HONEY-MOON WHEN WE'RE ALONE!
DON'T RUSH THINGS.

CAME BY BUS.

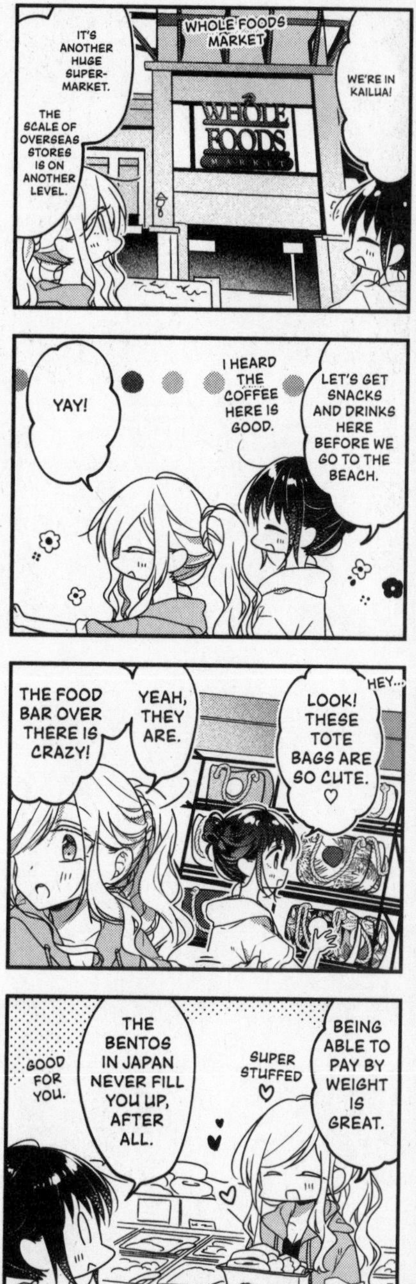
WE'RE IN KAILUA!
WHOLE FOODS MARKET
WHOLE FOODS MARKET
IT'S ANOTHER HUGE SUPER-MARKET.
THE SCALE OF OVERSEAS STORES IS ON ANOTHER LEVEL.
LET'S GET SNACKS AND DRINKS HERE BEFORE WE GO TO THE BEACH.
I HEARD THE COFFEE HERE IS GOOD.
YAY!
HEY...
LOOK! THESE TOTE BAGS ARE SO CUTE. ♡
YEAH, THEY ARE.
THE FOOD BAR OVER THERE IS CRAZY!
BEING ABLE TO PAY BY WEIGHT IS GREAT.
SUPER STUFFED ♡
THE BENTOS IN JAPAN NEVER FILL YOU UP, AFTER ALL.
GOOD FOR YOU.

I'M NOT SURE WHAT IT IS.

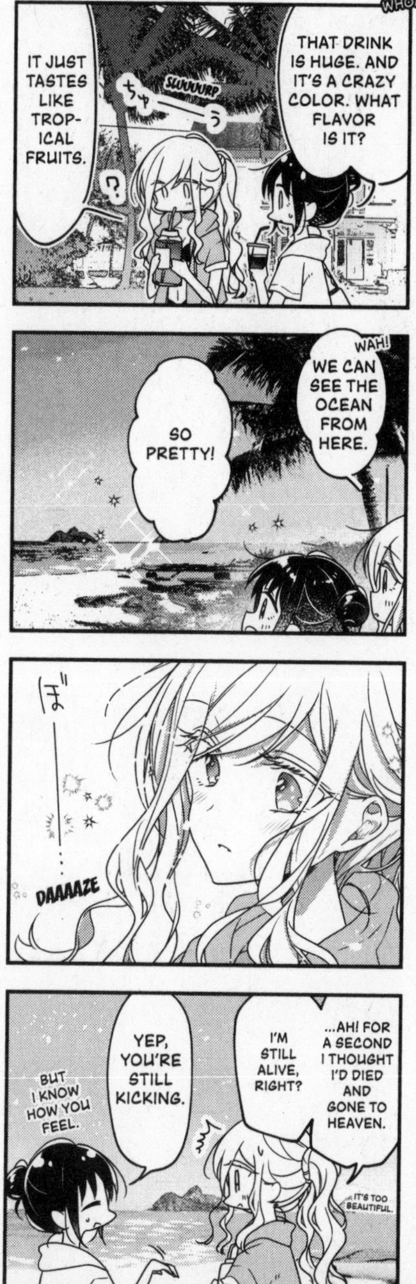
WHOA.
THAT DRINK IS HUGE. AND IT'S A CRAZY COLOR. WHAT FLAVOR IS IT?
SLUUUURP
ちゅーう
?
IT JUST TASTES LIKE TROP-ICAL FRUITS.
WAH!
WE CAN SEE THE OCEAN FROM HERE.
SO PRETTY!
ぼーー…
DAAAAZE
...AH! FOR A SECOND I THOUGHT I'D DIED AND GONE TO HEAVEN.
I'M STILL ALIVE, RIGHT?
IT'S TOO BEAUTIFUL.
YEP, YOU'RE STILL KICKING.
BUT I KNOW HOW YOU FEEL.

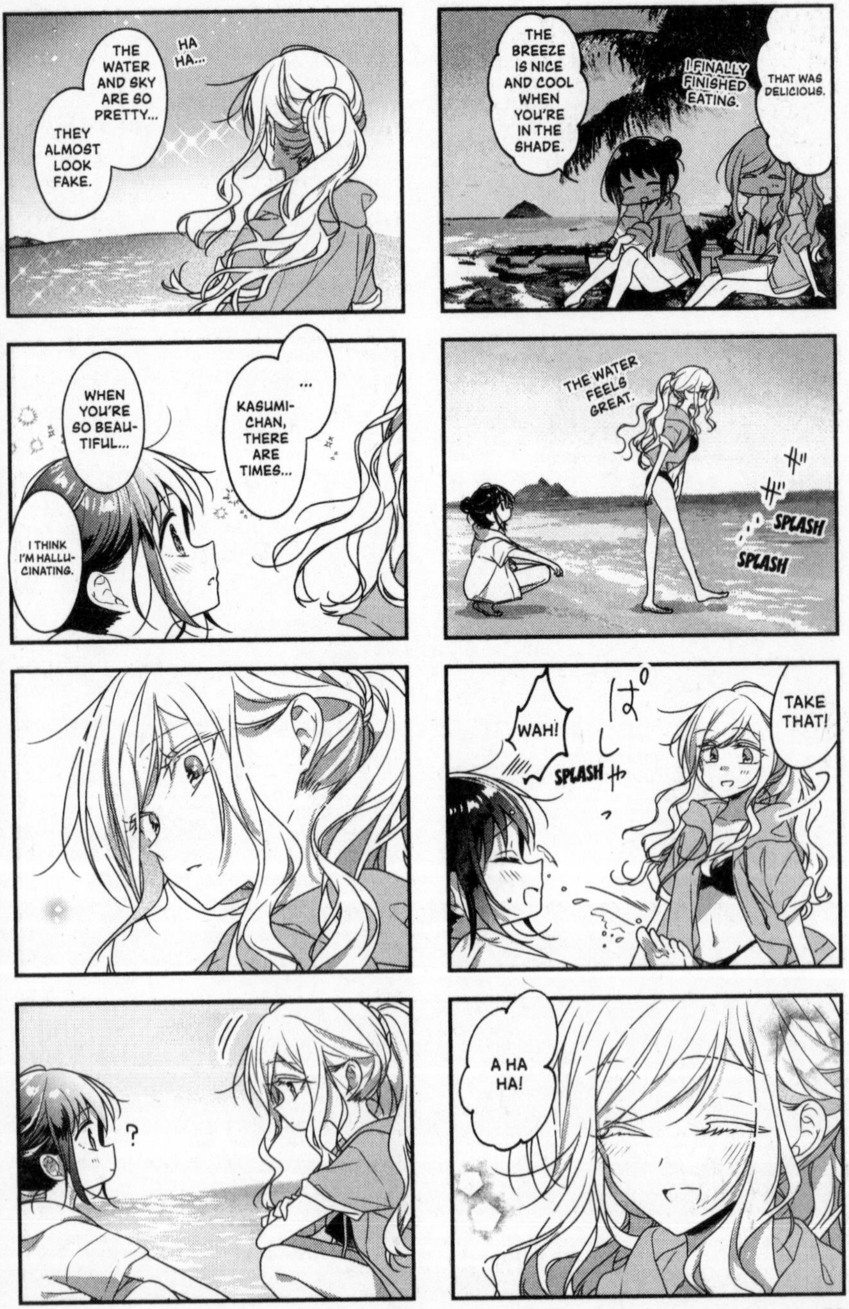

THAT WAS DELICIOUS.
I FINALLY FINISHED EATING.
THE BREEZE IS NICE AND COOL WHEN YOU'RE IN THE SHADE.
HA HA...
THE WATER AND SKY ARE SO PRETTY...
THEY ALMOST LOOK FAKE.
THE WATER FEELS GREAT.
SPLASH
SPLASH
...
KASUMI-CHAN, THERE ARE TIMES...
WHEN YOU'RE SO BEAU-TIFUL...
I THINK I'M HALLU-CINATING.
TAKE THAT!
ぱしゃっ
WAH!
SPLASH
A HA HA!
?

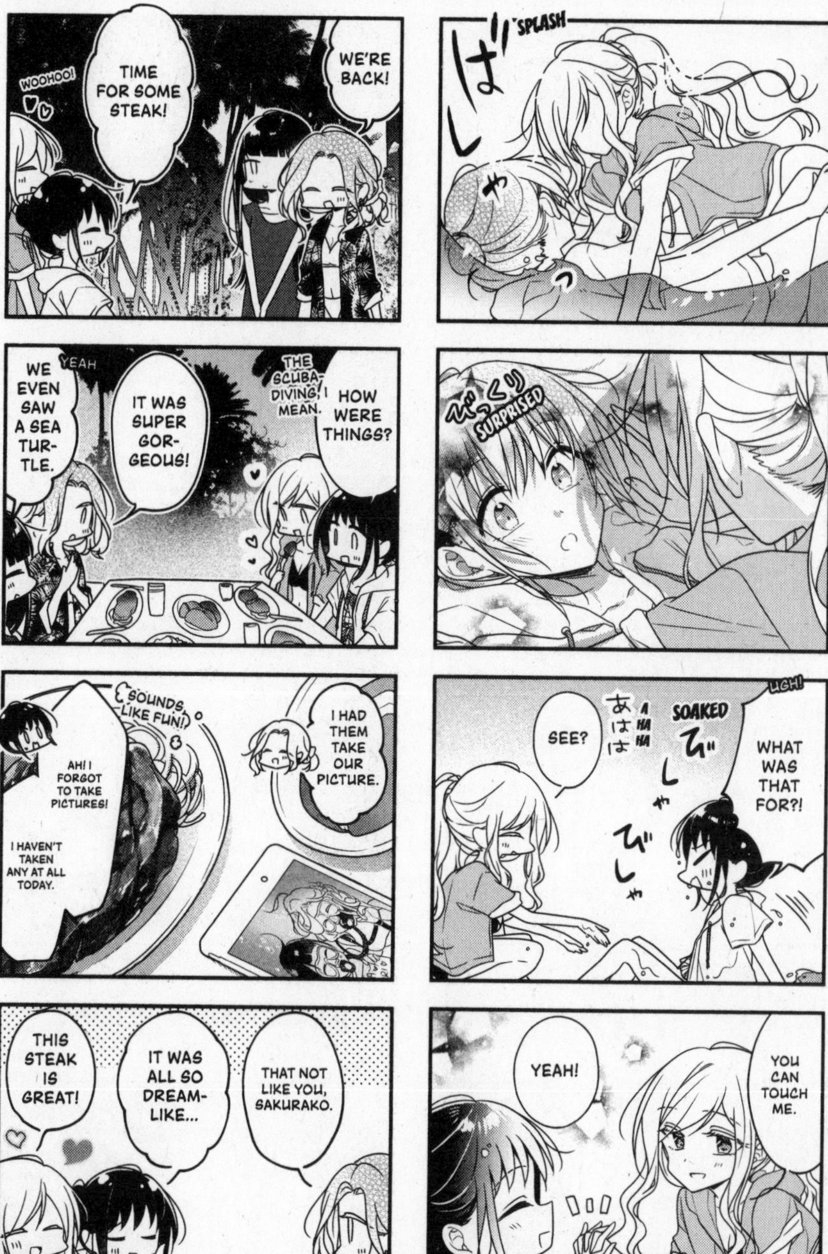
ばしゃ
SPLASH
SURPRISED
UGH!
WHAT WAS THAT FOR?!
SOAKED
びしゃ
びしゃ
あはは
A HA HA
SEE?
YOU CAN TOUCH ME.
YEAH!
WE'RE BACK!
TIME FOR SOME STEAK!
WOOHOO!
HOW WERE THINGS?
THE SCUBA-DIVING, I MEAN.
IT WAS SUPER GORGEOUS!
WE EVEN SAW A SEA TURTLE.
YEAH
I HAD THEM TAKE OUR PICTURE.
SOUNDS LIKE FUN!
AH! I FORGOT TO TAKE PICTURES!
I HAVEN'T TAKEN ANY AT ALL TODAY.
THAT NOT LIKE YOU, SAKURAKO.
IT WAS ALL SO DREAM-LIKE...
THIS STEAK IS GREAT!

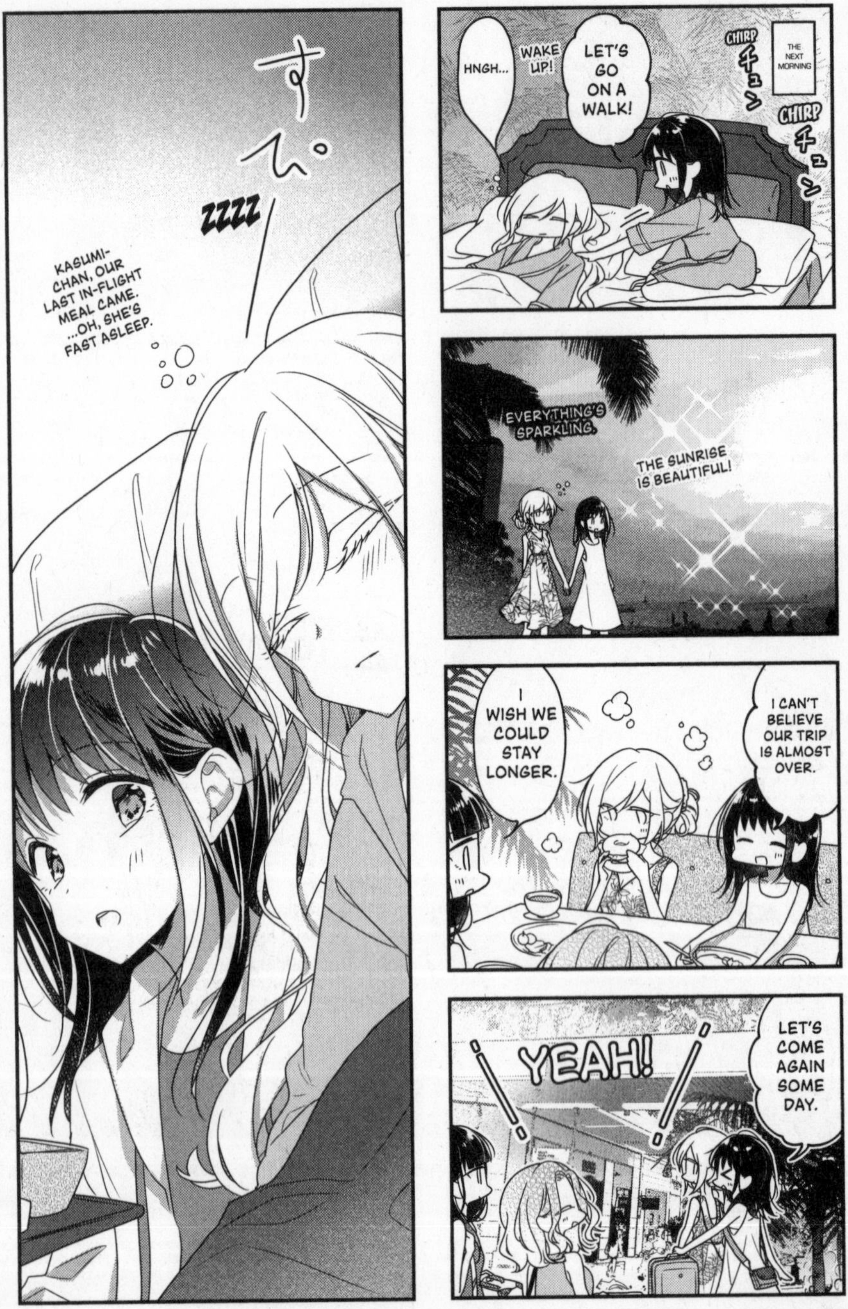

THE NEXT MORNING
CHIRP チュン
CHIRP チュン
LET'S GO ON A WALK!
WAKE UP!
HNGH...
THE SUNRISE IS BEAUTIFUL!
EVERYTHING'S SPARKLING.
I CAN'T BELIEVE OUR TRIP IS ALMOST OVER.
I WISH WE COULD STAY LONGER.
LET'S COME AGAIN SOME DAY.
YEAH!
すぴ
ZZZZ
KASUMI-CHAN, OUR LAST IN-FLIGHT MEAL CAME. ...OH, SHE'S FAST ASLEEP.

Illustration gallery of Yukiko

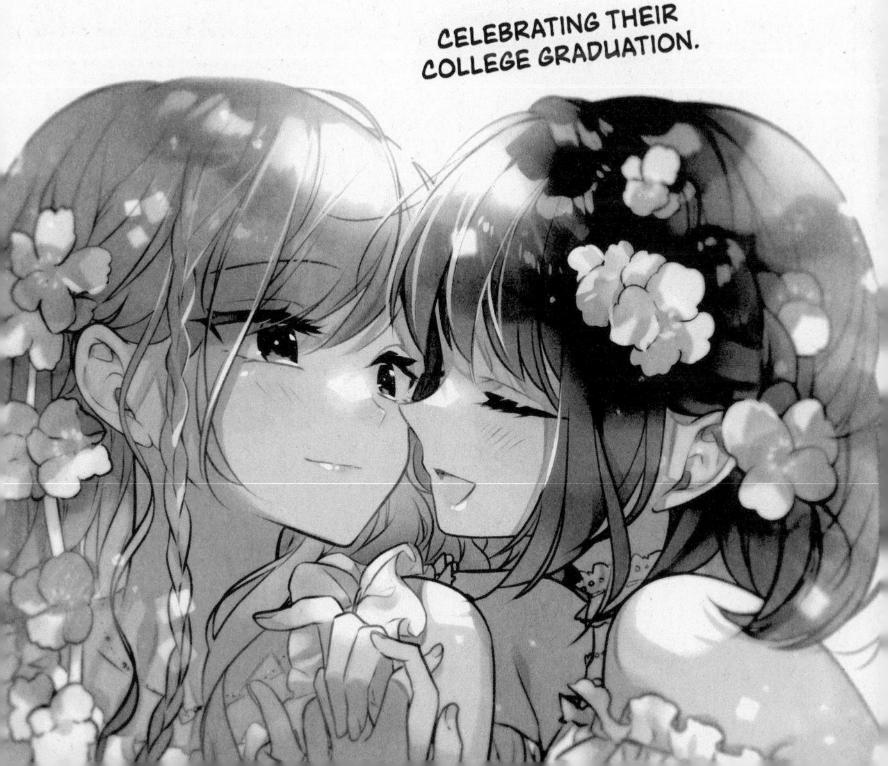
CELEBRATING THEIR
COLLEGE GRADUATION.

Futaribeya
A ROOM FOR TWO

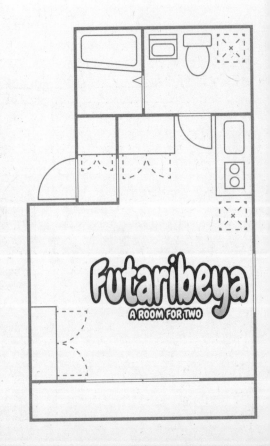

Chapter 71 (Part 1)

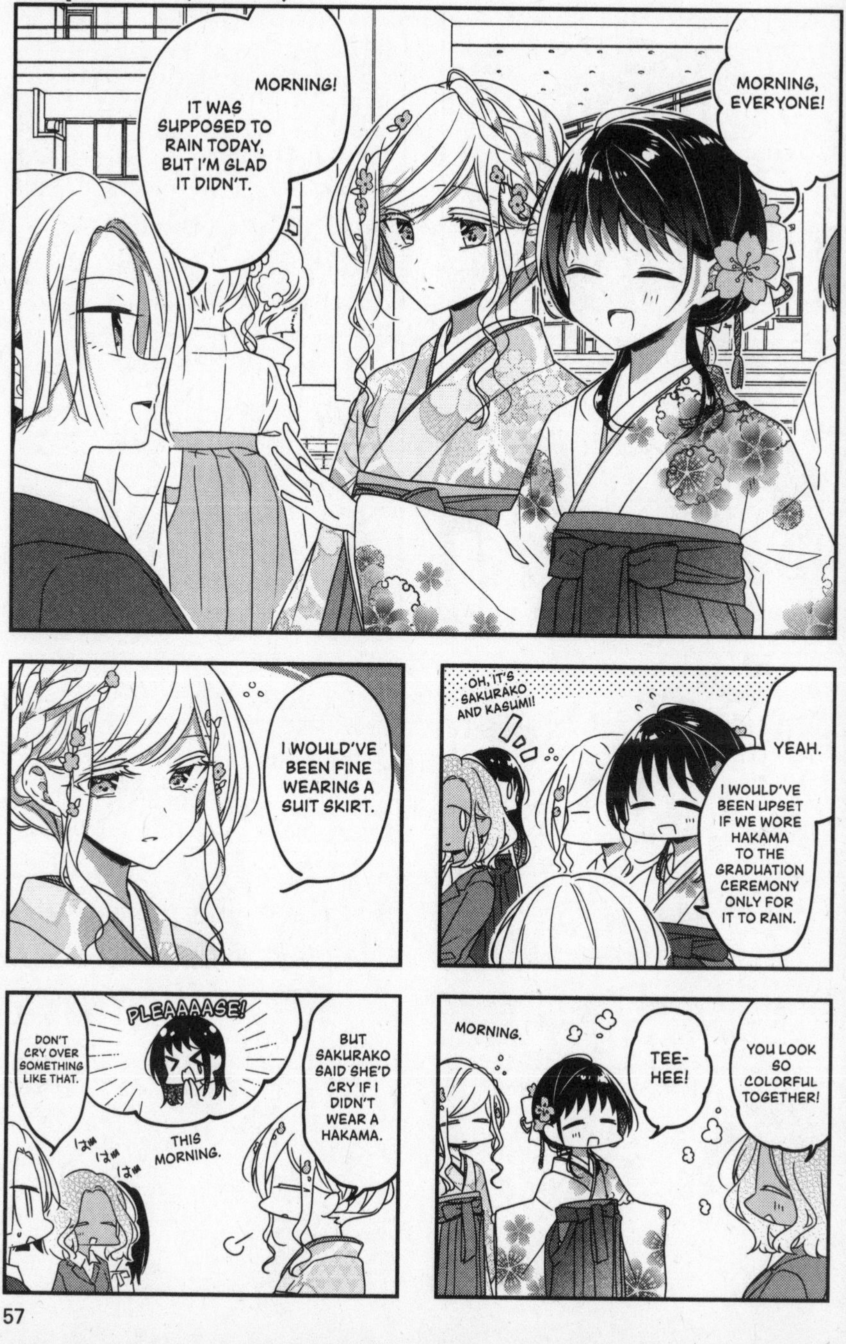
MORNING, EVERYONE!
MORNING!
IT WAS SUPPOSED TO RAIN TODAY, BUT I'M GLAD IT DIDN'T.
YEAH.
I WOULD'VE BEEN UPSET IF WE WORE HAKAMA TO THE GRADUATION CEREMONY ONLY FOR IT TO RAIN.
OH, IT'S SAKURAKO AND KASUMI!
I WOULD'VE BEEN FINE WEARING A SUIT SKIRT.
YOU LOOK SO COLORFUL TOGETHER!
TEE-HEE!
MORNING.
BUT SAKURAKO SAID SHE'D CRY IF I DIDN'T WEAR A HAKAMA.
PLEAAAASE!
THIS MORNING.
DON'T CRY OVER SOMETHING LIKE THAT.

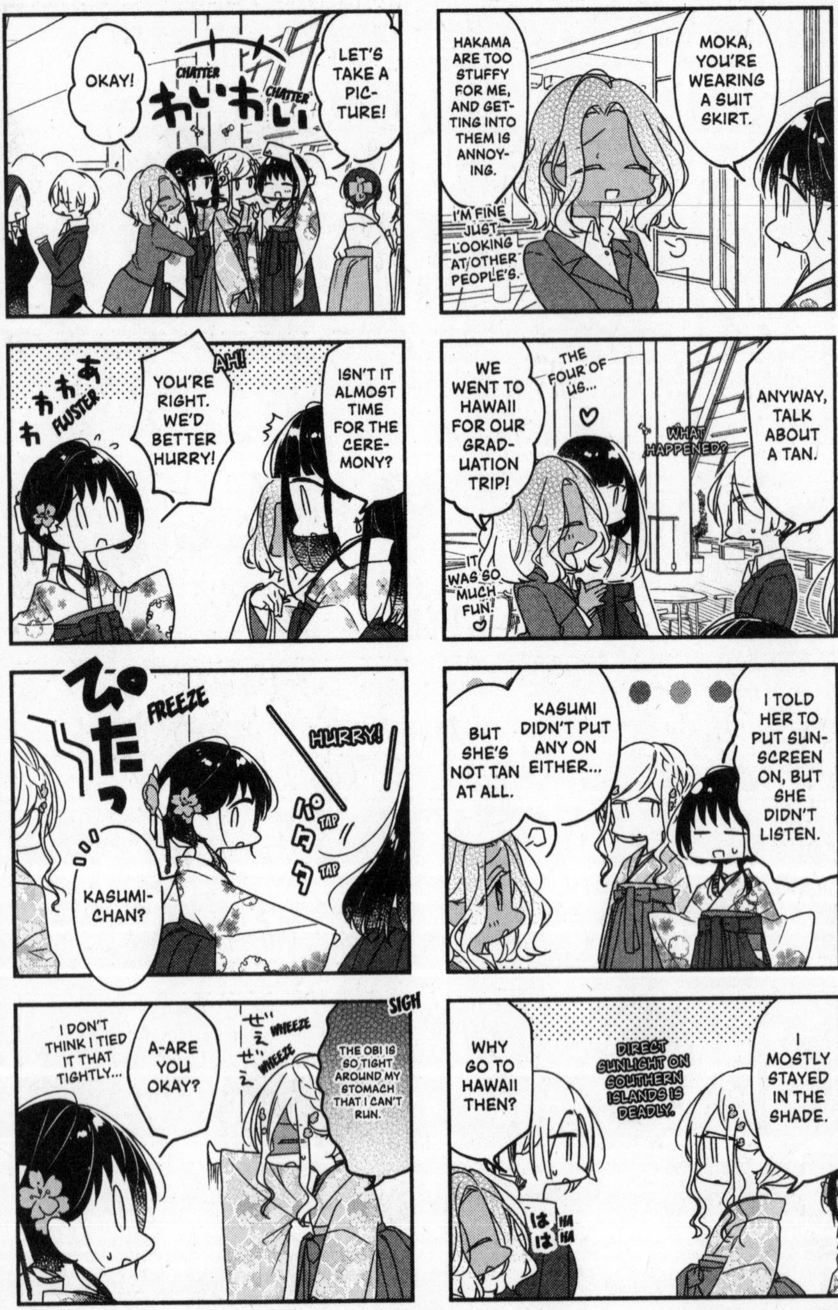
MOKA, YOU'RE WEARING A SUIT SKIRT.
HAKAMA ARE TOO STUFFY FOR ME, AND GETTING INTO THEM IS ANNOYING.
I'M FINE JUST LOOKING AT OTHER PEOPLE'S.
ANYWAY, TALK ABOUT A TAN.
WHAT HAPPENED?
THE FOUR OF US...
WE WENT TO HAWAII FOR OUR GRADUATION TRIP!
IT WAS SO MUCH FUN!
I TOLD HER TO PUT SUNSCREEN ON, BUT SHE DIDN'T LISTEN.
KASUMI DIDN'T PUT ANY ON EITHER...
BUT SHE'S NOT TAN AT ALL.
I MOSTLY STAYED IN THE SHADE.
DIRECT SUNLIGHT ON SOUTHERN ISLANDS IS DEADLY.
WHY GO TO HAWAII THEN?
はは HA HA
LET'S TAKE A PICTURE!
わいわい CHATTER CHATTER
OKAY!
ISN'T IT ALMOST TIME FOR THE CEREMONY?
AH!
YOU'RE RIGHT. WE'D BETTER HURRY!
あわあわ FLUSTER
HURRY!
パタタ TAP TAP
ぴたっ FREEZE
KASUMI-CHAN?
SIGH
THE OBI IS SO TIGHT AROUND MY STOMACH THAT I CAN'T RUN.
ぜぇぜぇ WHEEZE WHEEZE
A-ARE YOU OKAY?
I DON'T THINK I TIED IT THAT TIGHTLY...

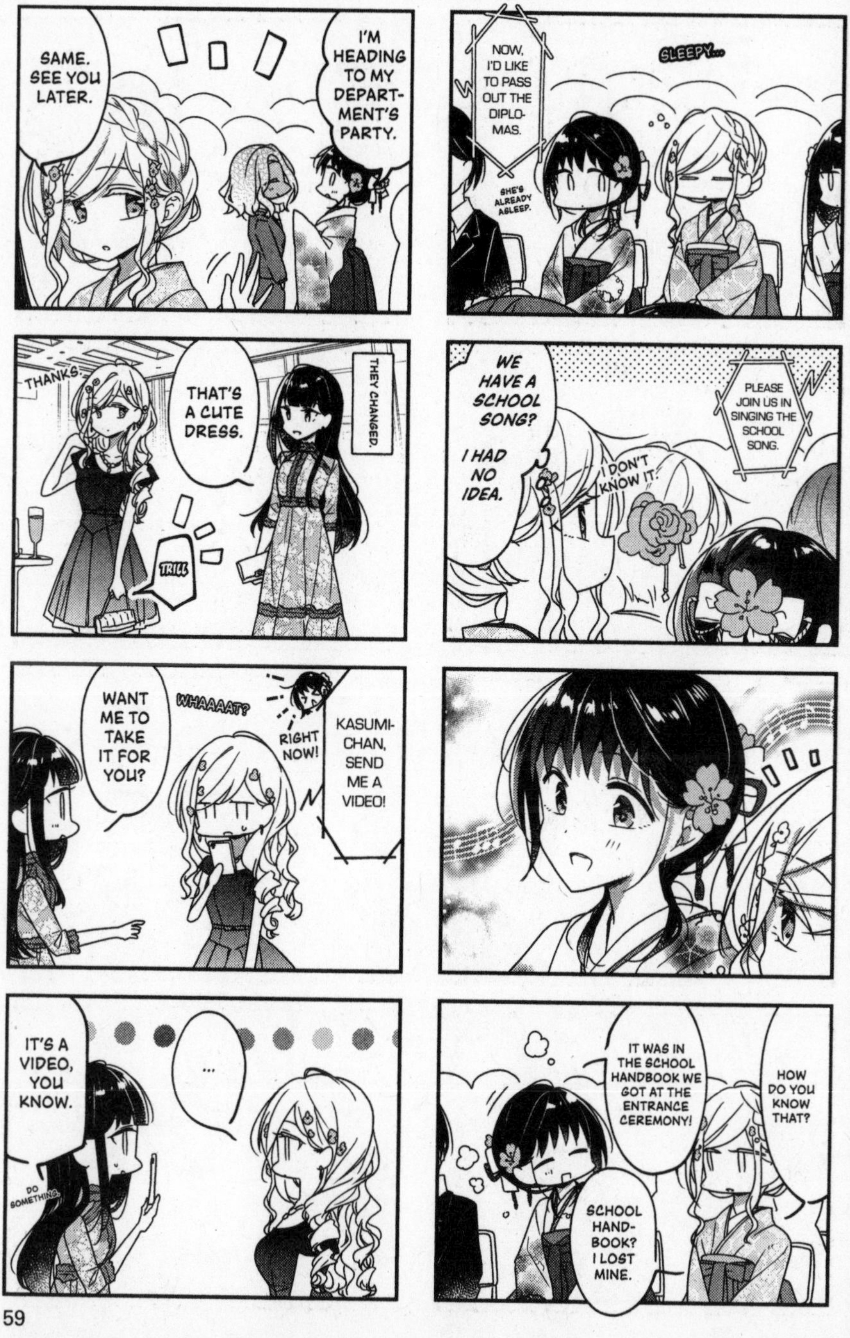
NOW, I'D LIKE TO PASS OUT THE DIPLOMAS.
SLEEPY...
SHE'S ALREADY ASLEEP.
PLEASE JOIN US IN SINGING THE SCHOOL SONG.
WE HAVE A SCHOOL SONG? I HAD NO IDEA.
I DON'T KNOW IT.
HOW DO YOU KNOW THAT?
IT WAS IN THE SCHOOL HANDBOOK WE GOT AT THE ENTRANCE CEREMONY!
SCHOOL HAND-BOOK? I LOST MINE.
I'M HEADING TO MY DEPART-MENT'S PARTY.
SAME. SEE YOU LATER.
THEY CHANGED.
THAT'S A CUTE DRESS.
THANKS.
TRILL
KASUMI-CHAN, SEND ME A VIDEO!
RIGHT NOW!
WHAAAAT?
WANT ME TO TAKE IT FOR YOU?
...
IT'S A VIDEO, YOU KNOW.
DO SOMETHING.

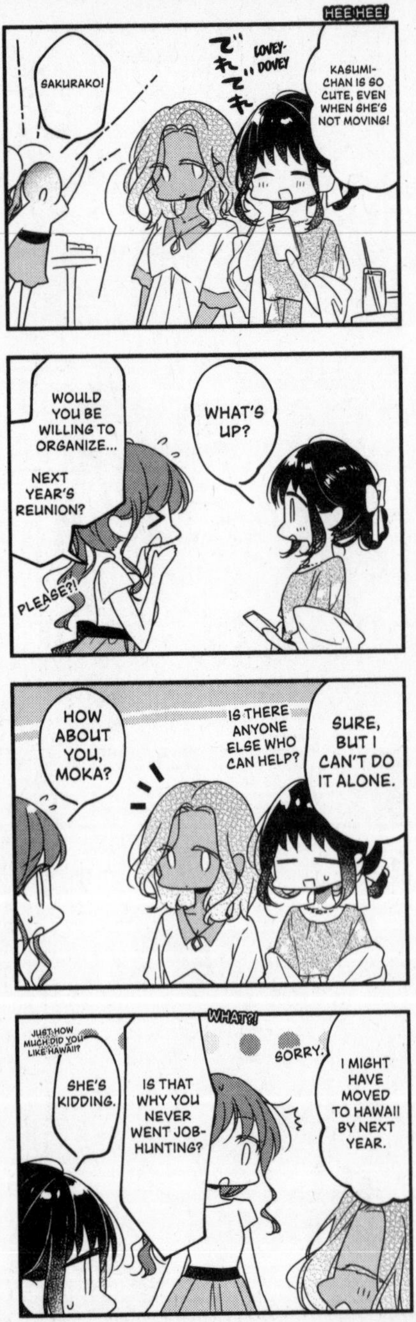
HEE HEE!
KASUMI-CHAN IS SO CUTE, EVEN WHEN SHE'S NOT MOVING!
でれでれ
LOVEY-DOVEY
SAKURAKO!
WHAT'S UP?
WOULD YOU BE WILLING TO ORGANIZE...
NEXT YEAR'S REUNION?
PLEASE?!
SURE, BUT I CAN'T DO IT ALONE.
IS THERE ANYONE ELSE WHO CAN HELP?
HOW ABOUT YOU, MOKA?
I MIGHT HAVE MOVED TO HAWAII BY NEXT YEAR.
SORRY.
WHAT?!
IS THAT WHY YOU NEVER WENT JOB-HUNTING?
SHE'S KIDDING.
JUST HOW MUCH DID YOU LIKE HAWAII?

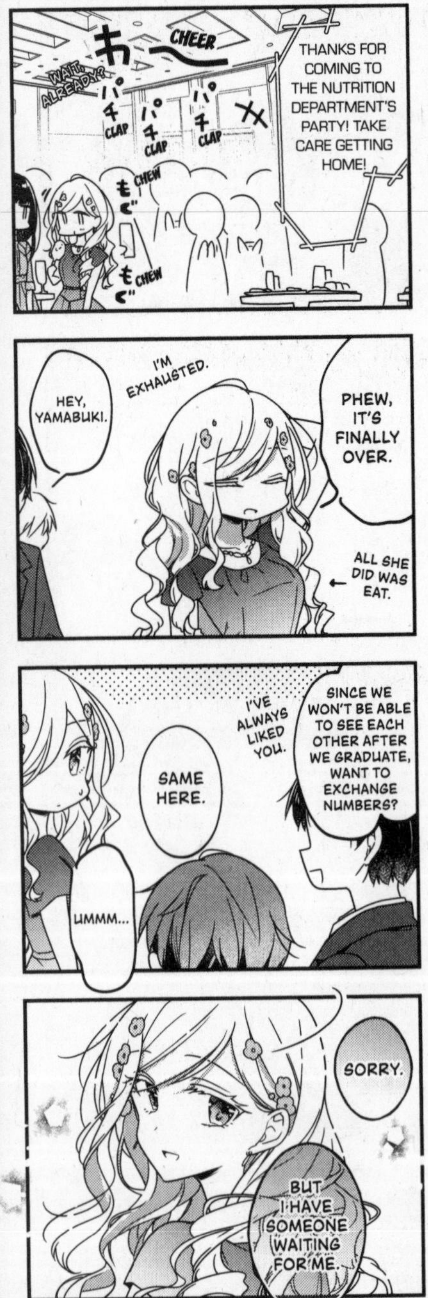
THANKS FOR COMING TO THE NUTRITION DEPARTMENT'S PARTY! TAKE CARE GETTING HOME!
わ〜
CHEER
パチ
CLAP
パチ
CLAP
パチ
CLAP
WAIT, ALREADY?
もぐ
CHEW
もぐ
CHEW
PHEW, IT'S FINALLY OVER.
I'M EXHAUSTED.
HEY, YAMABUKI.
ALL SHE DID WAS EAT.
SINCE WE WON'T BE ABLE TO SEE EACH OTHER AFTER WE GRADUATE, WANT TO EXCHANGE NUMBERS?
I'VE ALWAYS LIKED YOU.
SAME HERE.
UMMM...
SORRY.
BUT I HAVE SOMEONE WAITING FOR ME.

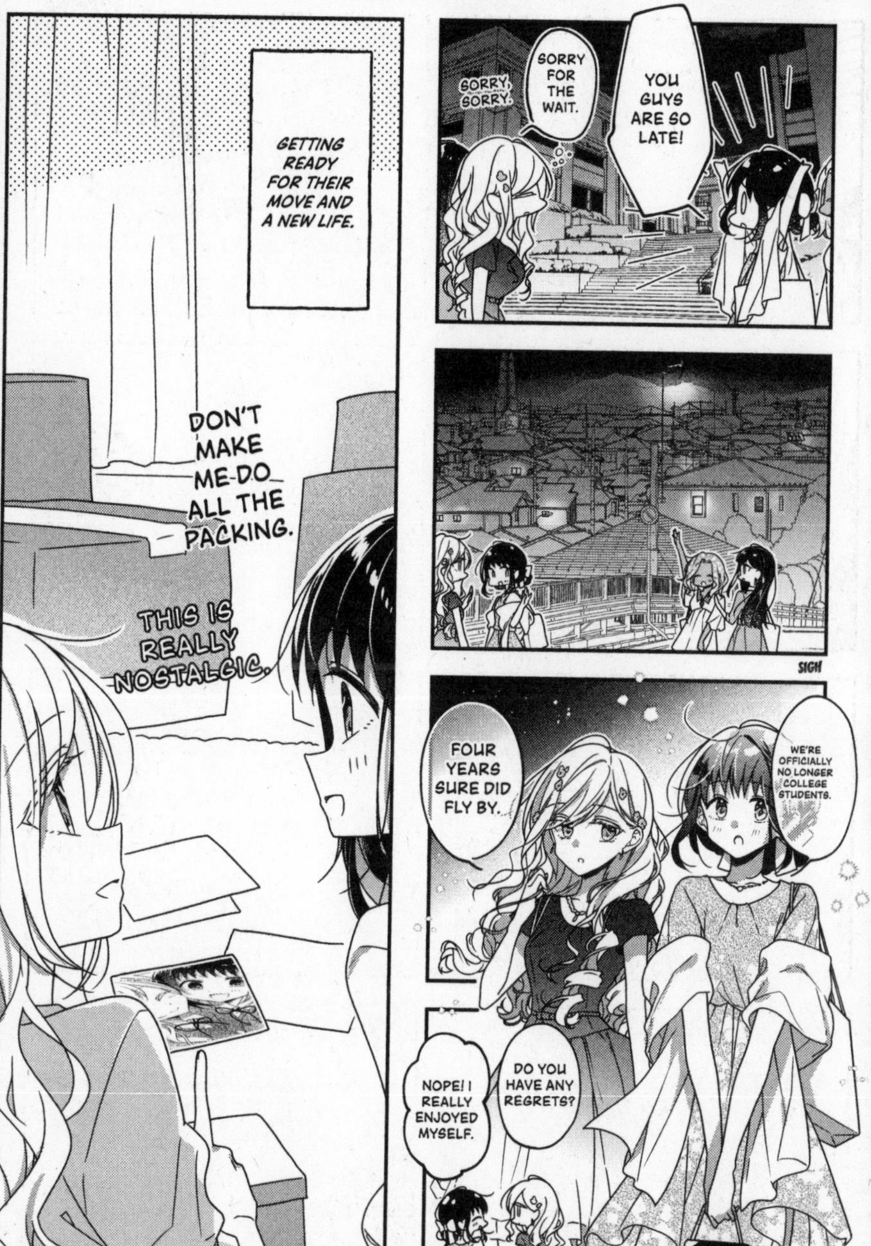
YOU GUYS ARE SO LATE!
SORRY FOR THE WAIT.
SORRY, SORRY.
SIGH
WE'RE OFFICIALLY NO LONGER COLLEGE STUDENTS.
FOUR YEARS SURE DID FLY BY.
DO YOU HAVE ANY REGRETS?
NOPE! I REALLY ENJOYED MYSELF.
GETTING READY FOR THEIR MOVE AND A NEW LIFE.
DON'T MAKE ME DO ALL THE PACKING.
THIS IS REALLY NOSTALGIC.

Illustration gallery of Yukiko

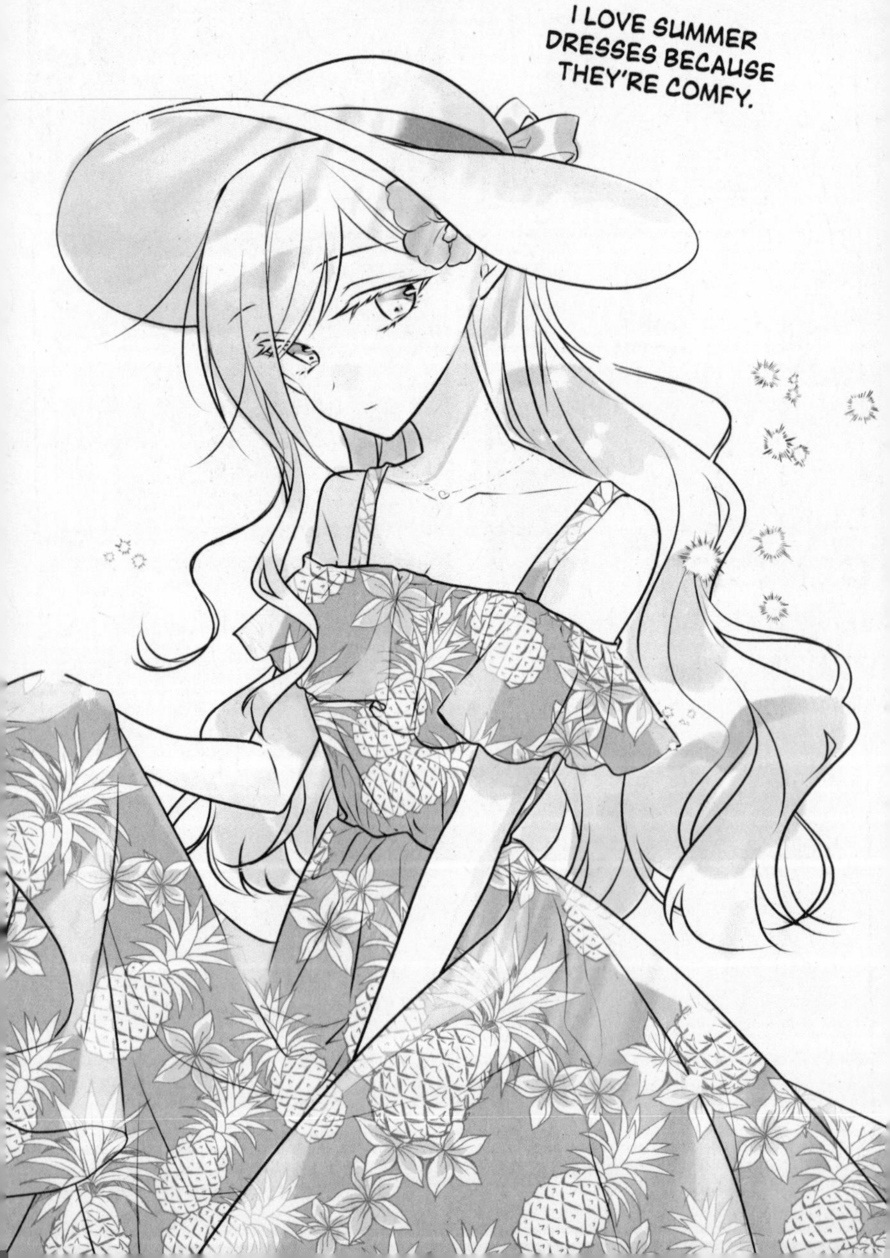
I LOVE SUMMER DRESSES BECAUSE THEY'RE COMFY.

Chapter 71.5

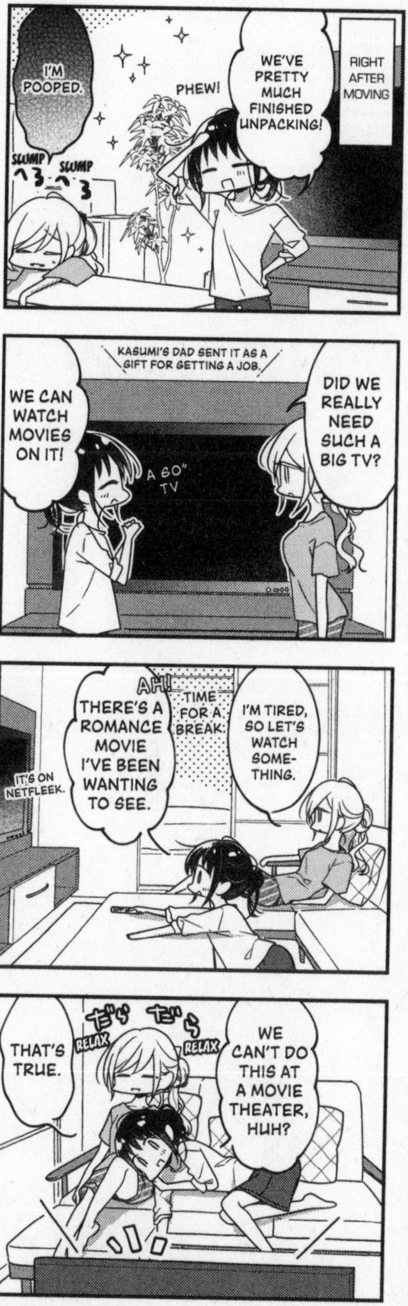
RIGHT AFTER MOVING
WE'VE PRETTY MUCH FINISHED UNPACKING!
PHEW!
I'M POOPED.
SLUMP
SLUMP
DID WE REALLY NEED SUCH A BIG TV?
KASUMI'S DAD SENT IT AS A GIFT FOR GETTING A JOB.
A 60" TV
WE CAN WATCH MOVIES ON IT!
I'M TIRED, SO LET'S WATCH SOMETHING.
TIME FOR A BREAK.
AH! THERE'S A ROMANCE MOVIE I'VE BEEN WANTING TO SEE.
IT'S ON NETFLEEK.
WE CAN'T DO THIS AT A MOVIE THEATER, HUH?
だら RELAX
だら RELAX
THAT'S TRUE.

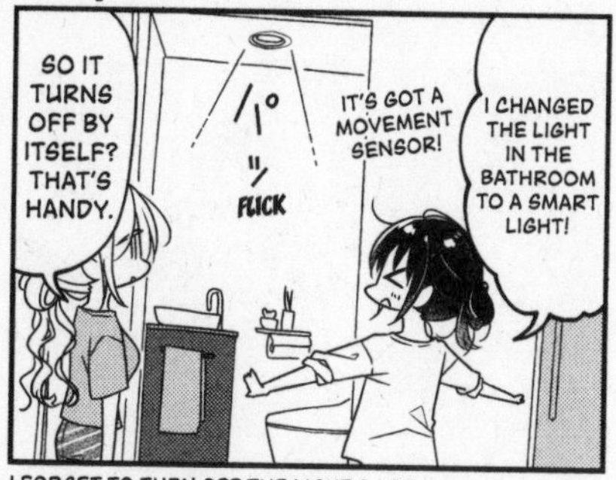
I CHANGED THE LIGHT IN THE BATHROOM TO A SMART LIGHT!
IT'S GOT A MOVEMENT SENSOR!
パッ FLICK
SO IT TURNS OFF BY ITSELF? THAT'S HANDY.

I FORGET TO TURN OFF THE LIGHT A LOT.

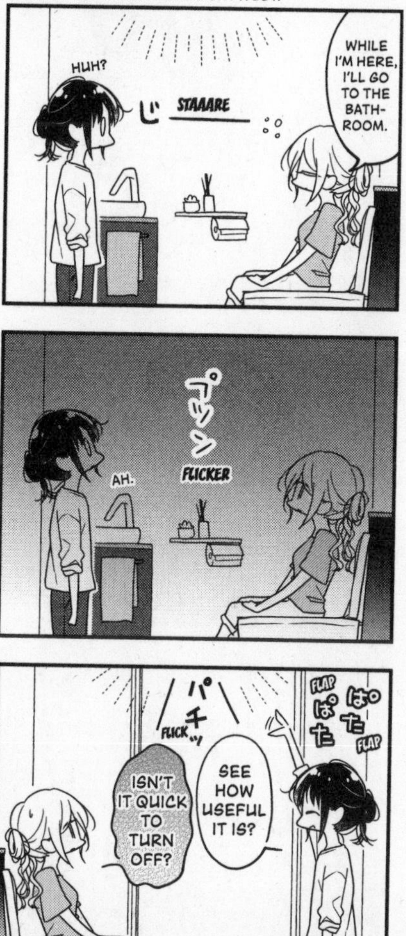
WHILE I'M HERE, I'LL GO TO THE BATH-ROOM.
じー STAAARE
HUH?
プツン FLICKER
AH.
はた ぱた FLAP FLAP
パチッ FLICK
SEE HOW USEFUL IT IS?
ISN'T IT QUICK TO TURN OFF?

AFTER THAT, THEY CHANGED THE SETTINGS.

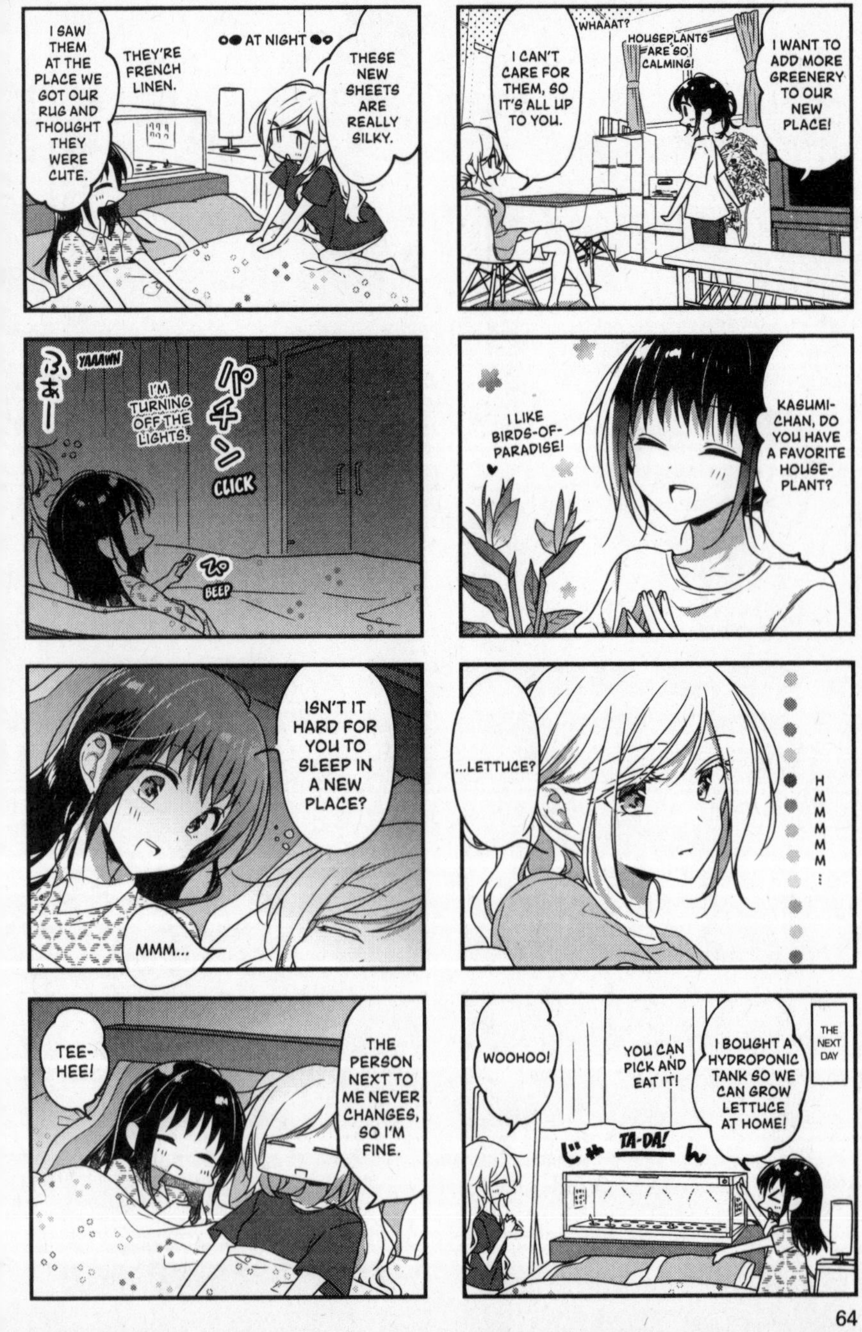
I WANT TO ADD MORE GREENERY TO OUR NEW PLACE!
HOUSEPLANTS ARE SO CALMING!
WHAAAT?
I CAN'T CARE FOR THEM, SO IT'S ALL UP TO YOU.
KASUMI-CHAN, DO YOU HAVE A FAVORITE HOUSE-PLANT?
I LIKE BIRDS-OF-PARADISE!
HMMMMM...
...LETTUCE?
THE NEXT DAY
I BOUGHT A HYDROPONIC TANK SO WE CAN GROW LETTUCE AT HOME!
YOU CAN PICK AND EAT IT!
WOOHOO!
じゃん
TA-DA!
AT NIGHT
THESE NEW SHEETS ARE REALLY SILKY.
THEY'RE FRENCH LINEN.
I SAW THEM AT THE PLACE WE GOT OUR RUG AND THOUGHT THEY WERE CUTE.
パチン
CLICK
I'M TURNING OFF THE LIGHTS.
YAAAWN
ふぁー
ぴっ
BEEP
ISN'T IT HARD FOR YOU TO SLEEP IN A NEW PLACE?
MMM...
THE PERSON NEXT TO ME NEVER CHANGES, SO I'M FINE.
TEE-HEE!

Futaribeya
A ROOM FOR TWO

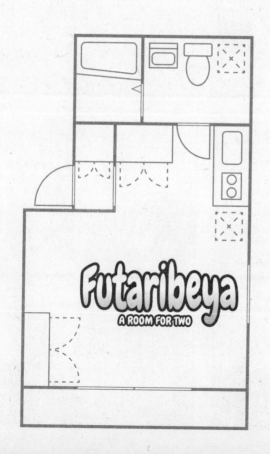

Chapter 71 (Part 2)

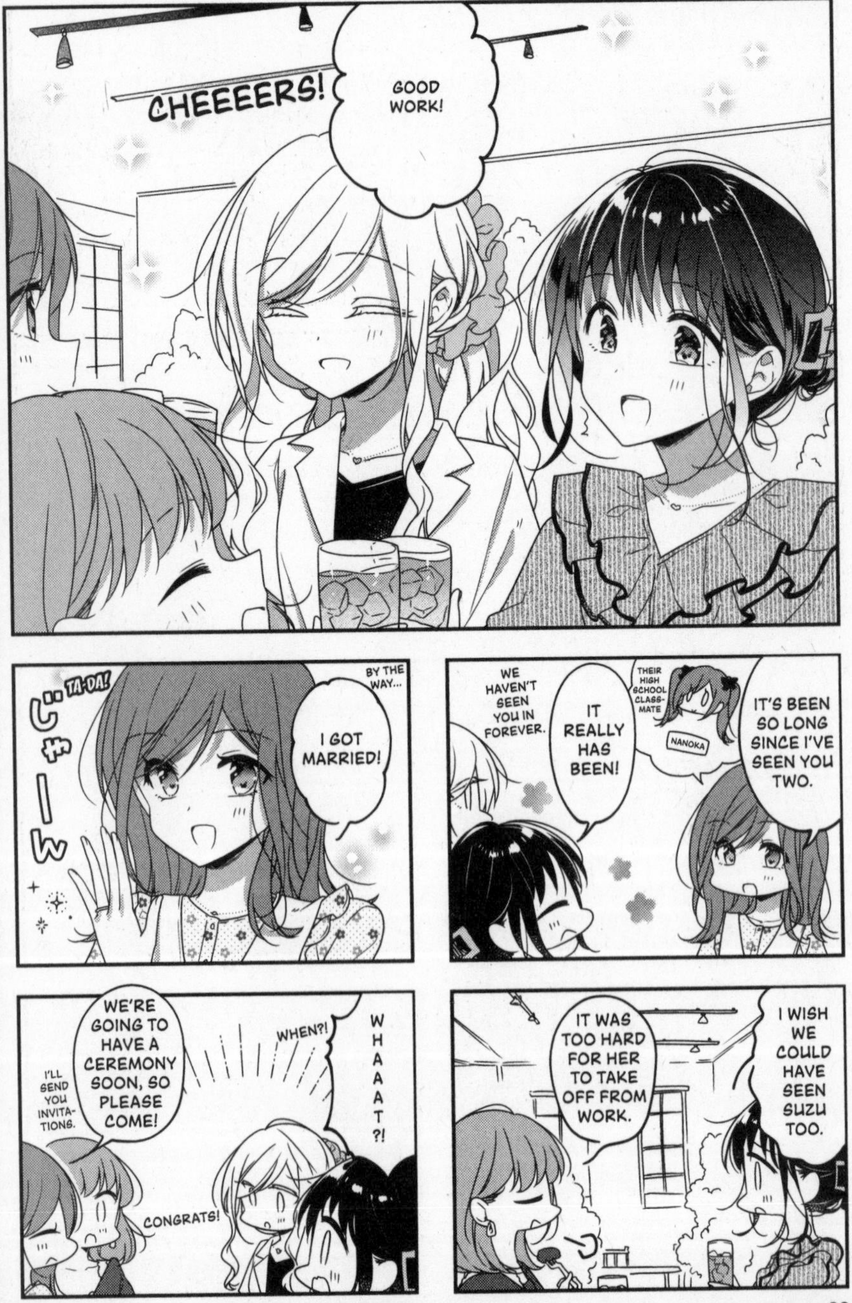
GOOD WORK!
CHEEEERS!
IT'S BEEN SO LONG SINCE I'VE SEEN YOU TWO.
THEIR HIGH SCHOOL CLASSMATE
NANOKA
IT REALLY HAS BEEN!
WE HAVEN'T SEEN YOU IN FOREVER.
BY THE WAY...
I GOT MARRIED!
TA-DA!
じゃーん
I WISH WE COULD HAVE SEEN SUZU TOO.
IT WAS TOO HARD FOR HER TO TAKE OFF FROM WORK.
WHAAAAT?!
WHEN?!
WE'RE GOING TO HAVE A CEREMONY SOON, SO PLEASE COME!
I'LL SEND YOU INVITATIONS.
CONGRATS!

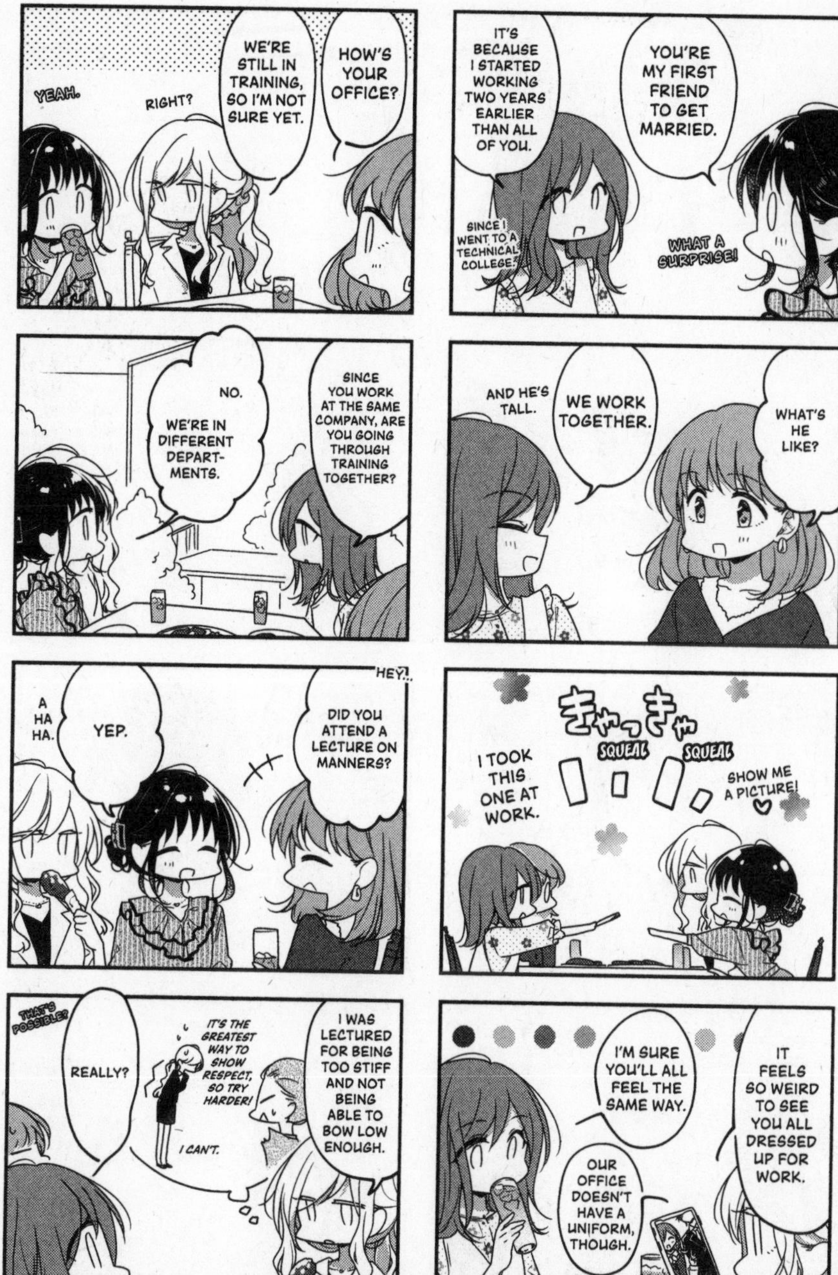
YOU'RE MY FIRST FRIEND TO GET MARRIED.
IT'S BECAUSE I STARTED WORKING TWO YEARS EARLIER THAN ALL OF YOU.
WHAT A SURPRISE!
SINCE I WENT TO A TECHNICAL COLLEGE.
HOW'S YOUR OFFICE?
WE'RE STILL IN TRAINING, SO I'M NOT SURE YET.
RIGHT?
YEAH.
WHAT'S HE LIKE?
WE WORK TOGETHER.
AND HE'S TALL.
SINCE YOU WORK AT THE SAME COMPANY, ARE YOU GOING THROUGH TRAINING TOGETHER?
NO.
WE'RE IN DIFFERENT DEPART-MENTS.
SHOW ME A PICTURE! ♡
きゃっきゃ
SQUEAL SQUEAL
I TOOK THIS ONE AT WORK.
HEY...
DID YOU ATTEND A LECTURE ON MANNERS?
YEP.
A HA HA.
IT FEELS SO WEIRD TO SEE YOU ALL DRESSED UP FOR WORK.
I'M SURE YOU'LL ALL FEEL THE SAME WAY.
OUR OFFICE DOESN'T HAVE A UNIFORM, THOUGH.
I WAS LECTURED FOR BEING TOO STIFF AND NOT BEING ABLE TO BOW LOW ENOUGH.
IT'S THE GREATEST WAY TO SHOW RESPECT, SO TRY HARDER!
I CAN'T.
REALLY?
THAT'S POSSIBLE?

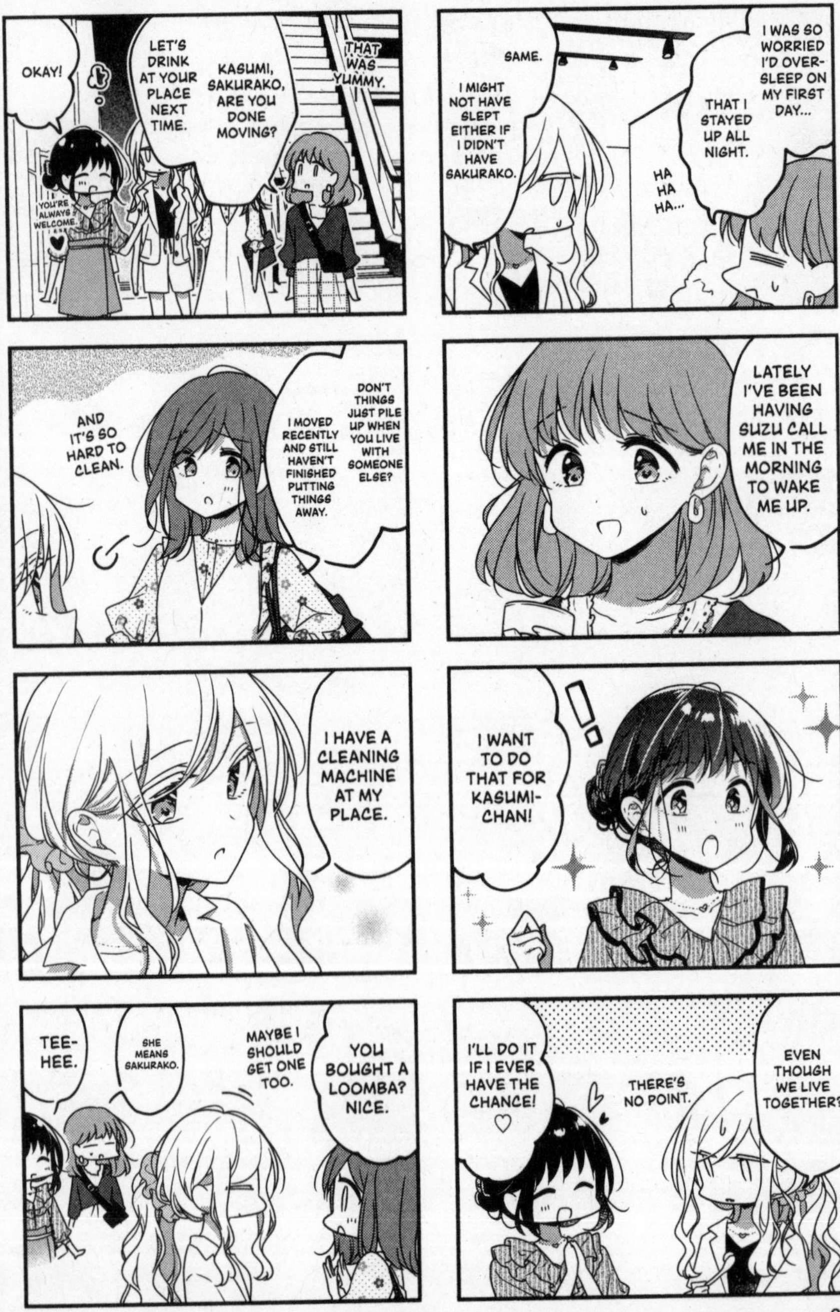
I WAS SO WORRIED I'D OVER-SLEEP ON MY FIRST DAY...
THAT I STAYED UP ALL NIGHT.
HA HA HA...
SAME.
I MIGHT NOT HAVE SLEPT EITHER IF I DIDN'T HAVE SAKURAKO.
LATELY I'VE BEEN HAVING SUZU CALL ME IN THE MORNING TO WAKE ME UP.
!
I WANT TO DO THAT FOR KASUMI-CHAN!
EVEN THOUGH WE LIVE TOGETHER?
THERE'S NO POINT.
I'LL DO IT IF I EVER HAVE THE CHANCE! ♡
THAT WAS YUMMY.
KASUMI, SAKURAKO, ARE YOU DONE MOVING?
LET'S DRINK AT YOUR PLACE NEXT TIME.
OKAY!
YOU'RE ALWAYS WELCOME. ♥
DON'T THINGS JUST PILE UP WHEN YOU LIVE WITH SOMEONE ELSE?
I MOVED RECENTLY AND STILL HAVEN'T FINISHED PUTTING THINGS AWAY.
AND IT'S SO HARD TO CLEAN.
I HAVE A CLEANING MACHINE AT MY PLACE.
YOU BOUGHT A LOOMBA? NICE.
MAYBE I SHOULD GET ONE TOO.
SHE MEANS SAKURAKO.
TEE-HEE.

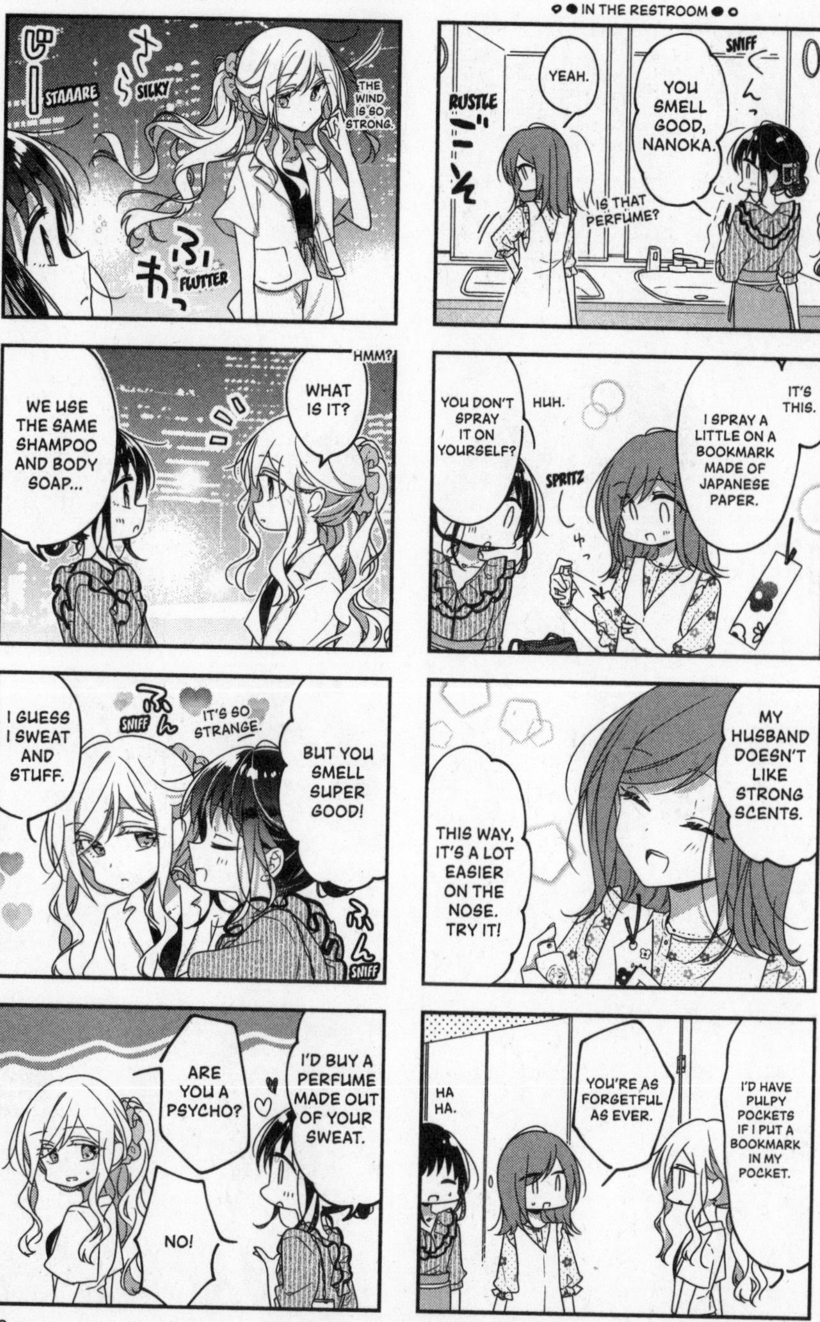
IN THE RESTROOM
RUSTLE
ごそ
SNIFF
くんっ
YOU SMELL GOOD, NANOKA.
IS THAT PERFUME?
YEAH.
IT'S THIS.
I SPRAY A LITTLE ON A BOOKMARK MADE OF JAPANESE PAPER.
HUH.
YOU DON'T SPRAY IT ON YOURSELF?
SPRITZ
MY HUSBAND DOESN'T LIKE STRONG SCENTS.
THIS WAY, IT'S A LOT EASIER ON THE NOSE. TRY IT!
I'D HAVE PULPY POCKETS IF I PUT A BOOKMARK IN MY POCKET.
YOU'RE AS FORGETFUL AS EVER.
HA HA.
じー
STAAARE
さら
SILKY
THE WIND IS SO STRONG.
ふわっ
FLUTTER
HMM?
WHAT IS IT?
WE USE THE SAME SHAMPOO AND BODY SOAP...
BUT YOU SMELL SUPER GOOD!
ふん
SNIFF
IT'S SO STRANGE.
I GUESS I SWEAT AND STUFF.
ふん
SNIFF
I'D BUY A PERFUME MADE OUT OF YOUR SWEAT.
ARE YOU A PSYCHO?
NO!

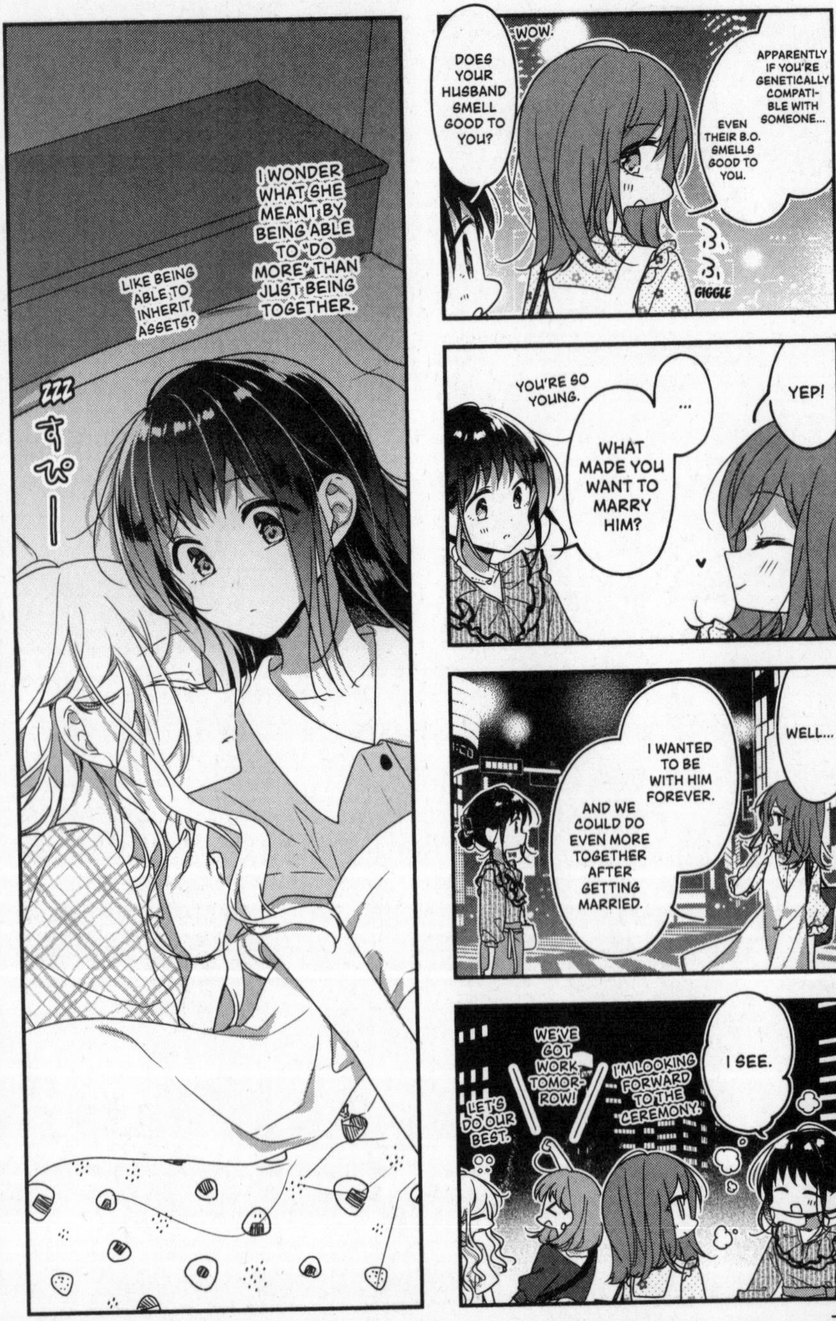
APPARENTLY IF YOU'RE GENETICALLY COMPATIBLE WITH SOMEONE...
EVEN THEIR B.O. SMELLS GOOD TO YOU.
ふふ
GIGGLE
WOW.
DOES YOUR HUSBAND SMELL GOOD TO YOU?
YEP!
YOU'RE SO YOUNG.
...
WHAT MADE YOU WANT TO MARRY HIM?
WELL...
I WANTED TO BE WITH HIM FOREVER.
AND WE COULD DO EVEN MORE TOGETHER AFTER GETTING MARRIED.
I SEE.
I'M LOOKING FORWARD TO THE CEREMONY.
WE'VE GOT WORK TOMORROW!
LET'S DO OUR BEST.
I WONDER WHAT SHE MEANT BY BEING ABLE TO "DO MORE" THAN JUST BEING TOGETHER.
LIKE BEING ABLE TO INHERIT ASSETS?
ZZZ
すぴー

Special Chapter #1 - "Time Sure Flies"

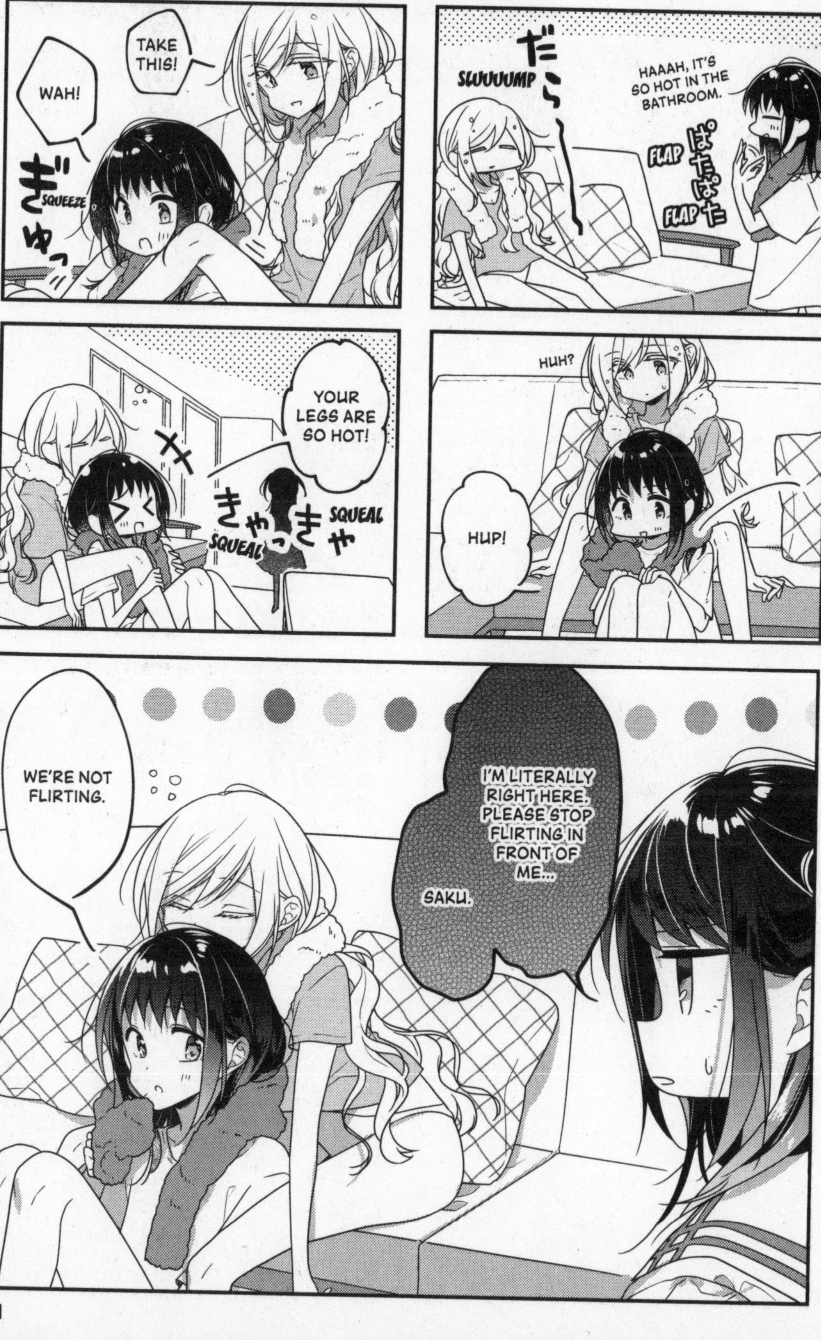

だら~
SLUUUUMP
HAAAH, IT'S SO HOT IN THE BATHROOM.
ぱたぱた
FLAP
FLAP
TAKE THIS!
WAH!
ぎゅっ
SQUEEZE
HUH?
HUP!
YOUR LEGS ARE SO HOT!
きゃっきゃ
SQUEAL
SQUEAL
I'M LITERALLY RIGHT HERE. PLEASE STOP FLIRTING IN FRONT OF ME...
SAKU.
WE'RE NOT FLIRTING.

SHE DOESN'T TAKE ME SERIOUSLY

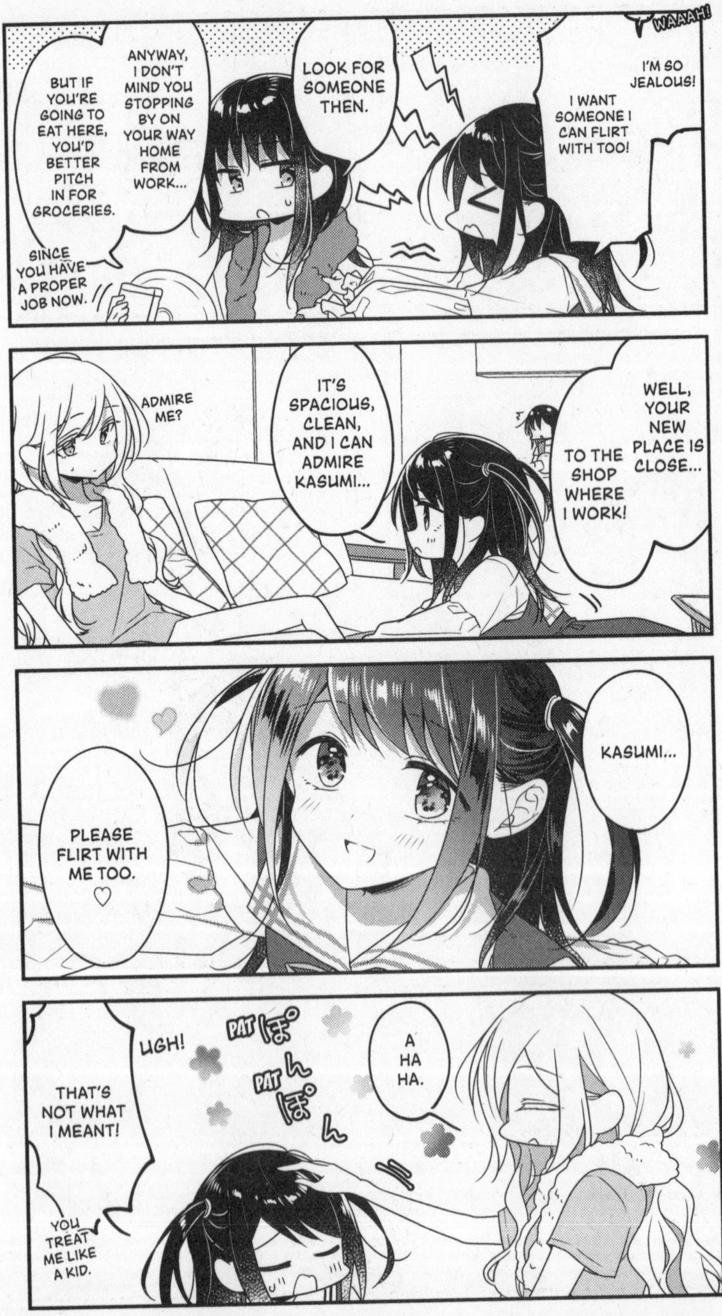

WAAAH!
I'M SO JEALOUS!
I WANT SOMEONE I CAN FLIRT WITH TOO!
LOOK FOR SOMEONE THEN.
ANYWAY, I DON'T MIND YOU STOPPING BY ON YOUR WAY HOME FROM WORK...
BUT IF YOU'RE GOING TO EAT HERE, YOU'D BETTER PITCH IN FOR GROCERIES.
SINCE YOU HAVE A PROPER JOB NOW.
WELL, YOUR NEW PLACE IS CLOSE...
TO THE SHOP WHERE I WORK!
IT'S SPACIOUS, CLEAN, AND I CAN ADMIRE KASUMI...
ADMIRE ME?
KASUMI...
PLEASE FLIRT WITH ME TOO. ♡
A HA HA.
PAT ぽん
PAT ぽん
UGH!
THAT'S NOT WHAT I MEANT!
YOU TREAT ME LIKE A KID.

NOT ONE TO TALK

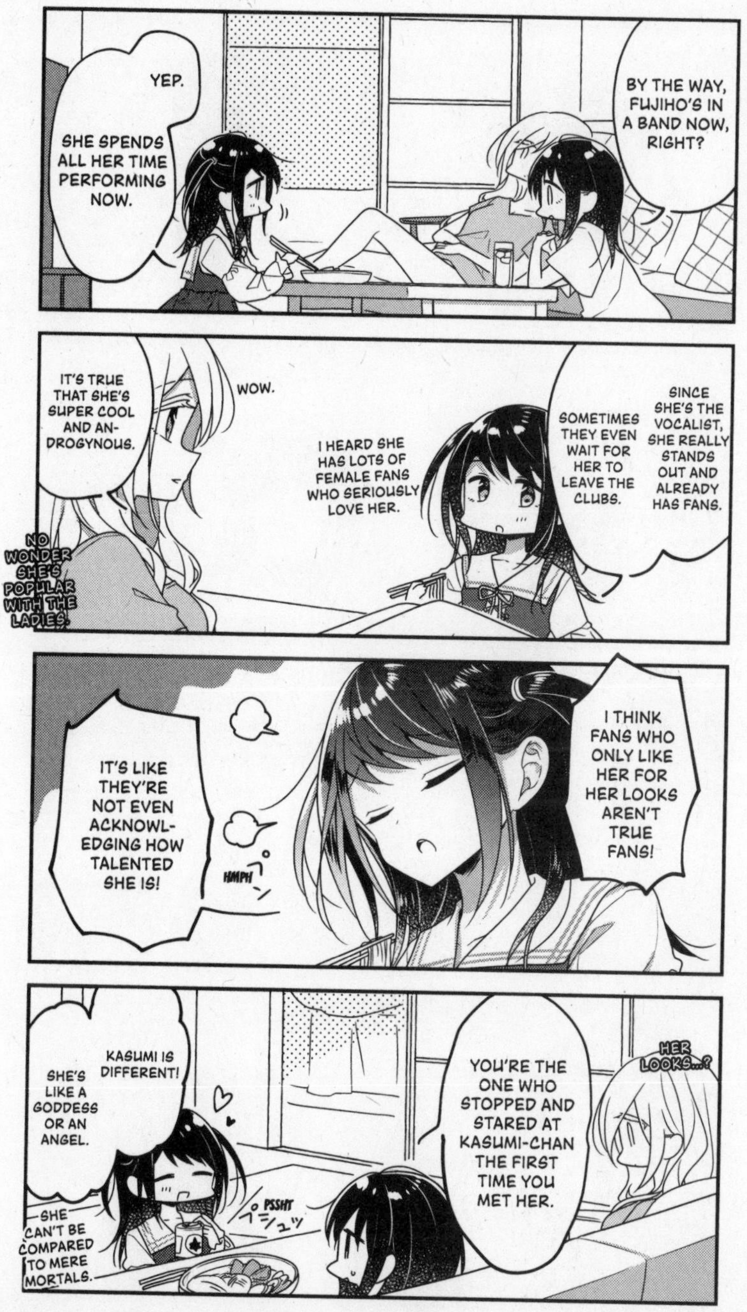
BY THE WAY, FUJIHO'S IN A BAND NOW, RIGHT?
YEP.
SHE SPENDS ALL HER TIME PERFORMING NOW.
SINCE SHE'S THE VOCALIST, SHE REALLY STANDS OUT AND ALREADY HAS FANS.
SOMETIMES THEY EVEN WAIT FOR HER TO LEAVE THE CLUBS.
I HEARD SHE HAS LOTS OF FEMALE FANS WHO SERIOUSLY LOVE HER.
WOW.
IT'S TRUE THAT SHE'S SUPER COOL AND ANDROGYNOUS.
NO WONDER SHE'S POPULAR WITH THE LADIES.
I THINK FANS WHO ONLY LIKE HER FOR HER LOOKS AREN'T TRUE FANS!
HMPH
IT'S LIKE THEY'RE NOT EVEN ACKNOWLEDGING HOW TALENTED SHE IS!
HER LOOKS...?
YOU'RE THE ONE WHO STOPPED AND STARED AT KASUMI-CHAN THE FIRST TIME YOU MET HER.
PSSHT
KASUMI IS DIFFERENT!
SHE'S LIKE A GODDESS OR AN ANGEL.
SHE CAN'T BE COMPARED TO MERE MORTALS.

THE MEMORY OF A GOLDFISH

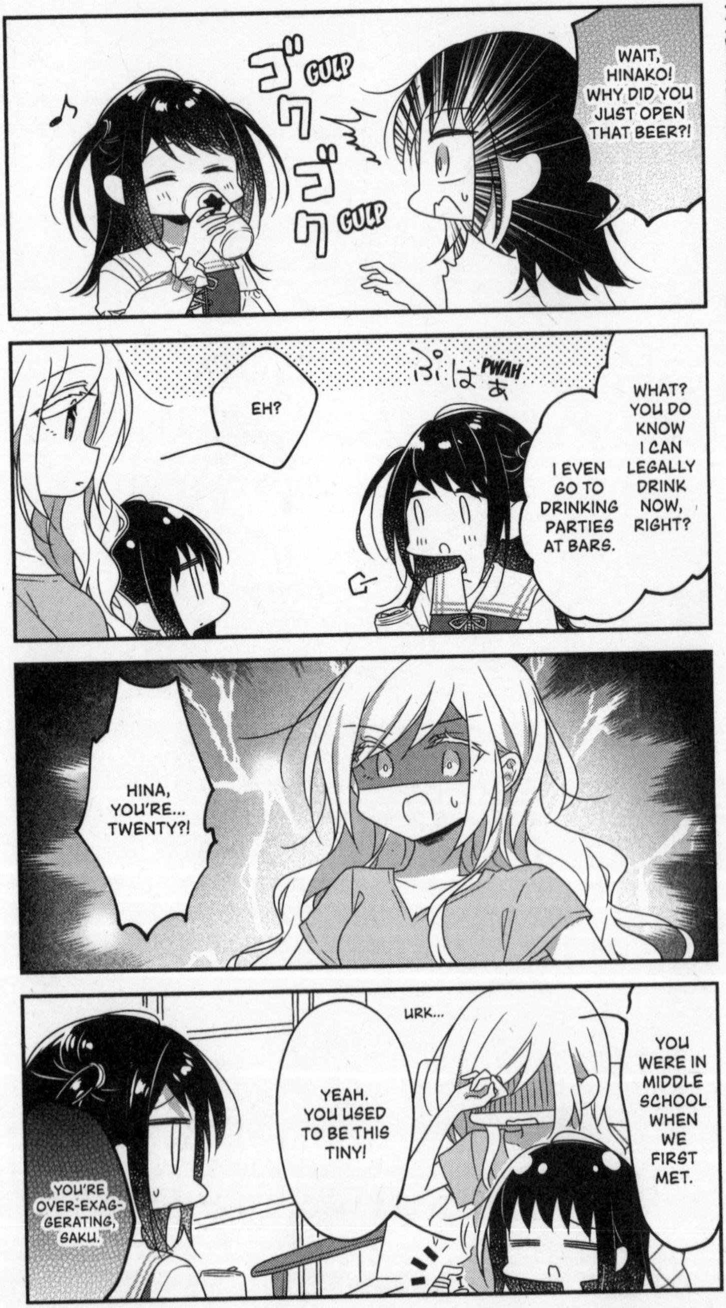
WAIT, HINAKO! WHY DID YOU JUST OPEN THAT BEER?!
ゴク GULP
ゴク GULP
ぷはぁ PWAH
WHAT? YOU DO KNOW I CAN LEGALLY DRINK NOW, RIGHT?
I EVEN GO TO DRINKING PARTIES AT BARS.
EH?
HINA, YOU'RE... TWENTY?!
YOU WERE IN MIDDLE SCHOOL WHEN WE FIRST MET.
URK...
YEAH. YOU USED TO BE THIS TINY!
YOU'RE OVER-EXAG-GERATING, SAKU.

DON'T WORRY ABOUT IT

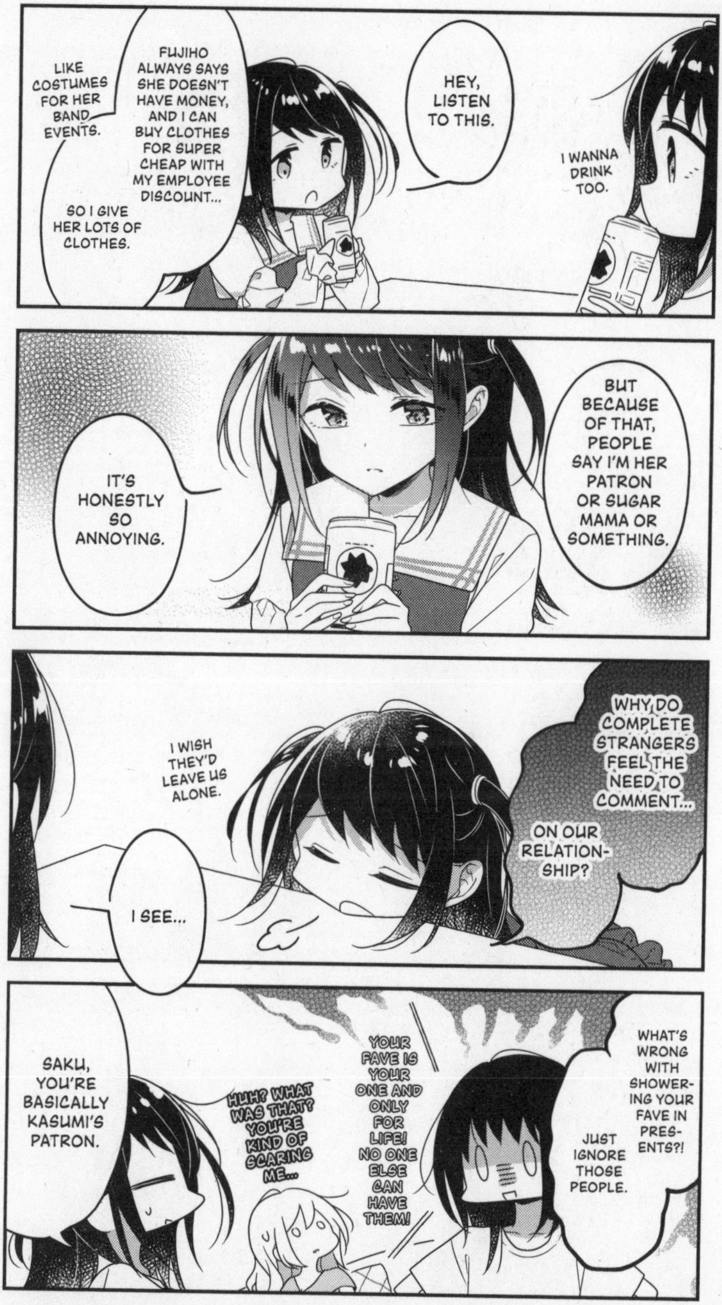
I WANNA DRINK TOO.
HEY, LISTEN TO THIS.
FUJIHO ALWAYS SAYS SHE DOESN'T HAVE MONEY, AND I CAN BUY CLOTHES FOR SUPER CHEAP WITH MY EMPLOYEE DISCOUNT...
LIKE COSTUMES FOR HER BAND EVENTS.
SO I GIVE HER LOTS OF CLOTHES.
BUT BECAUSE OF THAT, PEOPLE SAY I'M HER PATRON OR SUGAR MAMA OR SOMETHING.
IT'S HONESTLY SO ANNOYING.
WHY DO COMPLETE STRANGERS FEEL THE NEED TO COMMENT...
ON OUR RELATIONSHIP?
I WISH THEY'D LEAVE US ALONE.
I SEE...
WHAT'S WRONG WITH SHOWERING YOUR FAVE IN PRESENTS?!
JUST IGNORE THOSE PEOPLE.
YOUR FAVE IS YOUR ONE AND ONLY FOR LIFE! NO ONE ELSE CAN HAVE THEM!
HUH? WHAT WAS THAT? YOU'RE KIND OF SCARING ME...
SAKU, YOU'RE BASICALLY KASUMI'S PATRON.

VARIOUS EXPRESSIONS

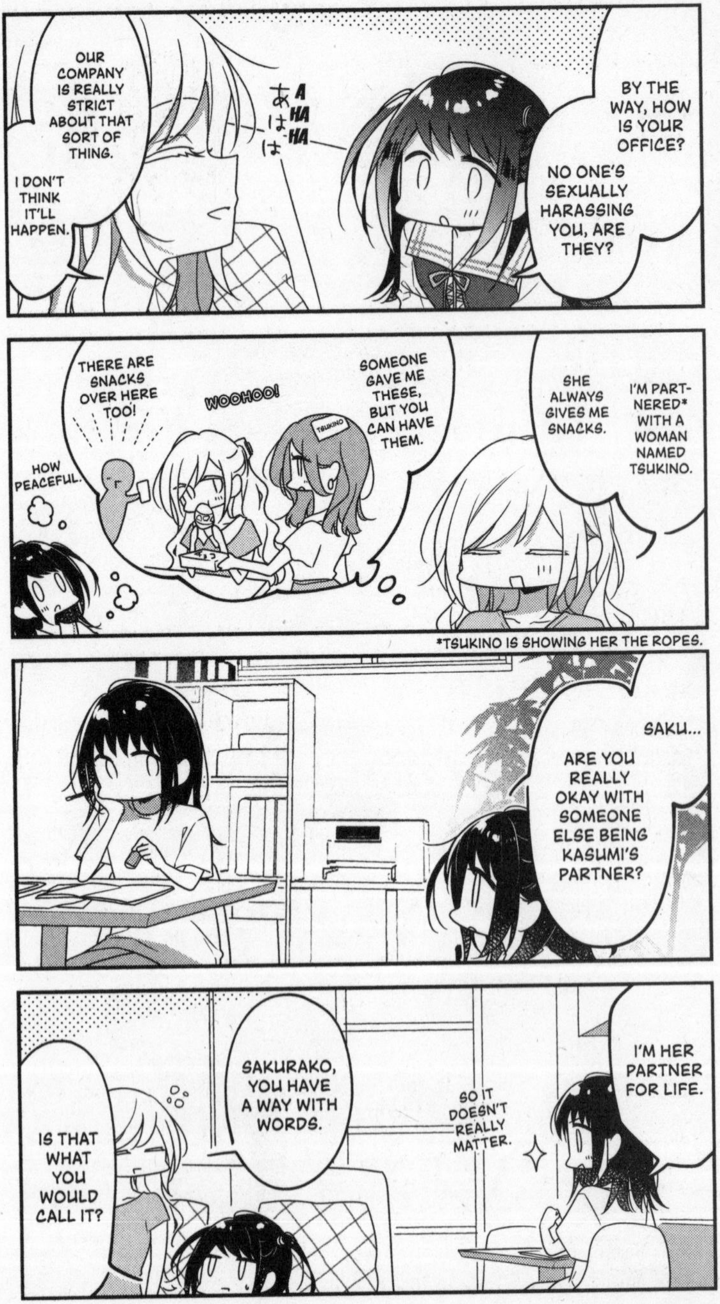

BY THE WAY, HOW IS YOUR OFFICE?
NO ONE'S SEXUALLY HARASSING YOU, ARE THEY?
A HA HA あはは
OUR COMPANY IS REALLY STRICT ABOUT THAT SORT OF THING.
I DON'T THINK IT'LL HAPPEN.
I'M PARTNERED* WITH A WOMAN NAMED TSUKINO.
SHE ALWAYS GIVES ME SNACKS.
SOMEONE GAVE ME THESE, BUT YOU CAN HAVE THEM.
TSUKINO
WOOHOO!
THERE ARE SNACKS OVER HERE TOO!
HOW PEACEFUL.
*TSUKINO IS SHOWING HER THE ROPES.
SAKU...
ARE YOU REALLY OKAY WITH SOMEONE ELSE BEING KASUMI'S PARTNER?
I'M HER PARTNER FOR LIFE.
SO IT DOESN'T REALLY MATTER.
SAKURAKO, YOU HAVE A WAY WITH WORDS.
IS THAT WHAT YOU WOULD CALL IT?

SINCE IT'S THE RAINY SEASON

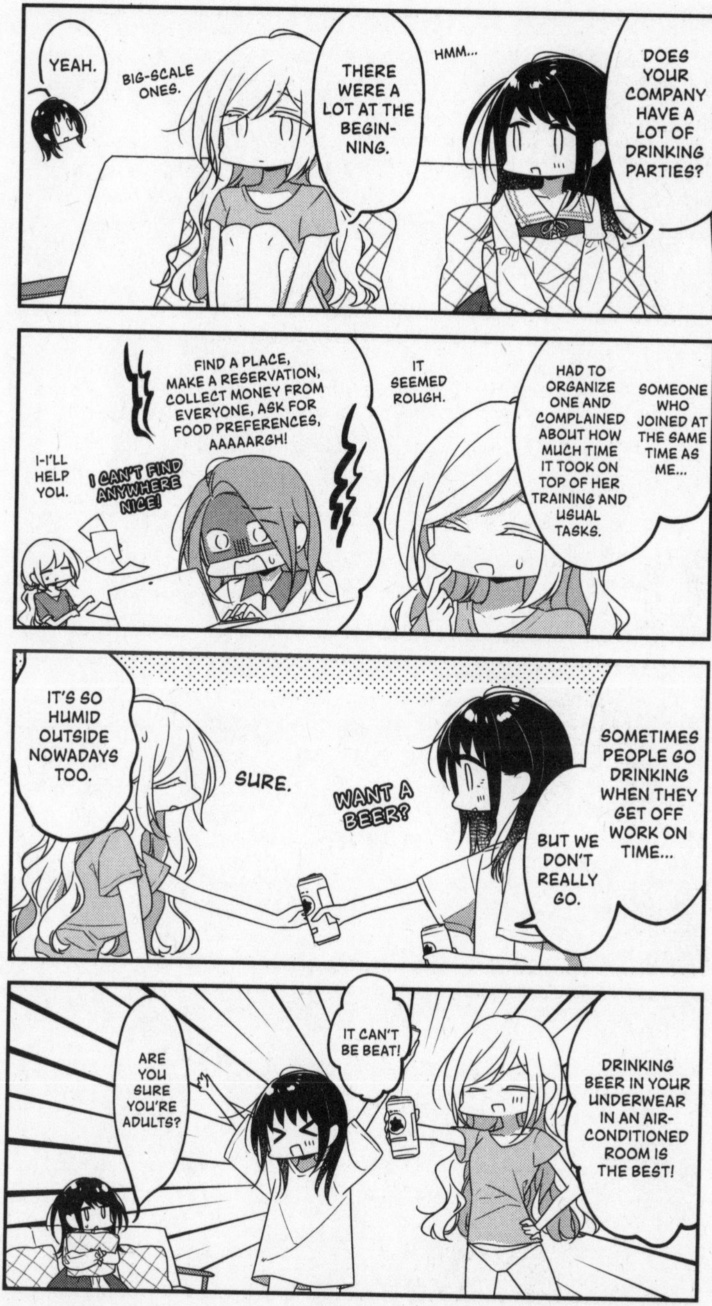
DOES YOUR COMPANY HAVE A LOT OF DRINKING PARTIES?
HMM...
THERE WERE A LOT AT THE BEGIN-NING.
BIG-SCALE ONES.
YEAH.
SOMEONE WHO JOINED AT THE SAME TIME AS ME...
HAD TO ORGANIZE ONE AND COMPLAINED ABOUT HOW MUCH TIME IT TOOK ON TOP OF HER TRAINING AND USUAL TASKS.
IT SEEMED ROUGH.
FIND A PLACE, MAKE A RESERVATION, COLLECT MONEY FROM EVERYONE, ASK FOR FOOD PREFERENCES, AAAAARGH!
I CAN'T FIND ANYWHERE NICE!
I-I'LL HELP YOU.
SOMETIMES PEOPLE GO DRINKING WHEN THEY GET OFF WORK ON TIME...
BUT WE DON'T REALLY GO.
WANT A BEER?
SURE.
IT'S SO HUMID OUTSIDE NOWADAYS TOO.
DRINKING BEER IN YOUR UNDERWEAR IN AN AIR-CONDITIONED ROOM IS THE BEST!
IT CAN'T BE BEAT!
ARE YOU SURE YOU'RE ADULTS?

SELFISH

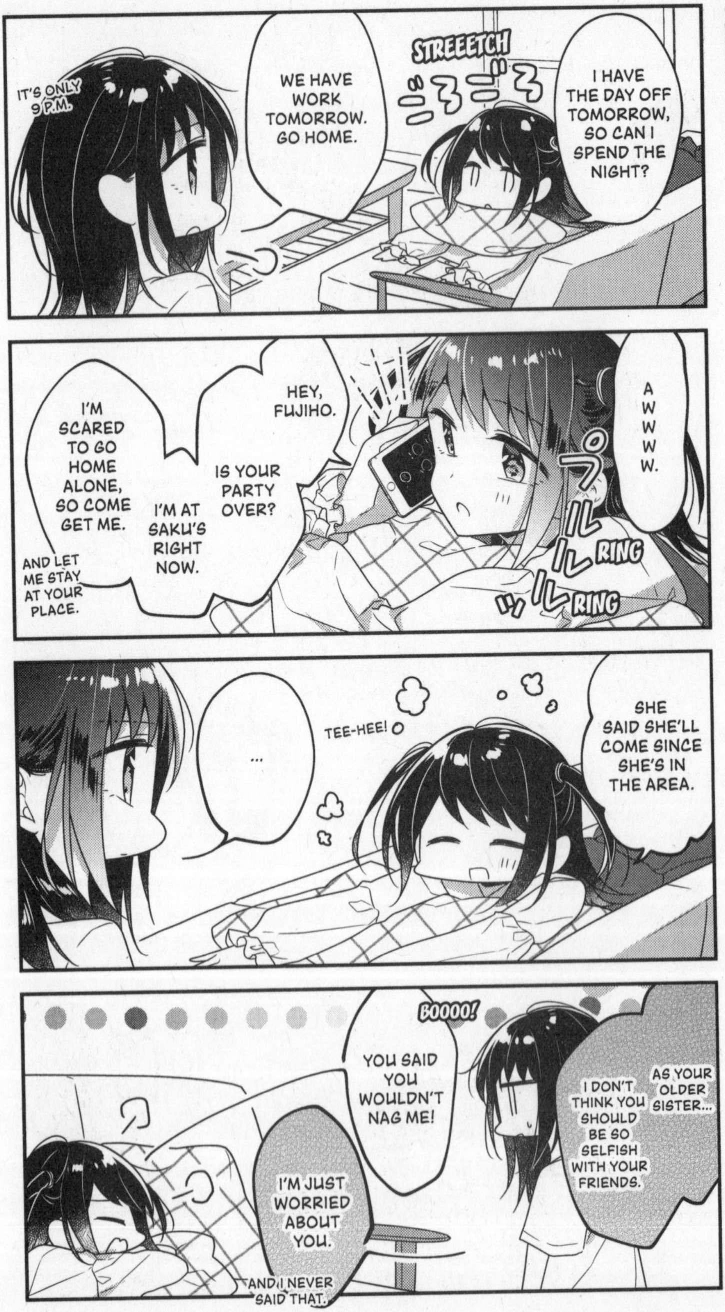
I HAVE THE DAY OFF TOMORROW, SO CAN I SPEND THE NIGHT?
STREEETCH
ごろごろ
WE HAVE WORK TOMORROW. GO HOME.
IT'S ONLY 9 P.M.
AWWWW.
プルルル
RING RING
HEY, FUJIHO.
IS YOUR PARTY OVER?
I'M AT SAKU'S RIGHT NOW.
I'M SCARED TO GO HOME ALONE, SO COME GET ME.
AND LET ME STAY AT YOUR PLACE.
SHE SAID SHE'LL COME SINCE SHE'S IN THE AREA.
TEE-HEE!
...
AS YOUR OLDER SISTER...
I DON'T THINK YOU SHOULD BE SO SELFISH WITH YOUR FRIENDS.
BOOOO!
YOU SAID YOU WOULDN'T NAG ME!
I'M JUST WORRIED ABOUT YOU.
AND I NEVER SAID THAT.

SURPRISED

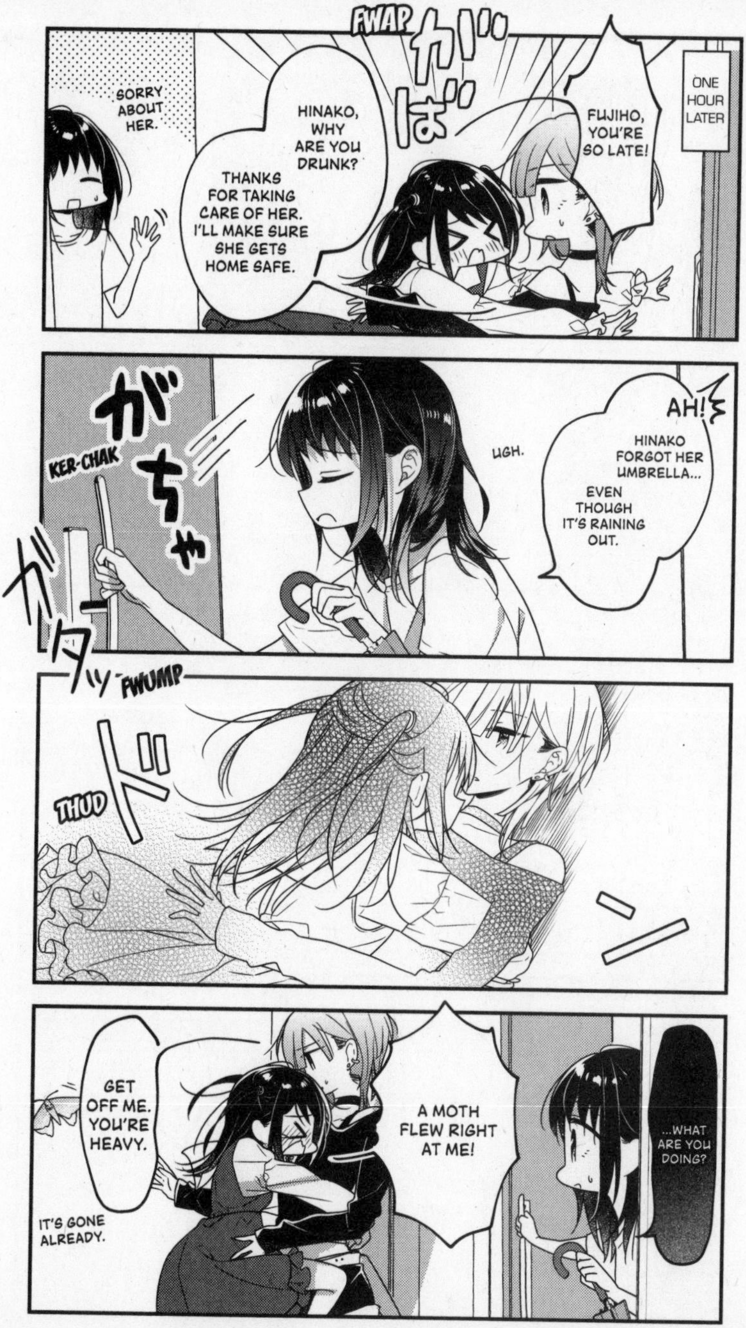
ONE HOUR LATER
FUJIHO, YOU'RE SO LATE!
FWAP
がばっ
HINAKO, WHY ARE YOU DRUNK?
THANKS FOR TAKING CARE OF HER. I'LL MAKE SURE SHE GETS HOME SAFE.
SORRY ABOUT HER.
AH!
HINAKO FORGOT HER UMBRELLA...
EVEN THOUGH IT'S RAINING OUT.
UGH.
がちゃ
KER-CHAK
ガタッ
FWUMP
ドッ
THUD
...WHAT ARE YOU DOING?
A MOTH FLEW RIGHT AT ME!
GET OFF ME. YOU'RE HEAVY.
IT'S GONE ALREADY.

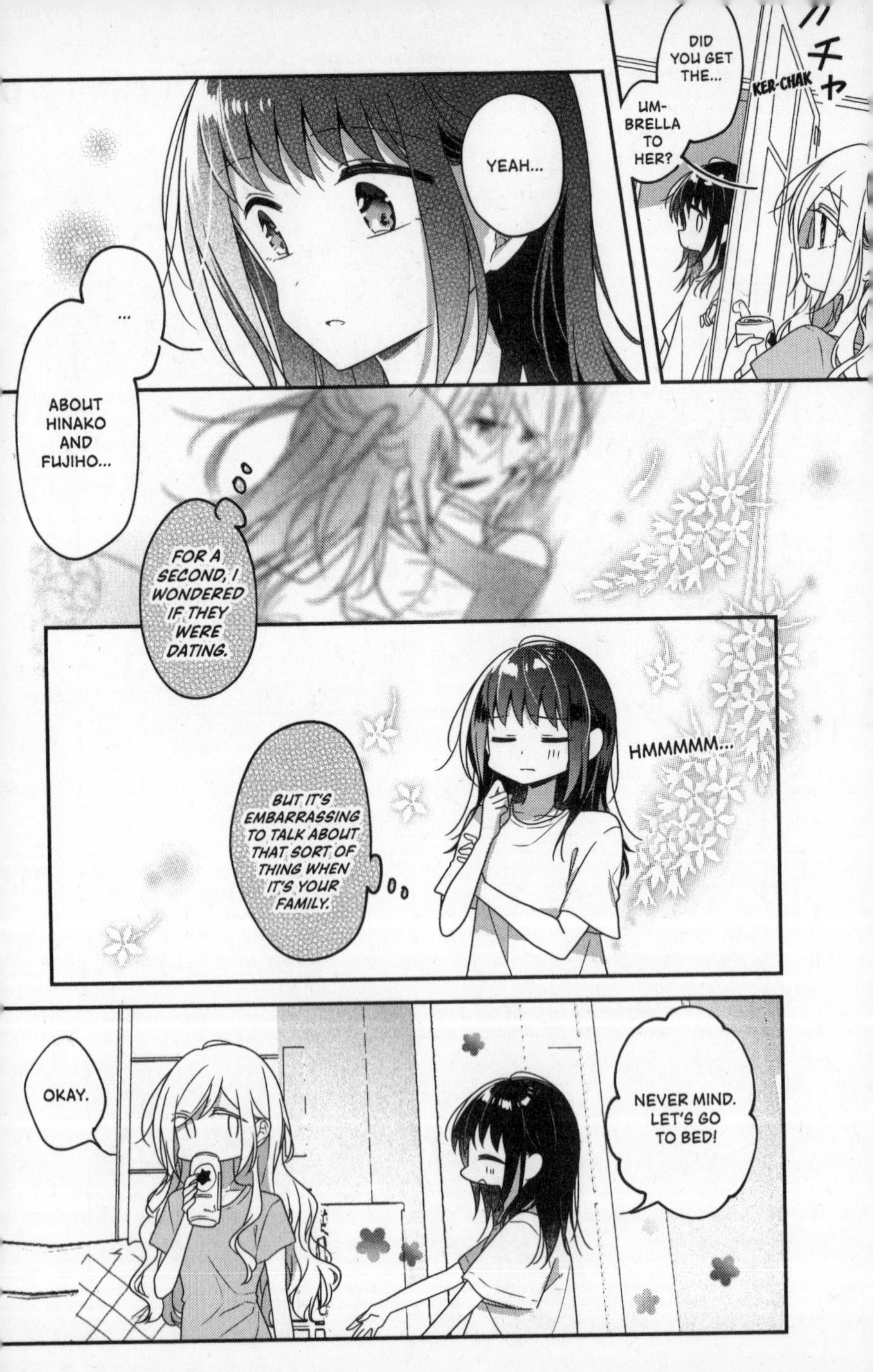
DID YOU GET THE... UM-BRELLA TO HER?
KER-CHAK
YEAH...
...
ABOUT HINAKO AND FUJIHO...
FOR A SECOND, I WONDERED IF THEY WERE DATING.
HMMMMM...
BUT IT'S EMBARRASSING TO TALK ABOUT THAT SORT OF THING WHEN IT'S YOUR FAMILY.
NEVER MIND. LET'S GO TO BED!
OKAY.

Illustration gallery of Yukiko

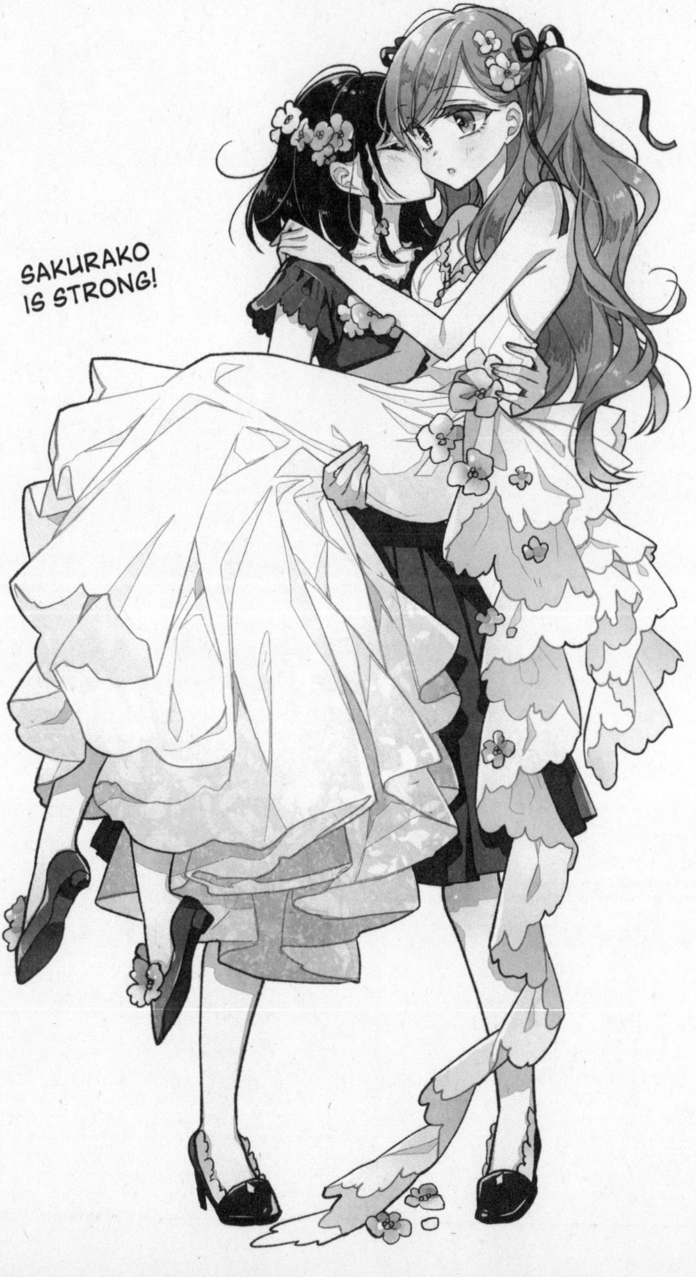
SAKURAKO
IS STRONG!

Futaribeya
A ROOM FOR TWO

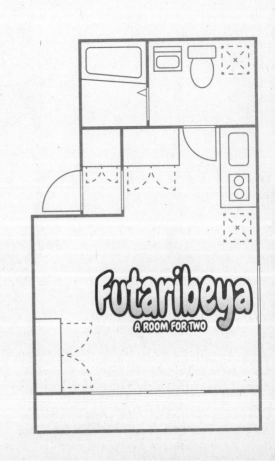

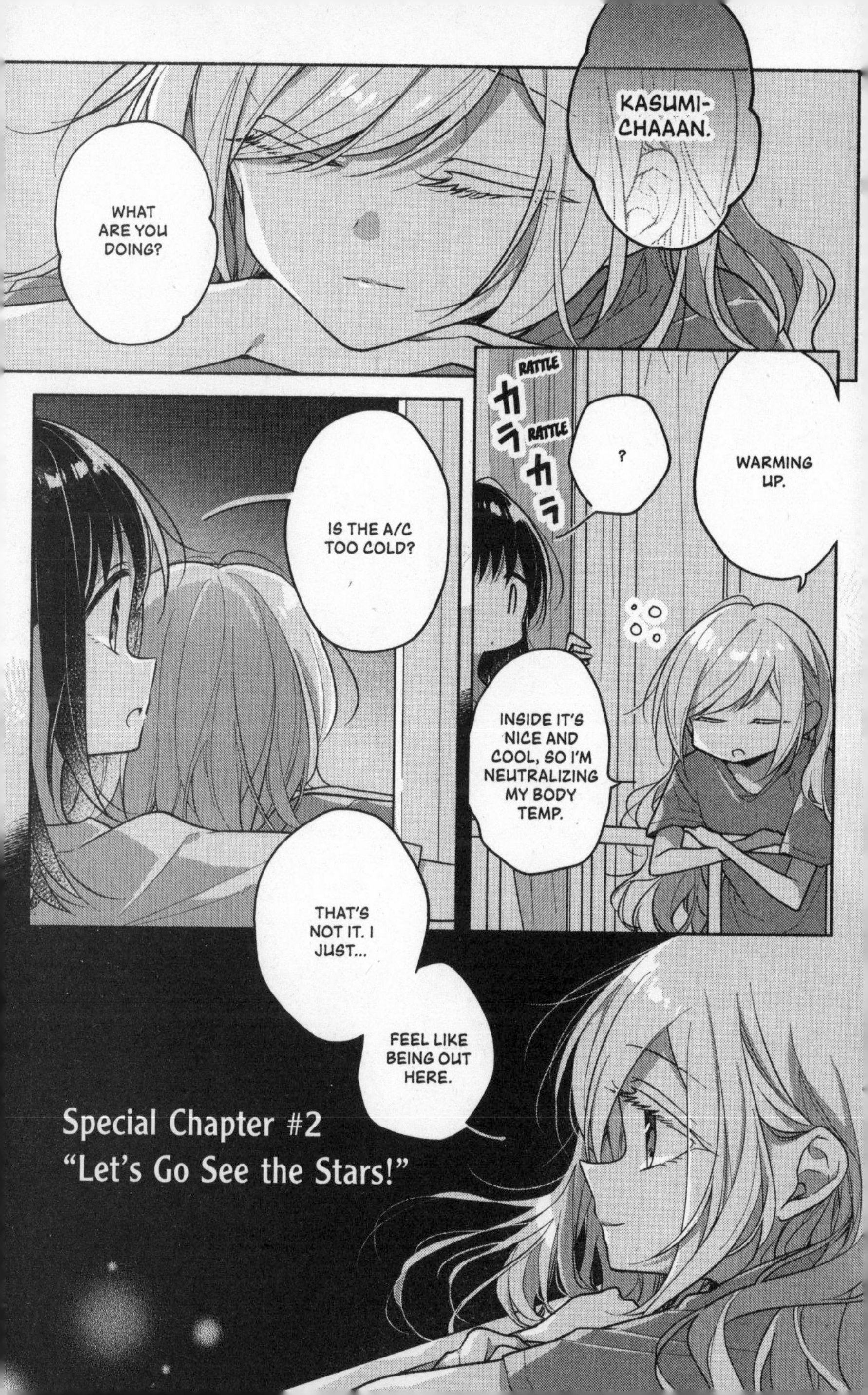
KASUMI-CHAAAN.
WHAT ARE YOU DOING?
WARMING UP.
?
RATTLE カラ
RATTLE カラ
INSIDE IT'S NICE AND COOL, SO I'M NEUTRALIZING MY BODY TEMP.
IS THE A/C TOO COLD?
THAT'S NOT IT. I JUST...
FEEL LIKE BEING OUT HERE.
Special Chapter #2
"Let's Go See the Stars!"

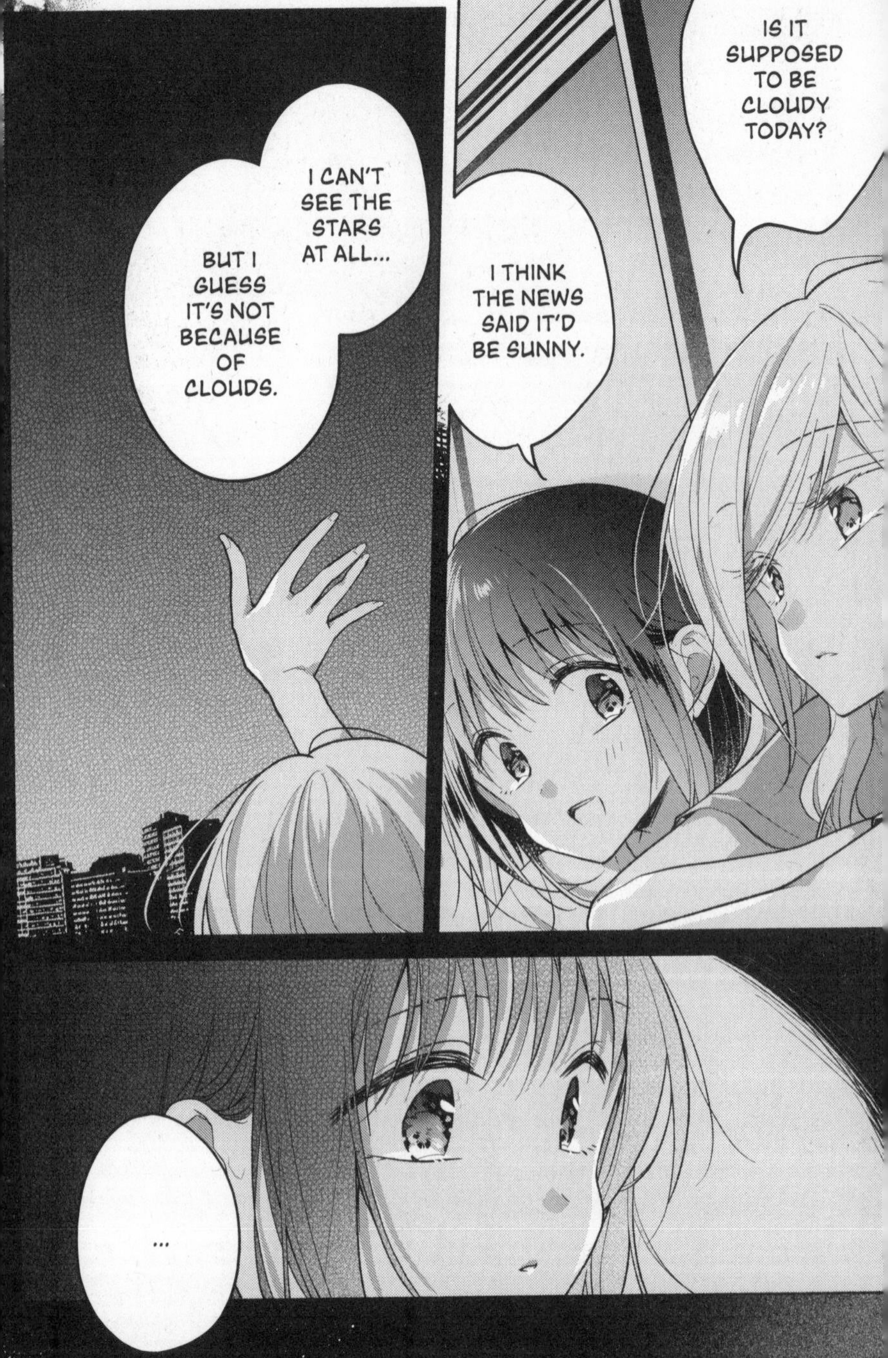
IS IT SUPPOSED TO BE CLOUDY TODAY?
I THINK THE NEWS SAID IT'D BE SUNNY.
I CAN'T SEE THE STARS AT ALL...
BUT I GUESS IT'S NOT BECAUSE OF CLOUDS.
...

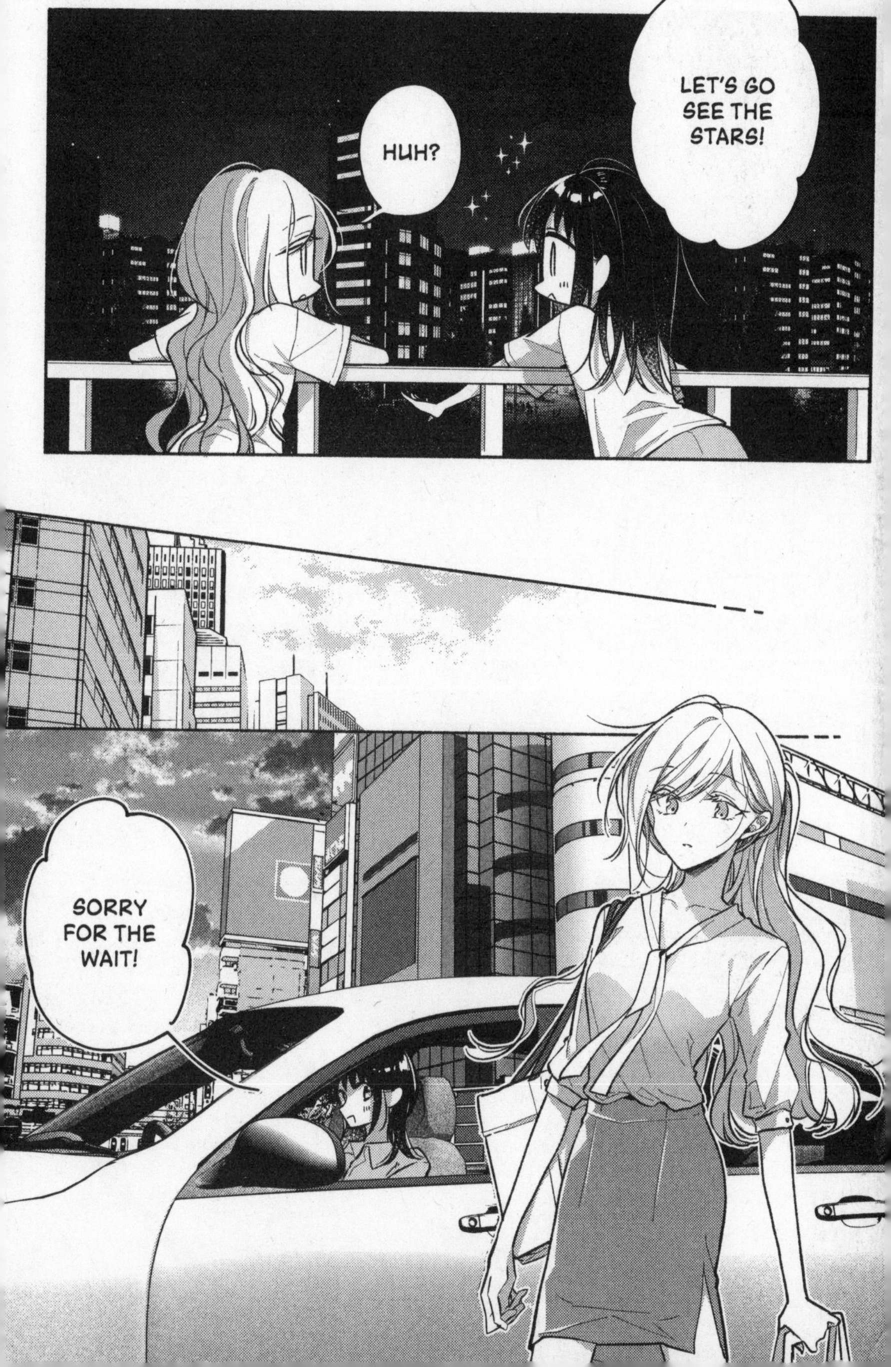
LET'S GO SEE THE STARS!
HUH?
SORRY FOR THE WAIT!

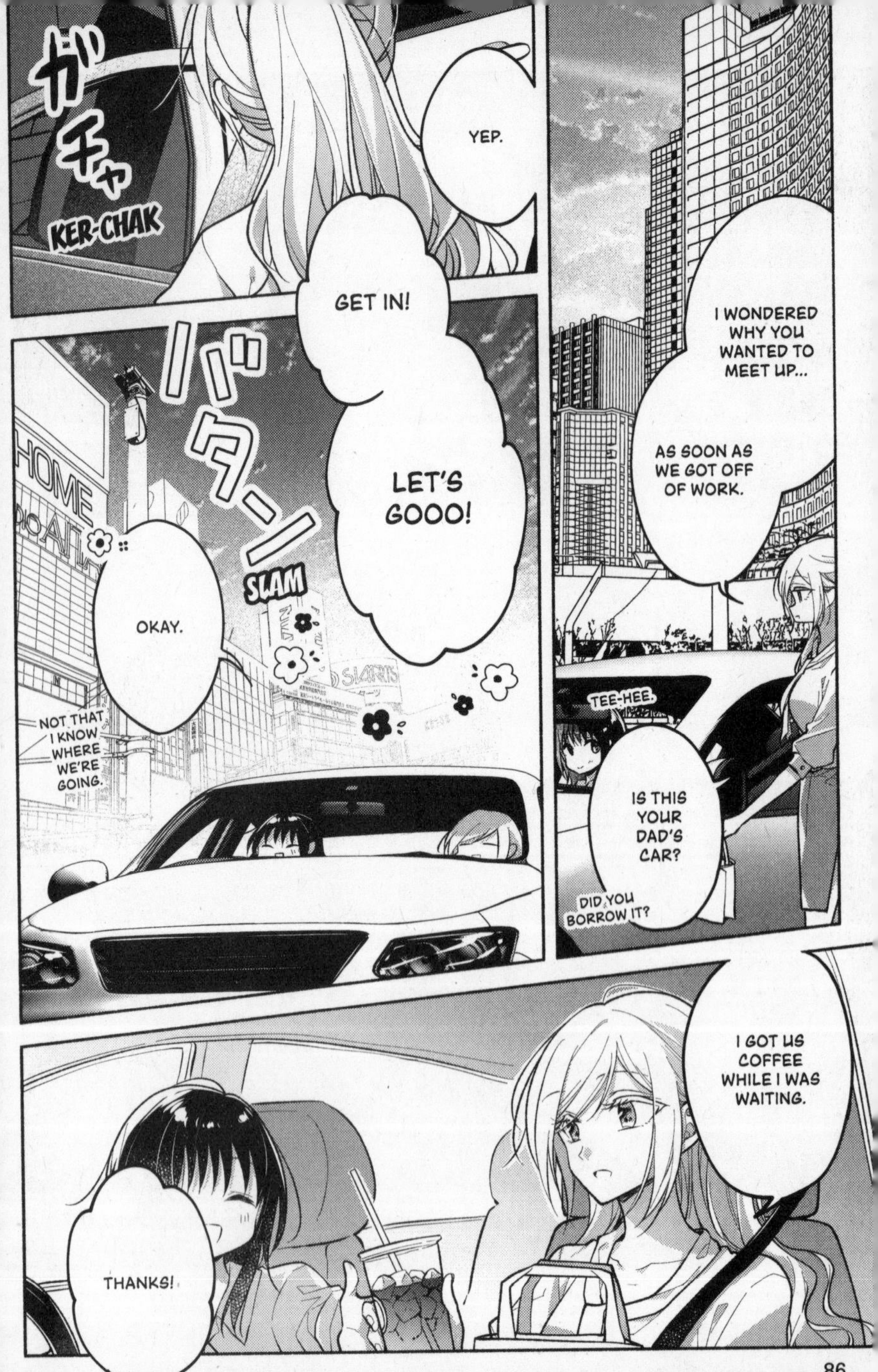
I WONDERED WHY YOU WANTED TO MEET UP...
AS SOON AS WE GOT OFF OF WORK.
TEE-HEE.
IS THIS YOUR DAD'S CAR?
DID YOU BORROW IT?
ガチャ
KER-CHAK
YEP.
GET IN!
LET'S GOOO!
バターン
SLAM
OKAY.
NOT THAT I KNOW WHERE WE'RE GOING.
I GOT US COFFEE WHILE I WAS WAITING.
THANKS!

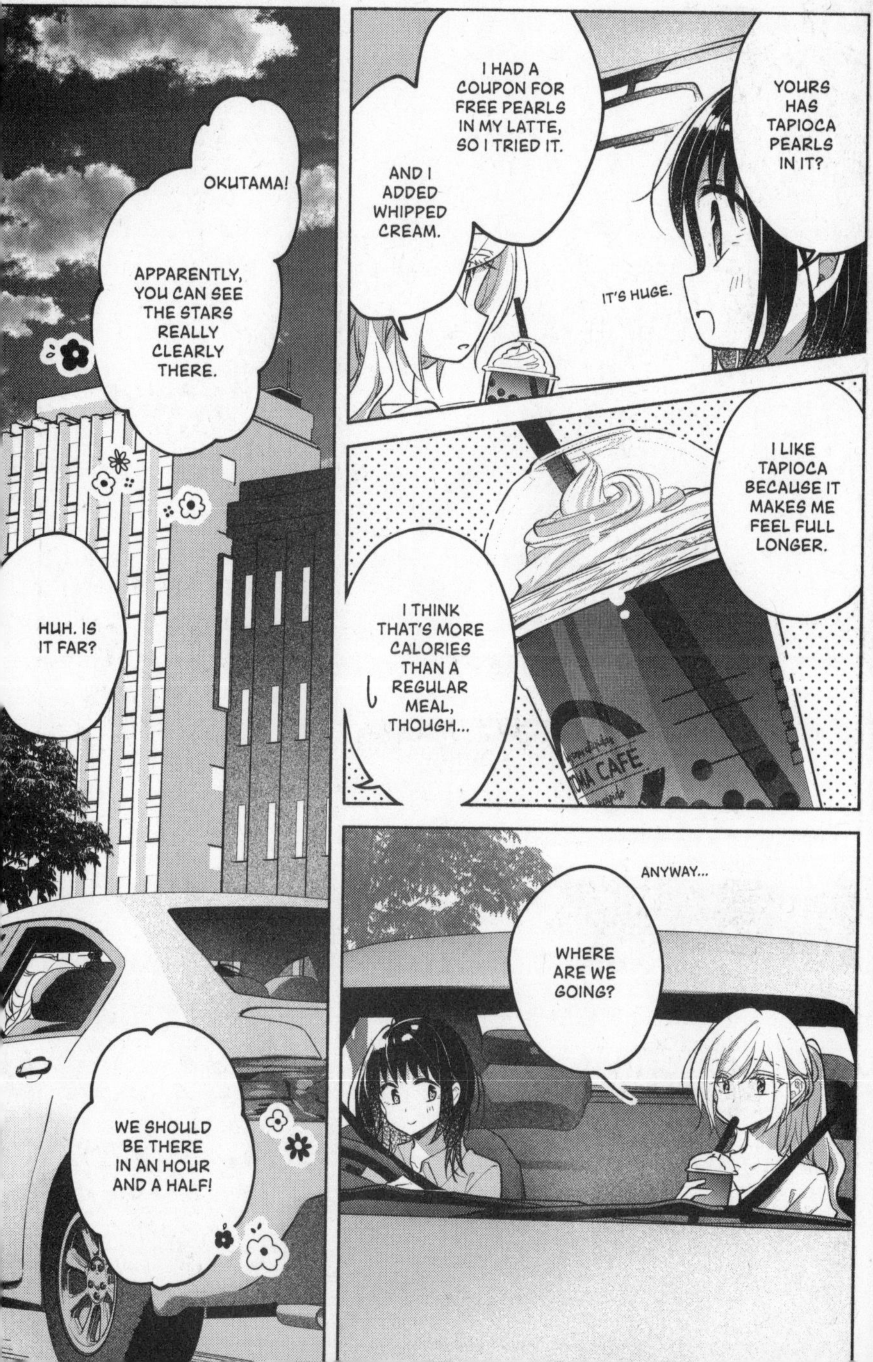
YOURS HAS TAPIOCA PEARLS IN IT?
IT'S HUGE.
I HAD A COUPON FOR FREE PEARLS IN MY LATTE, SO I TRIED IT.
AND I ADDED WHIPPED CREAM.
I LIKE TAPIOCA BECAUSE IT MAKES ME FEEL FULL LONGER.
I THINK THAT'S MORE CALORIES THAN A REGULAR MEAL, THOUGH...
ANYWAY...
WHERE ARE WE GOING?
OKUTAMA!
APPARENTLY, YOU CAN SEE THE STARS REALLY CLEARLY THERE.
HUH. IS IT FAR?
WE SHOULD BE THERE IN AN HOUR AND A HALF!

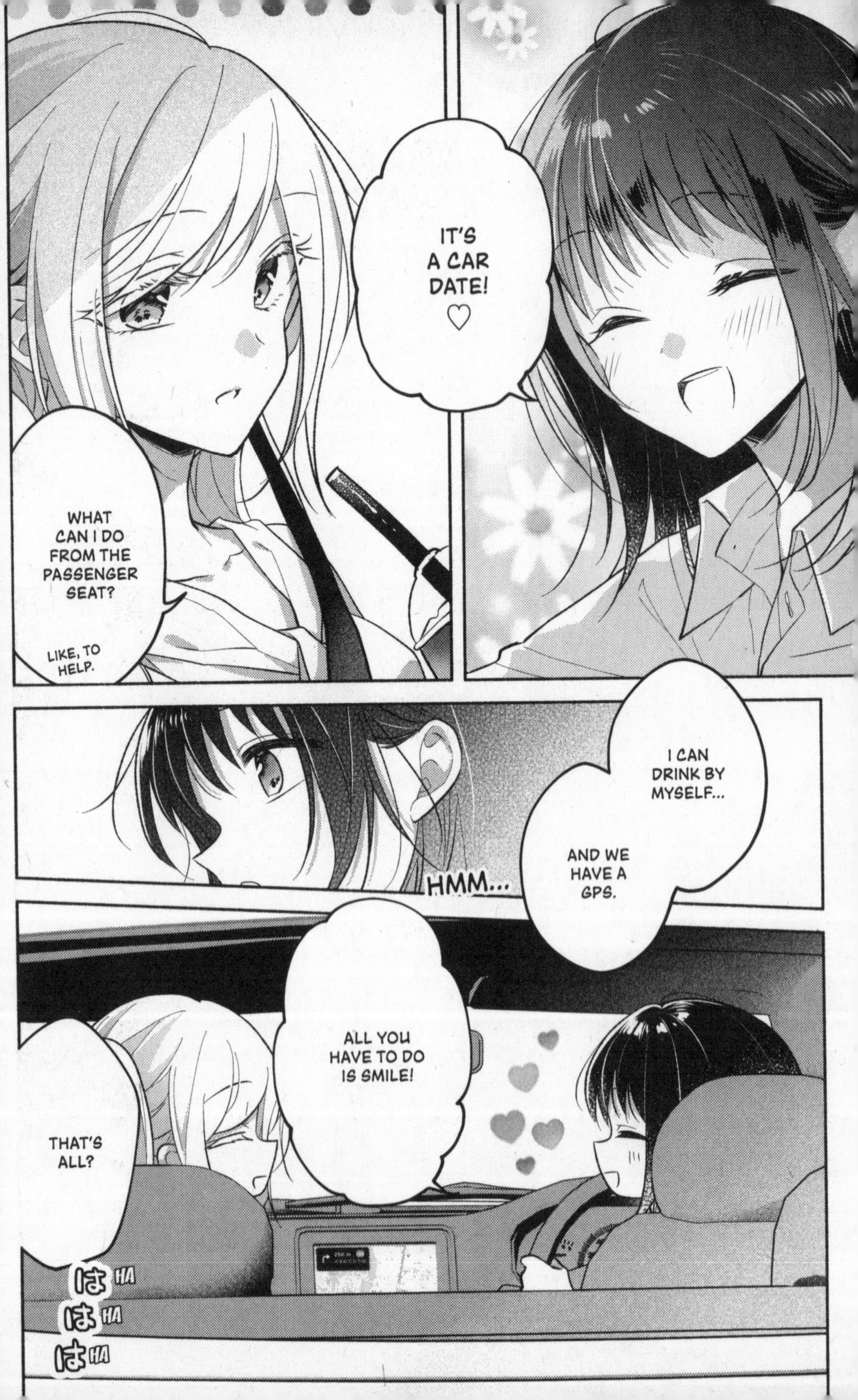
IT'S A CAR DATE! ♡
WHAT CAN I DO FROM THE PASSENGER SEAT?
LIKE, TO HELP.
I CAN DRINK BY MYSELF...
AND WE HAVE A GPS.
HMM...
ALL YOU HAVE TO DO IS SMILE!
THAT'S ALL?
は HA
は HA
は HA

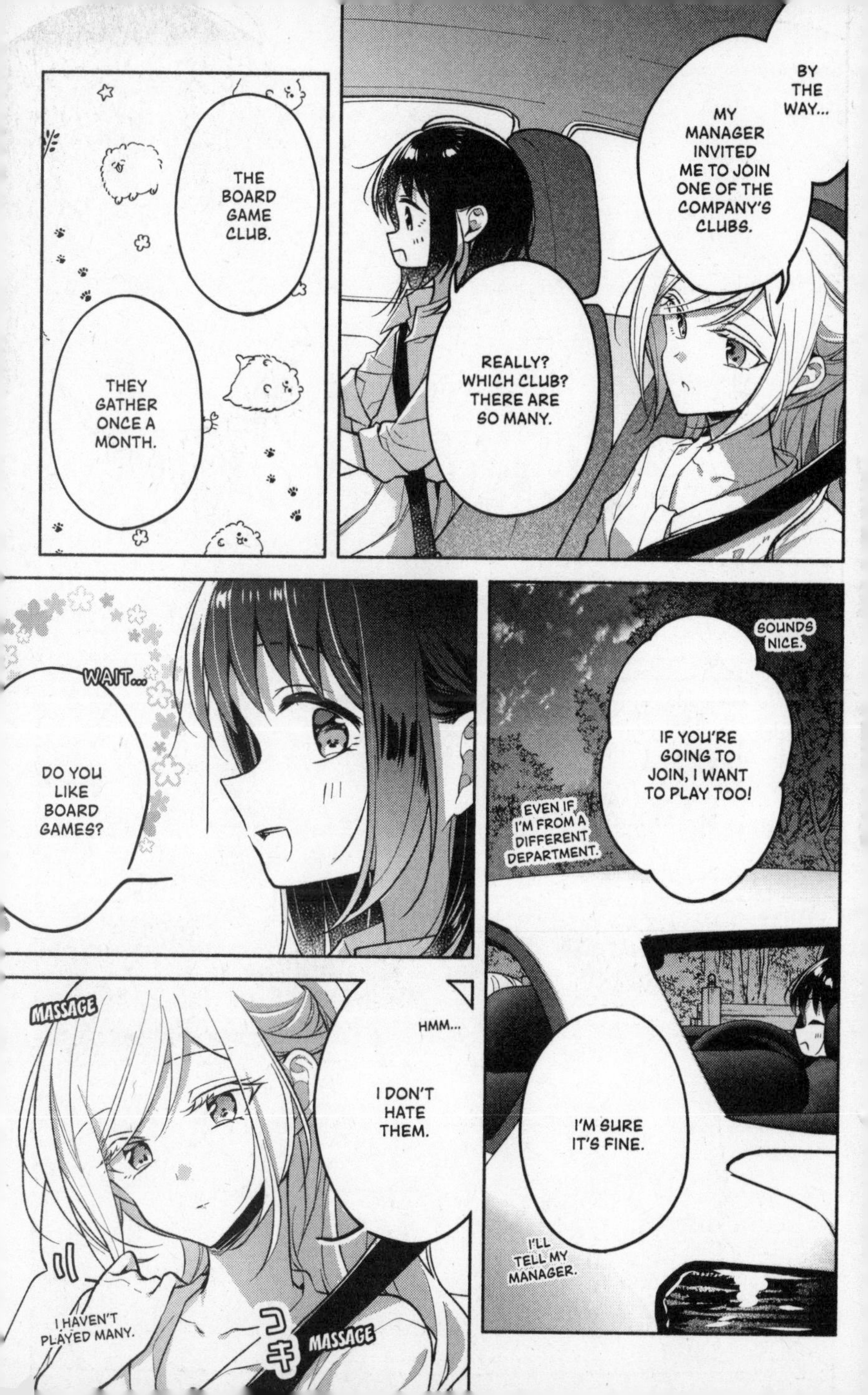
BY THE WAY...
MY MANAGER INVITED ME TO JOIN ONE OF THE COMPANY'S CLUBS.
REALLY? WHICH CLUB? THERE ARE SO MANY.
THE BOARD GAME CLUB.
THEY GATHER ONCE A MONTH.
SOUNDS NICE.
IF YOU'RE GOING TO JOIN, I WANT TO PLAY TOO!
EVEN IF I'M FROM A DIFFERENT DEPARTMENT.
I'M SURE IT'S FINE.
I'LL TELL MY MANAGER.
WAIT...
DO YOU LIKE BOARD GAMES?
MASSAGE
HMM...
I DON'T HATE THEM.
I HAVEN'T PLAYED MANY.
MASSAGE

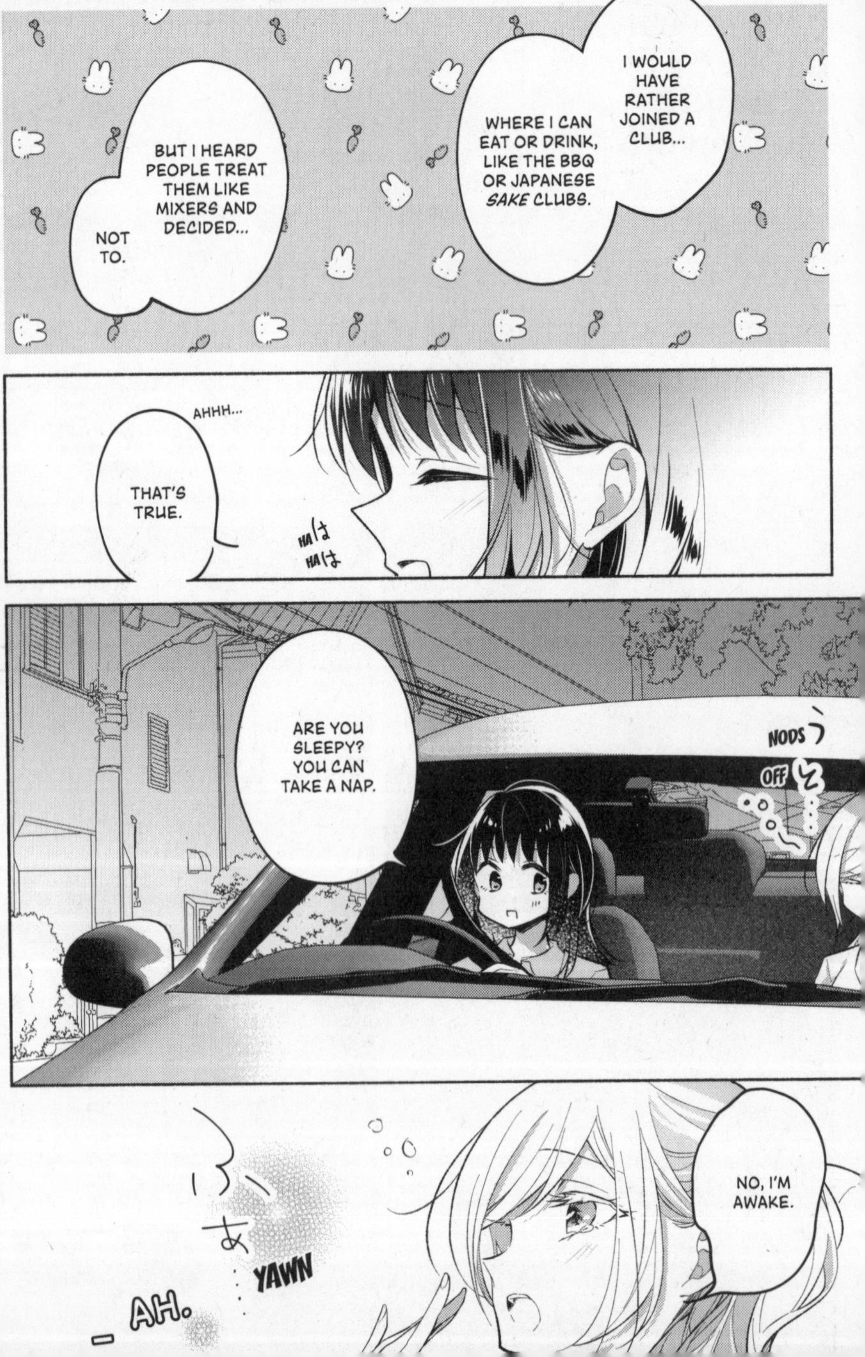
I WOULD HAVE RATHER JOINED A CLUB...
WHERE I CAN EAT OR DRINK, LIKE THE BBQ OR JAPANESE *SAKE* CLUBS.
BUT I HEARD PEOPLE TREAT THEM LIKE MIXERS AND DECIDED...
NOT TO.
HA は HA は
AHHH...
THAT'S TRUE.
NODS う
OFF と...
ARE YOU SLEEPY? YOU CAN TAKE A NAP.
NO, I'M AWAKE.
ふぁ
YAWN
AH.

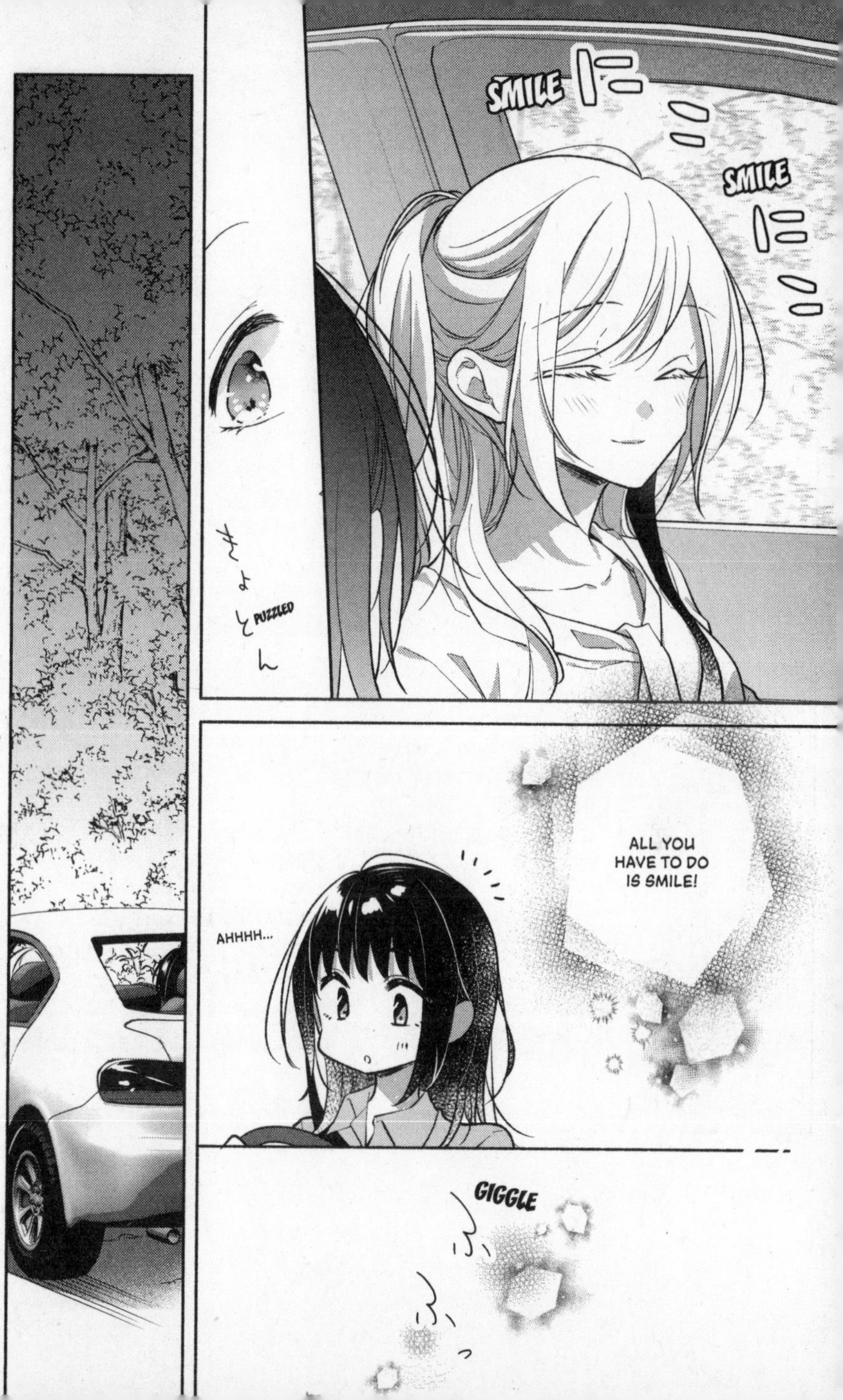
SMILE
SMILE
きょとん
PUZZLED
ALL YOU HAVE TO DO IS SMILE!
AHHHH...
GIGGLE
ふふっ

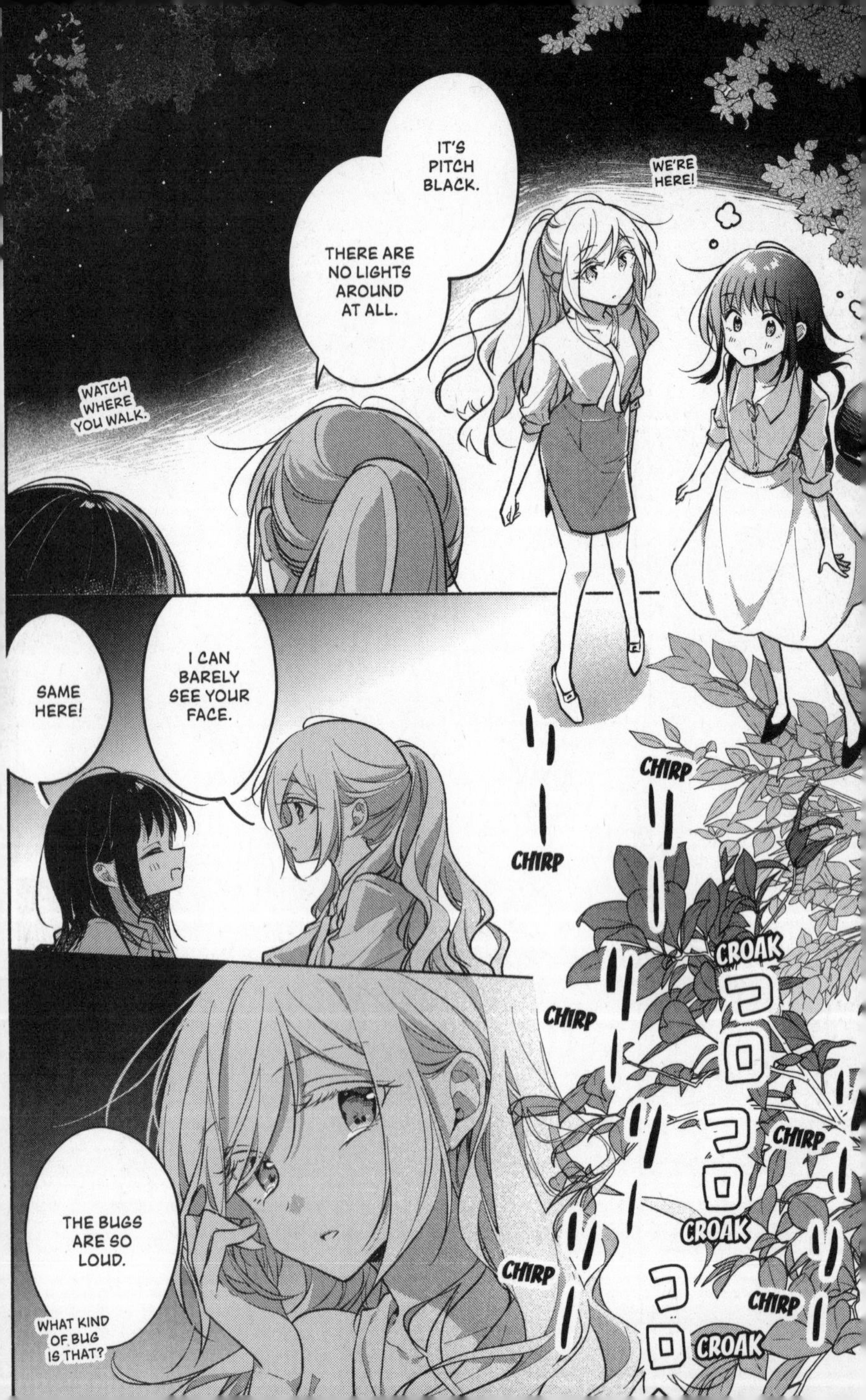

WE'RE HERE!
IT'S PITCH BLACK.
THERE ARE NO LIGHTS AROUND AT ALL.
WATCH WHERE YOU WALK.
CHIRP
CHIRP
CROAK
コロ
コロ
CHIRP
CHIRP
CROAK
CHIRP
CHIRP
CROAK
I CAN BARELY SEE YOUR FACE.
SAME HERE!
THE BUGS ARE SO LOUD.
WHAT KIND OF BUG IS THAT?

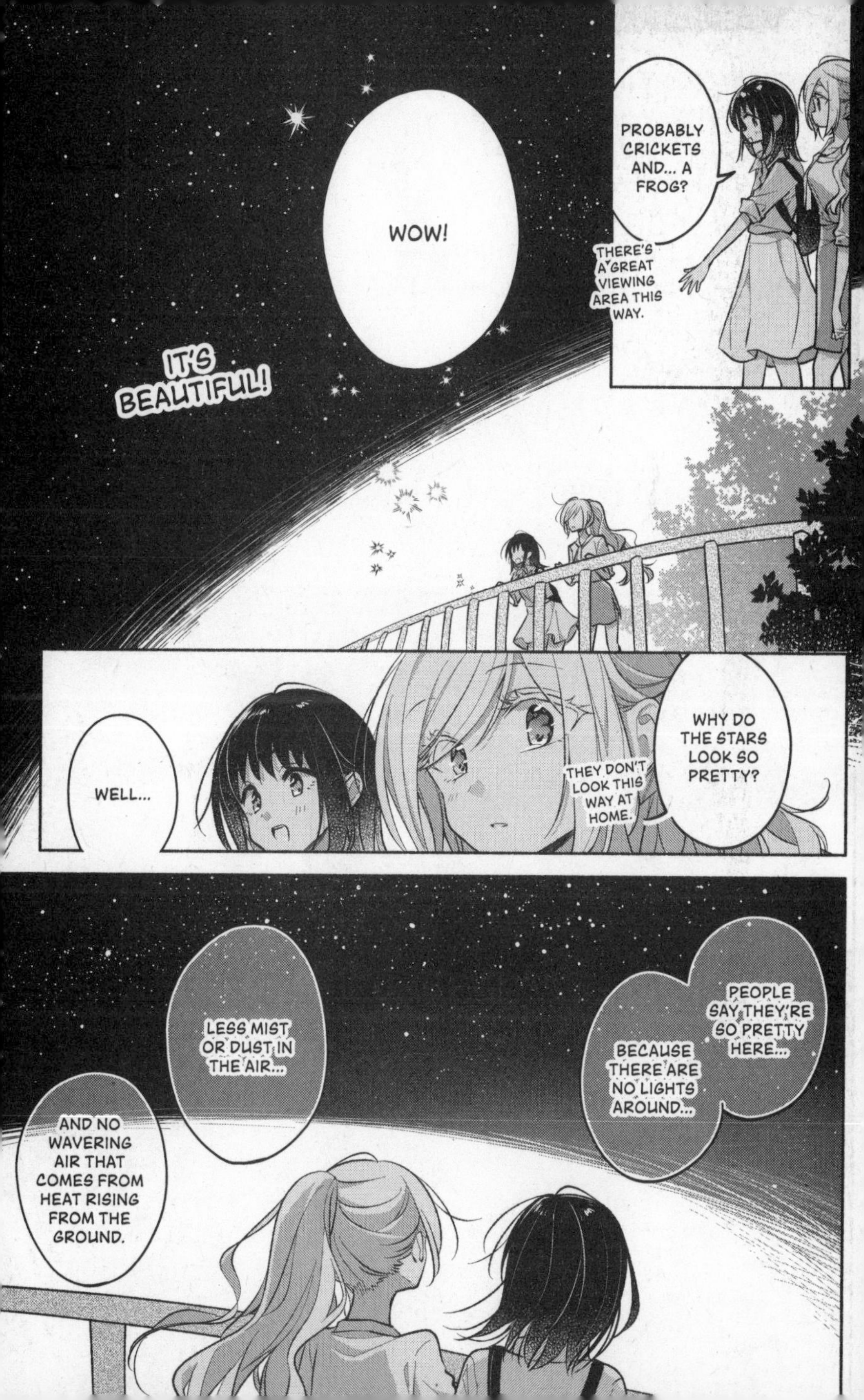
PROBABLY CRICKETS AND... A FROG?
THERE'S A GREAT VIEWING AREA THIS WAY.
WOW!
IT'S BEAUTIFUL!
WHY DO THE STARS LOOK SO PRETTY?
THEY DON'T LOOK THIS WAY AT HOME.
WELL...
PEOPLE SAY THEY'RE SO PRETTY HERE...
BECAUSE THERE ARE NO LIGHTS AROUND...
LESS MIST OR DUST IN THE AIR...
AND NO WAVERING AIR THAT COMES FROM HEAT RISING FROM THE GROUND.

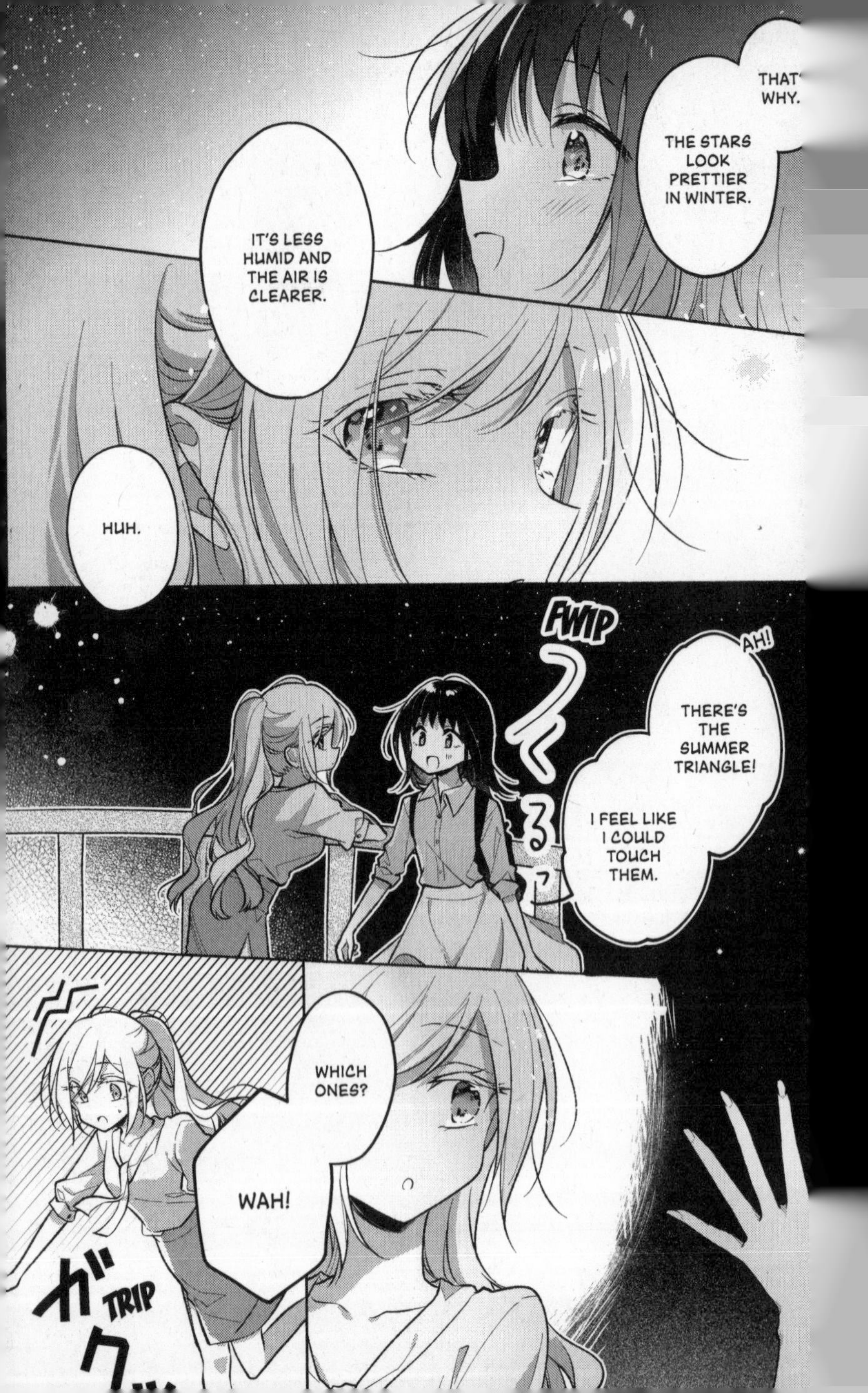
THAT'
WHY.
THE STARS LOOK PRETTIER IN WINTER.
IT'S LESS HUMID AND THE AIR IS CLEARER.
HUH.
FWIP
AH!
THERE'S THE SUMMER TRIANGLE!
I FEEL LIKE I COULD TOUCH THEM.
WHICH ONES?
WAH!
TRIP

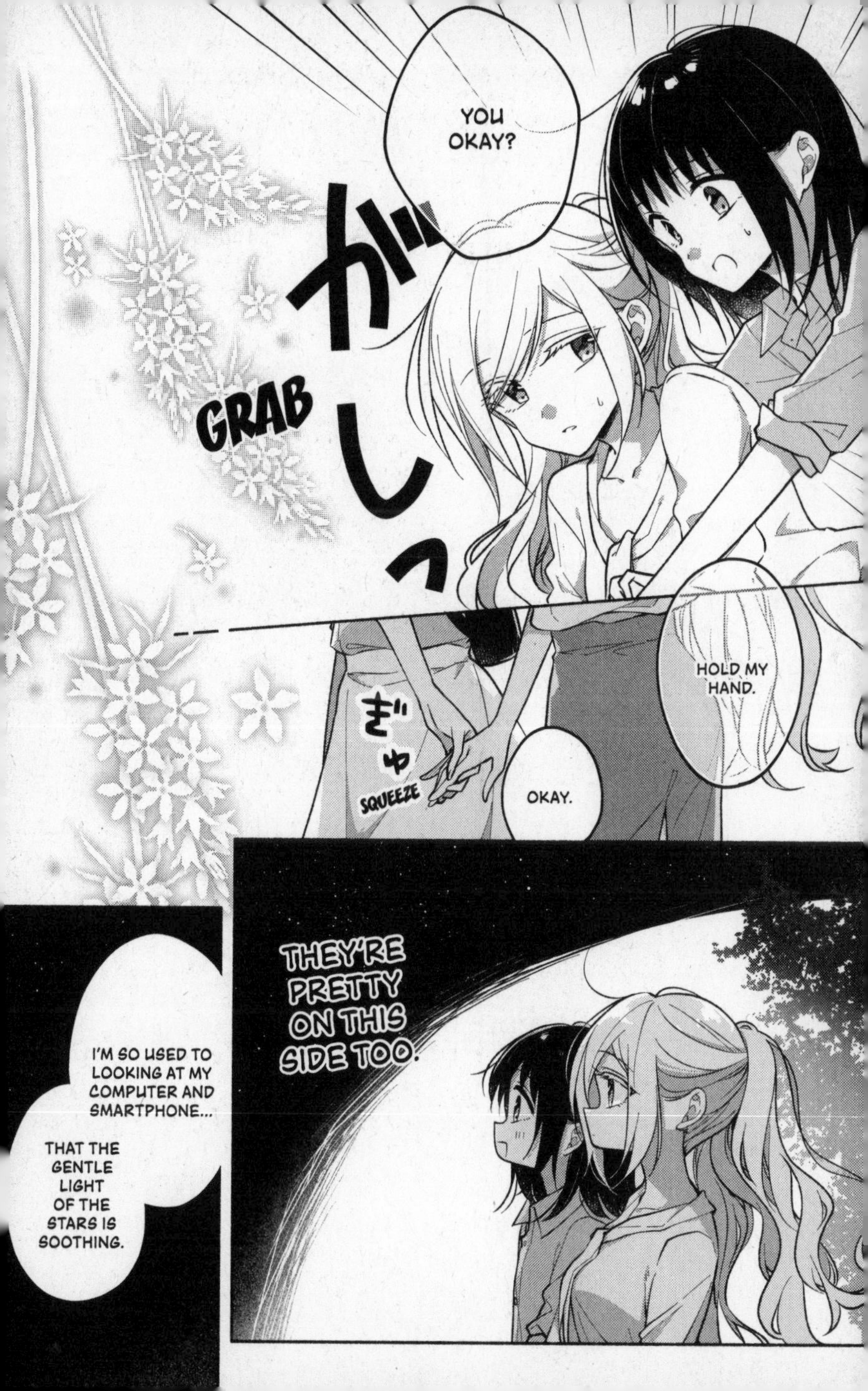
YOU OKAY?
がしっ
GRAB
HOLD MY HAND.
OKAY.
ぎゅ
SQUEEZE
THEY'RE PRETTY ON THIS SIDE TOO.
I'M SO USED TO LOOKING AT MY COMPUTER AND SMARTPHONE...
THAT THE GENTLE LIGHT OF THE STARS IS SOOTHING.

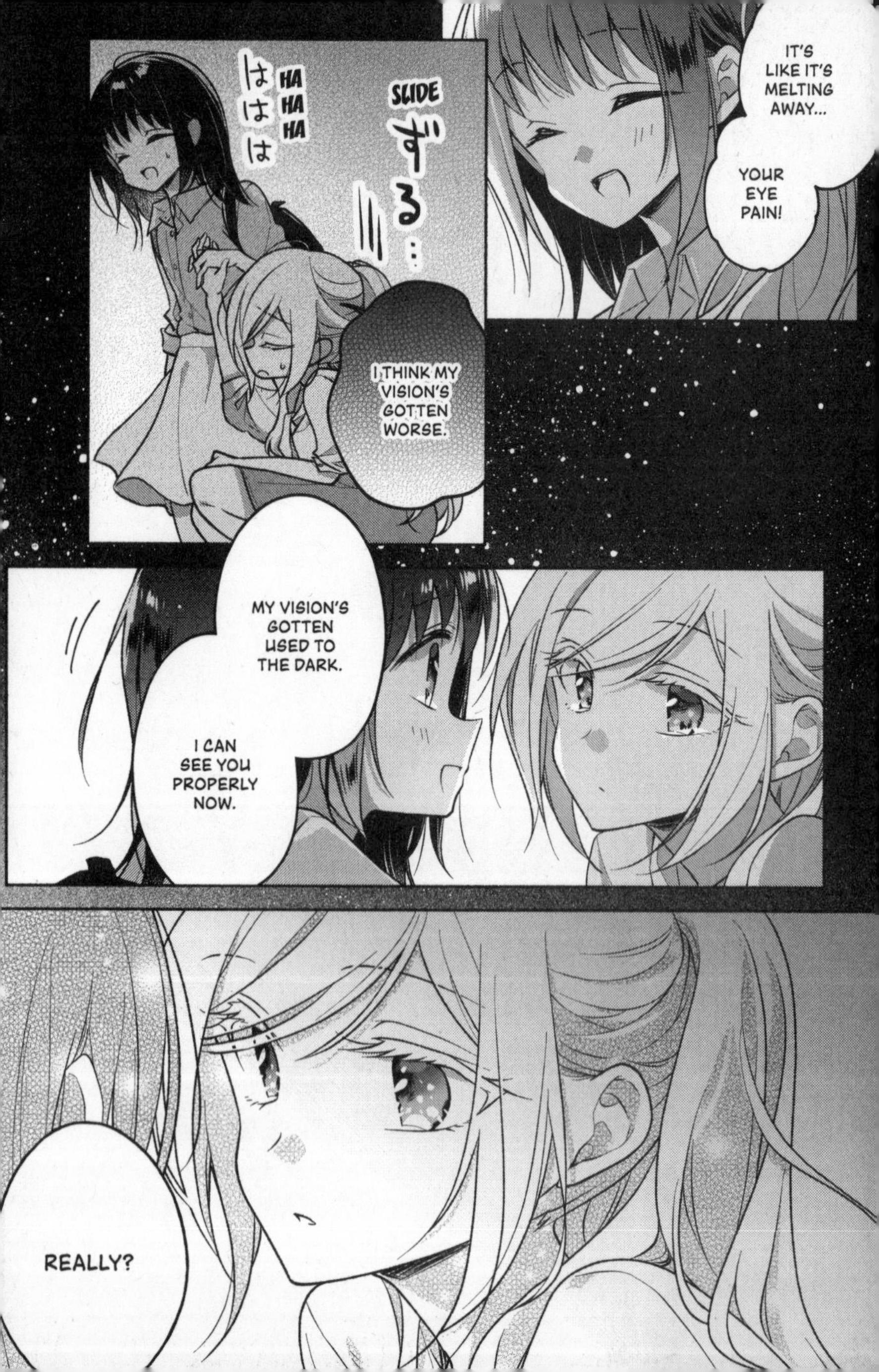
IT'S LIKE IT'S MELTING AWAY...
YOUR EYE PAIN!
SLIDE ずる…
HA HA HA ははは
I THINK MY VISION'S GOTTEN WORSE.
MY VISION'S GOTTEN USED TO THE DARK.
I CAN SEE YOU PROPERLY NOW.
REALLY?

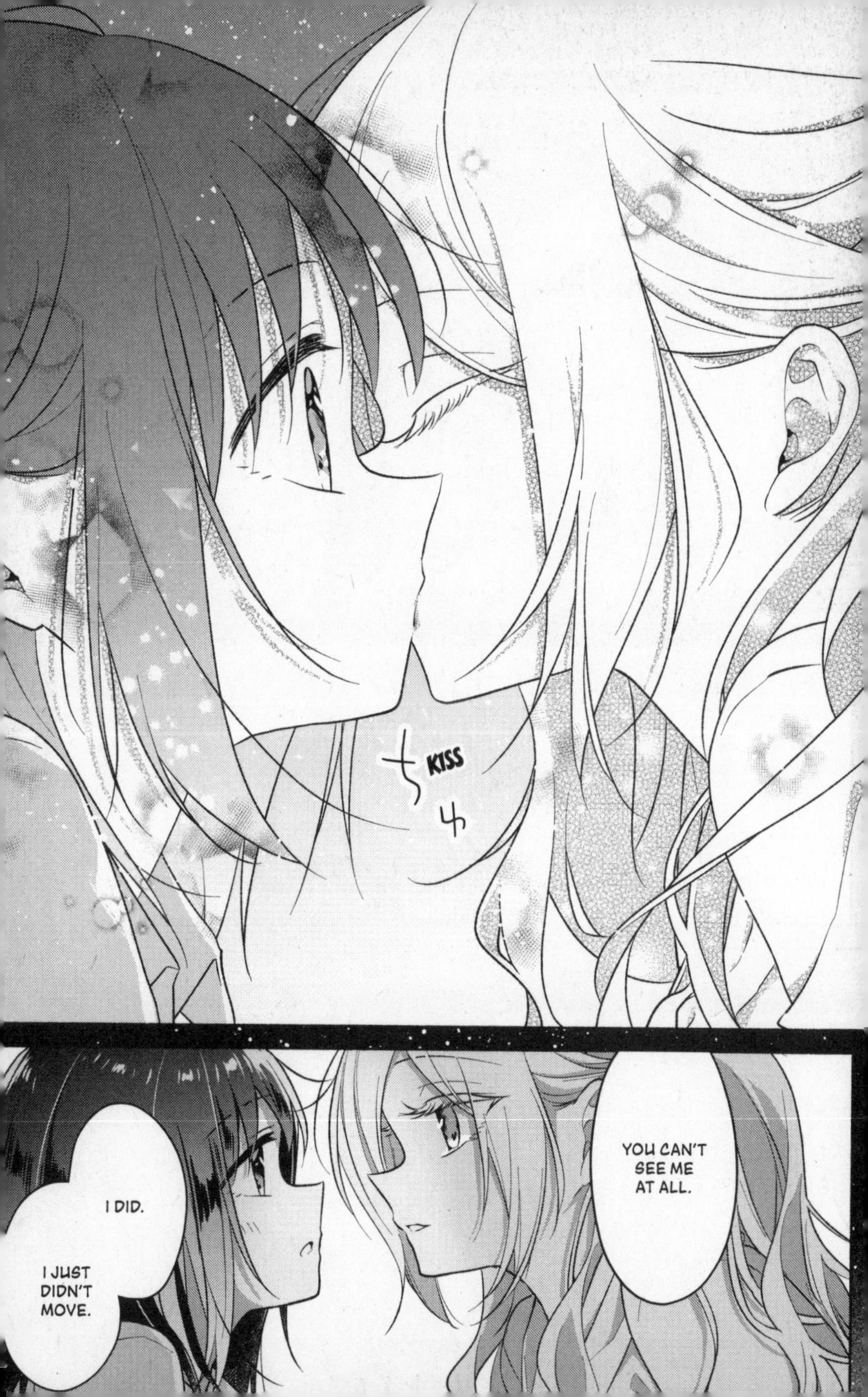
KISS
YOU CAN'T SEE ME AT ALL.
I DID.
I JUST DIDN'T MOVE.

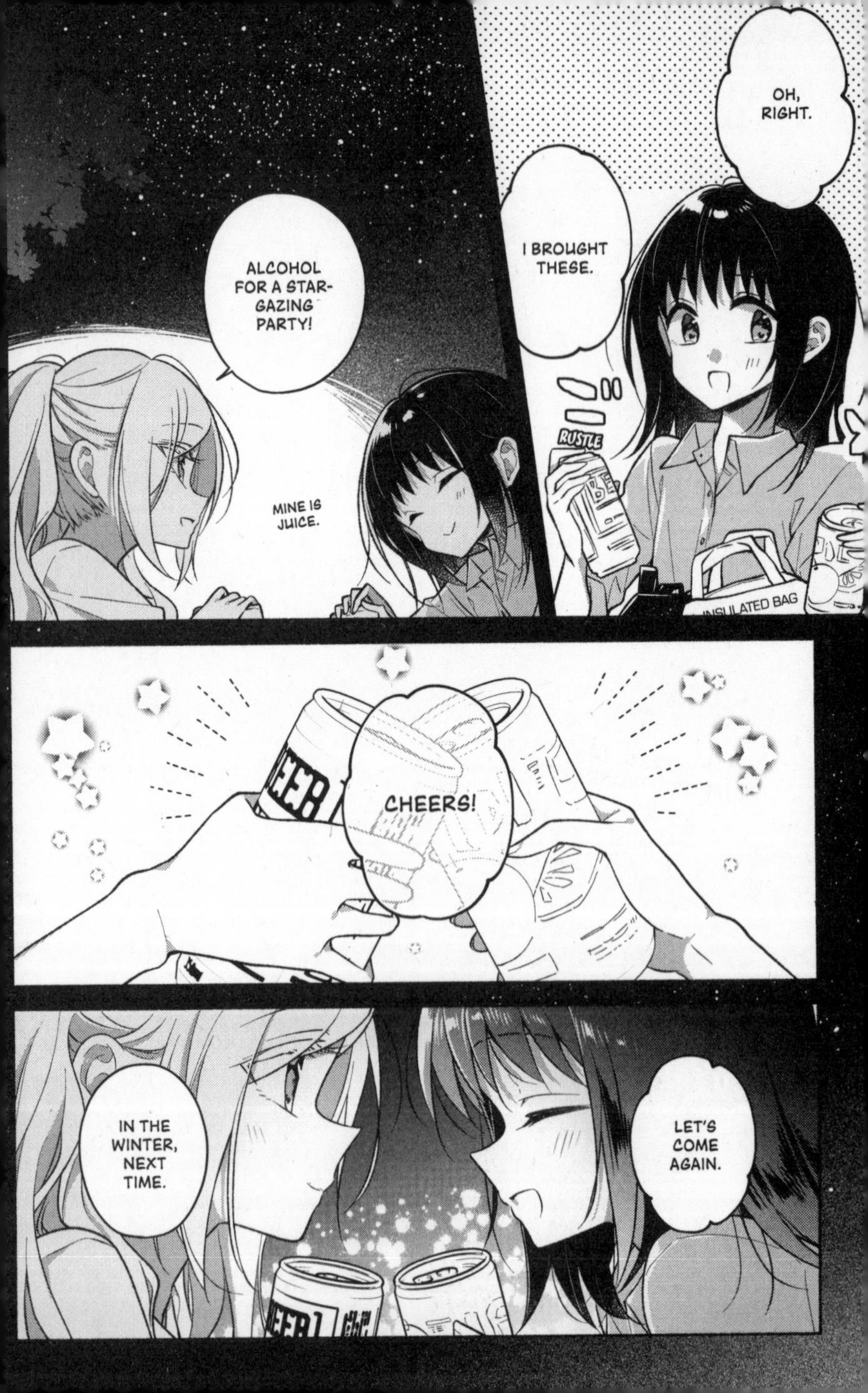
OH, RIGHT.
I BROUGHT THESE.
RUSTLE
INSULATED BAG
ALCOHOL FOR A STAR-GAZING PARTY!
MINE IS JUICE.
CHEERS!
LET'S COME AGAIN.
IN THE WINTER, NEXT TIME.

Illustration gallery of Yukiko

I MADE THIS ILLUSTRATION INTO A PORTABLE PHONE CHARGER!

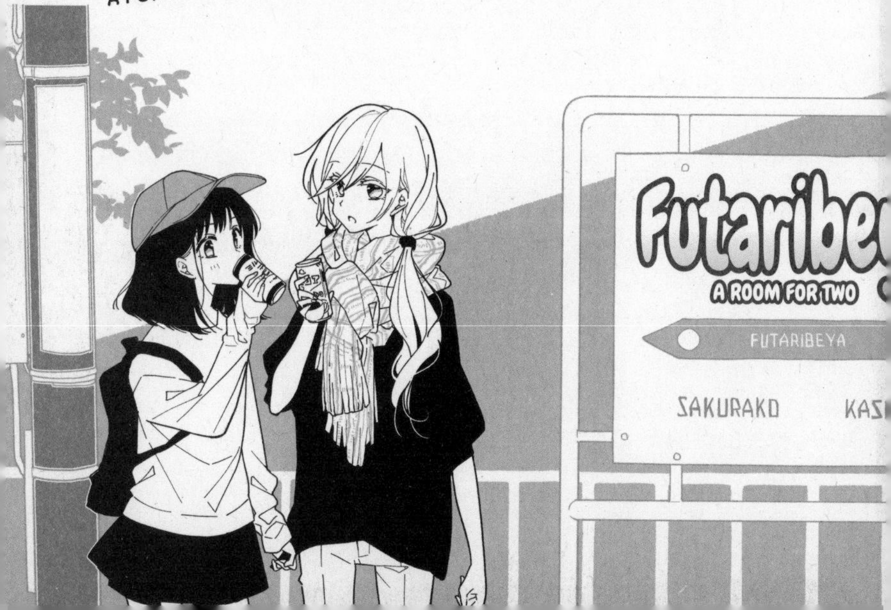
Futaribe
A ROOM FOR TWO
FUTARIBEYA
SAKURAKO
KAS

Futaribeya
A ROOM FOR TWO

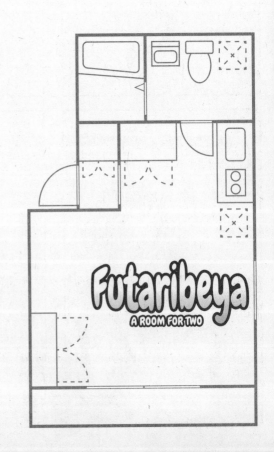

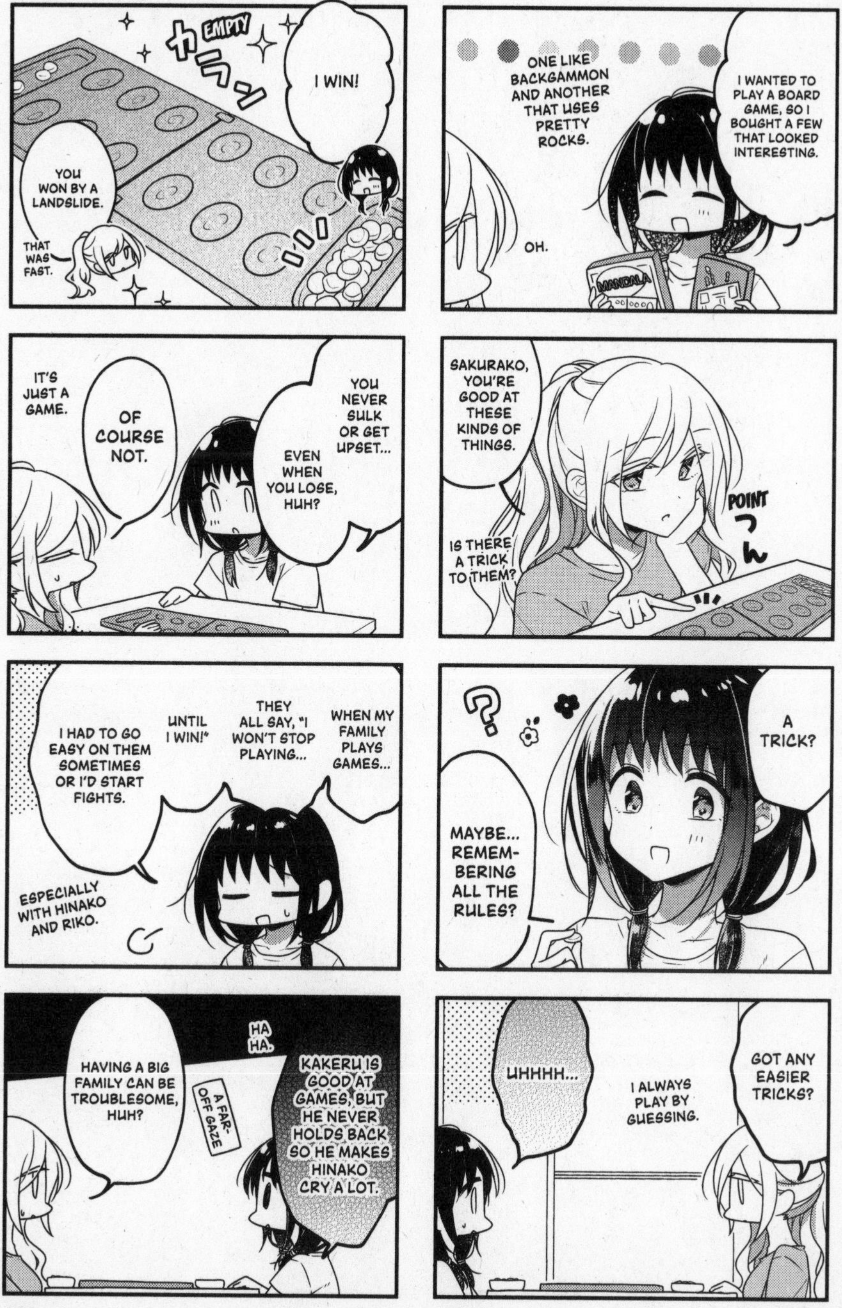
I WANTED TO PLAY A BOARD GAME, SO I BOUGHT A FEW THAT LOOKED INTERESTING.
ONE LIKE BACKGAMMON AND ANOTHER THAT USES PRETTY ROCKS.
OH.
MANDALA
EMPTY
I WIN!
YOU WON BY A LANDSLIDE.
THAT WAS FAST.
SAKURAKO, YOU'RE GOOD AT THESE KINDS OF THINGS.
POINT
IS THERE A TRICK TO THEM?
YOU NEVER SULK OR GET UPSET...
EVEN WHEN YOU LOSE, HUH?
OF COURSE NOT.
IT'S JUST A GAME.
A TRICK?
MAYBE... REMEMBERING ALL THE RULES?
WHEN MY FAMILY PLAYS GAMES...
THEY ALL SAY, "I WON'T STOP PLAYING...
UNTIL I WIN!"
I HAD TO GO EASY ON THEM SOMETIMES OR I'D START FIGHTS.
ESPECIALLY WITH HINAKO AND RIKO.
GOT ANY EASIER TRICKS?
I ALWAYS PLAY BY GUESSING.
UHHHH...
HA HA.
KAKERU IS GOOD AT GAMES, BUT HE NEVER HOLDS BACK SO HE MAKES HINAKO CRY A LOT.
A FAR-OFF GAZE
HAVING A BIG FAMILY CAN BE TROUBLESOME, HUH?

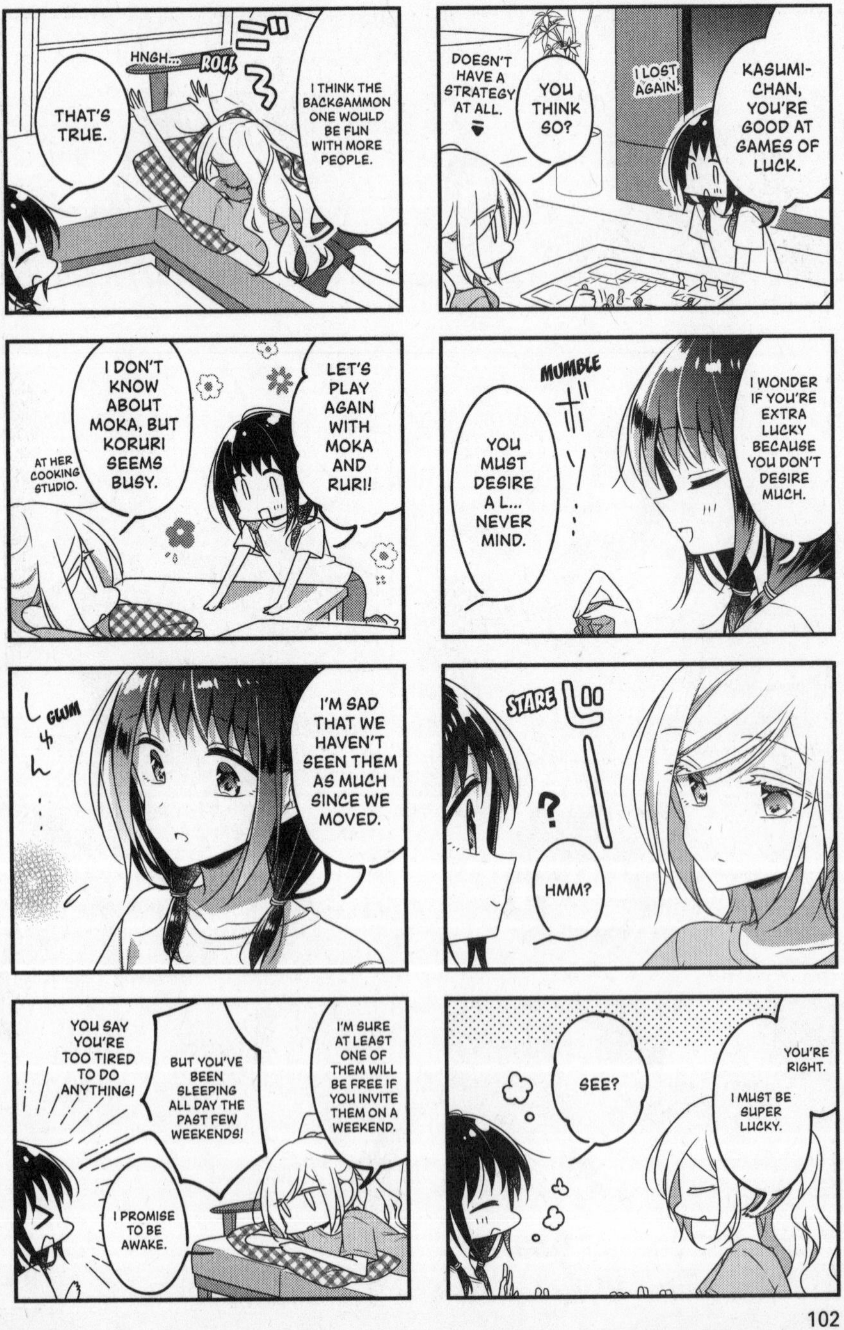
KASUMI-CHAN, YOU'RE GOOD AT GAMES OF LUCK.
I LOST AGAIN.
YOU THINK SO?
DOESN'T HAVE A STRATEGY AT ALL.
I WONDER IF YOU'RE EXTRA LUCKY BECAUSE YOU DON'T DESIRE MUCH.
MUMBLE
YOU MUST DESIRE A L... NEVER MIND.
STARE
HMM?
YOU'RE RIGHT.
I MUST BE SUPER LUCKY.
SEE?
I THINK THE BACKGAMMON ONE WOULD BE FUN WITH MORE PEOPLE.
ROLL
HNGH...
THAT'S TRUE.
LET'S PLAY AGAIN WITH MOKA AND RURI!
I DON'T KNOW ABOUT MOKA, BUT KORURI SEEMS BUSY.
AT HER COOKING STUDIO.
I'M SAD THAT WE HAVEN'T SEEN THEM AS MUCH SINCE WE MOVED.
GLUM
I'M SURE AT LEAST ONE OF THEM WILL BE FREE IF YOU INVITE THEM ON A WEEKEND.
BUT YOU'VE BEEN SLEEPING ALL DAY THE PAST FEW WEEKENDS!
YOU SAY YOU'RE TOO TIRED TO DO ANYTHING!
I PROMISE TO BE AWAKE.

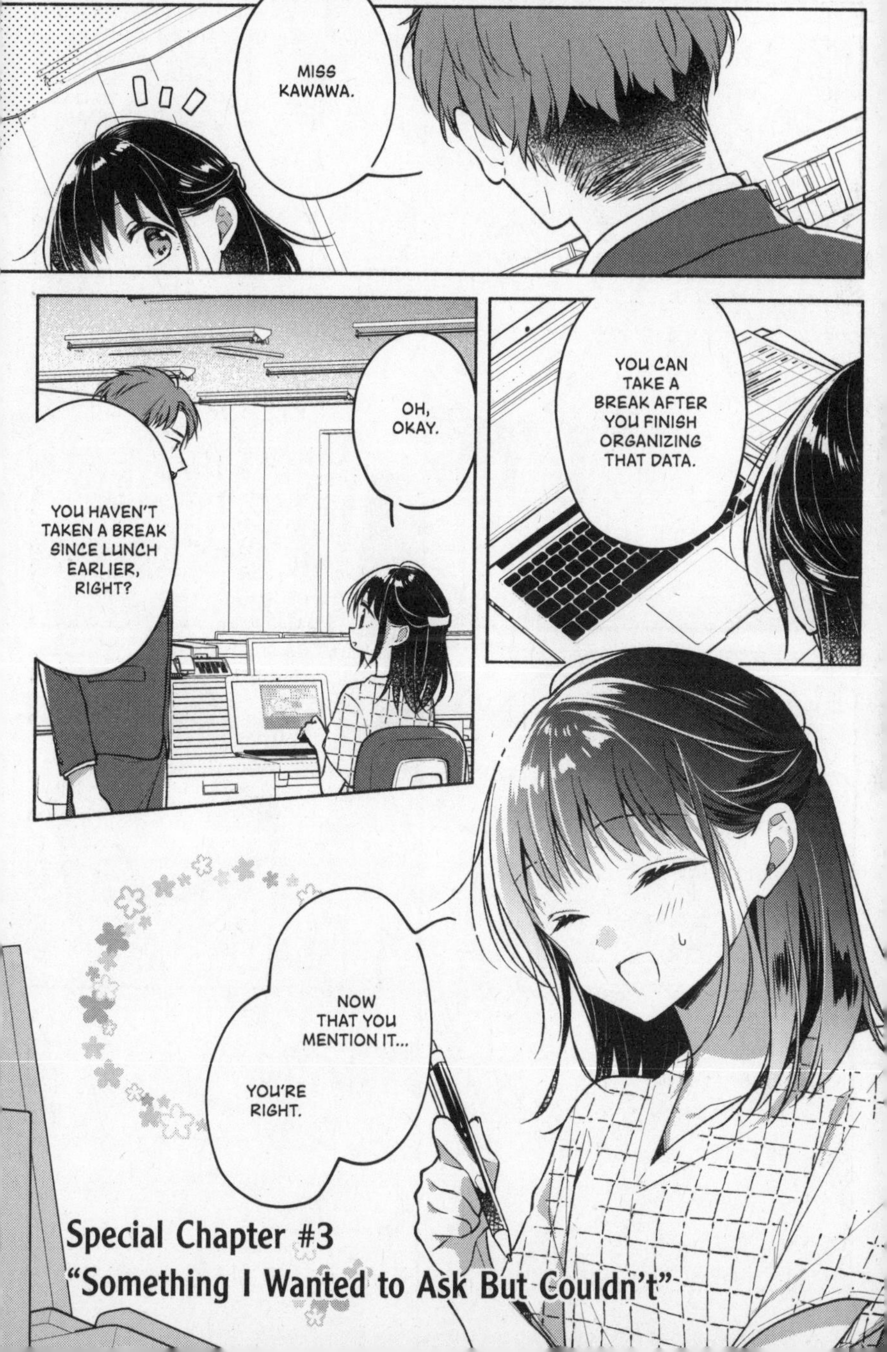
MISS KAWAWA.
YOU CAN TAKE A BREAK AFTER YOU FINISH ORGANIZING THAT DATA.
OH, OKAY.
YOU HAVEN'T TAKEN A BREAK SINCE LUNCH EARLIER, RIGHT?
NOW THAT YOU MENTION IT...
YOU'RE RIGHT.

Special Chapter #3
"Something I Wanted to Ask But Couldn't"

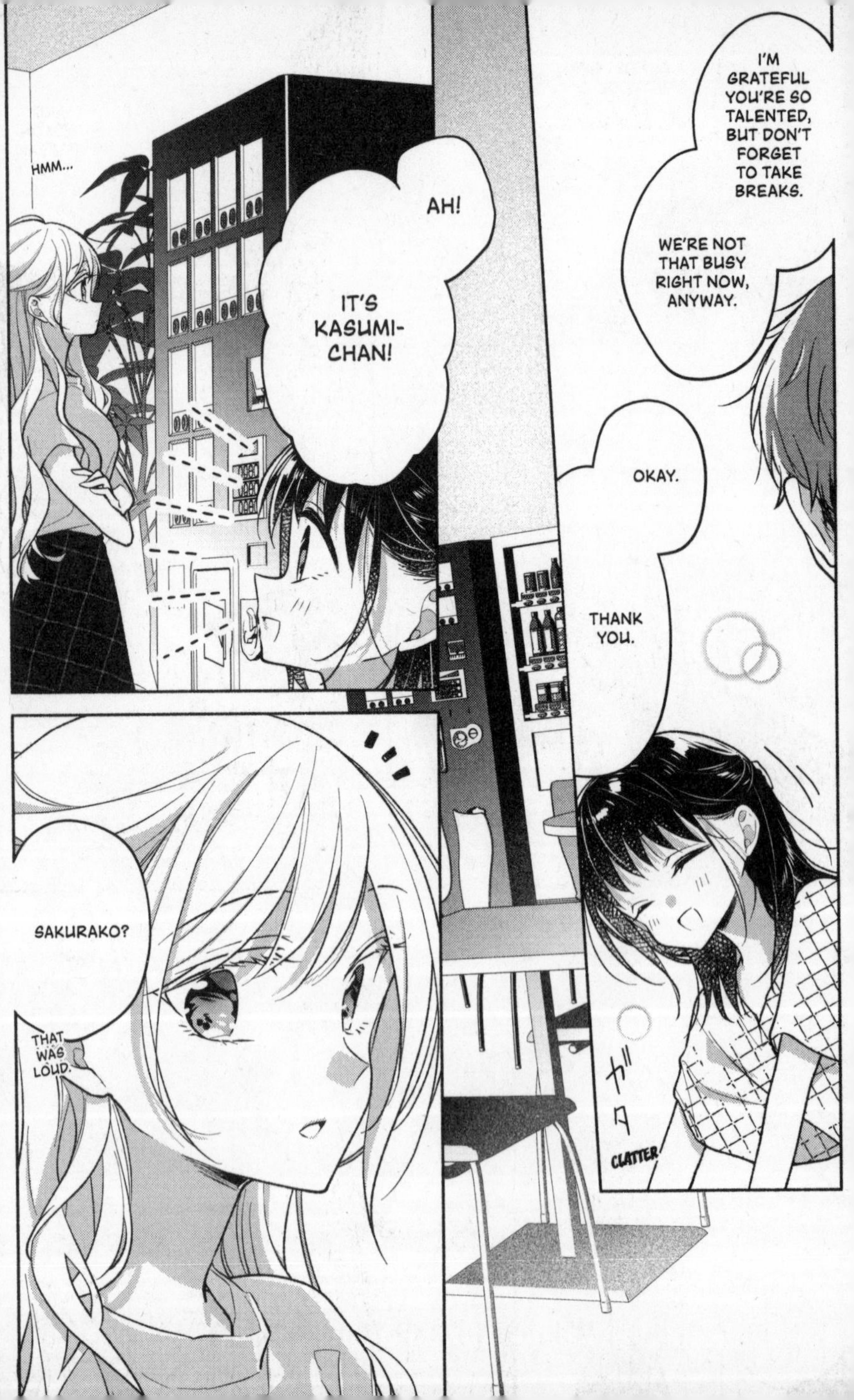
I'M GRATEFUL YOU'RE SO TALENTED, BUT DON'T FORGET TO TAKE BREAKS.
WE'RE NOT THAT BUSY RIGHT NOW, ANYWAY.
OKAY.
THANK YOU.
ガタ
CLATTER
AH!
IT'S KASUMI-CHAN!
HMM...
SAKURAKO?
THAT WAS LOUD.

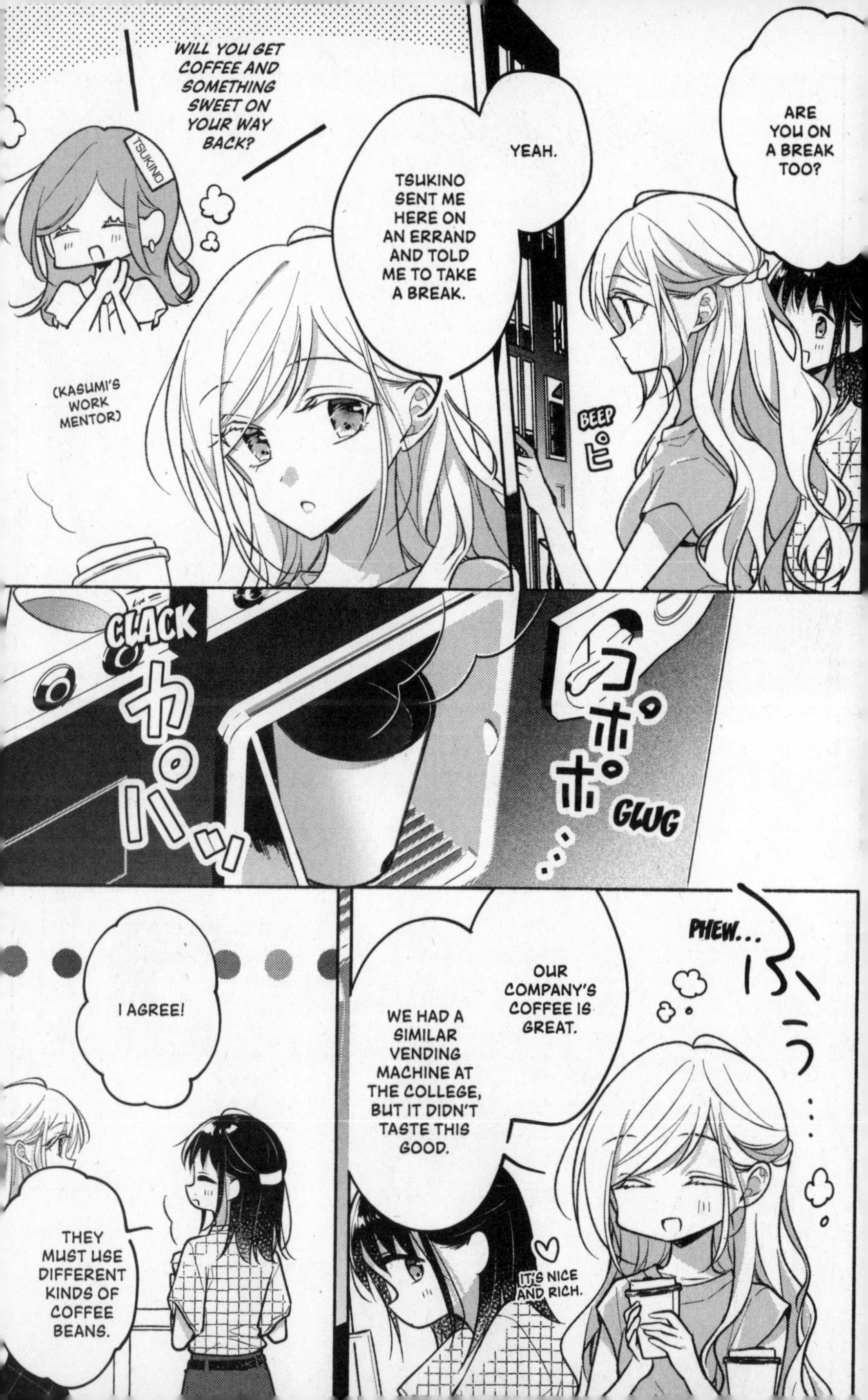
ARE YOU ON A BREAK TOO?
BEEP
ピ
YEAH.
TSUKINO SENT ME HERE ON AN ERRAND AND TOLD ME TO TAKE A BREAK.
WILL YOU GET COFFEE AND SOMETHING SWEET ON YOUR WAY BACK?
TSUKINO
(KASUMI'S WORK MENTOR)
コポポ
GLUG
CLACK
PHEW...
ふぅ...
OUR COMPANY'S COFFEE IS GREAT.
WE HAD A SIMILAR VENDING MACHINE AT THE COLLEGE, BUT IT DIDN'T TASTE THIS GOOD.
IT'S NICE AND RICH.
I AGREE!
THEY MUST USE DIFFERENT KINDS OF COFFEE BEANS.

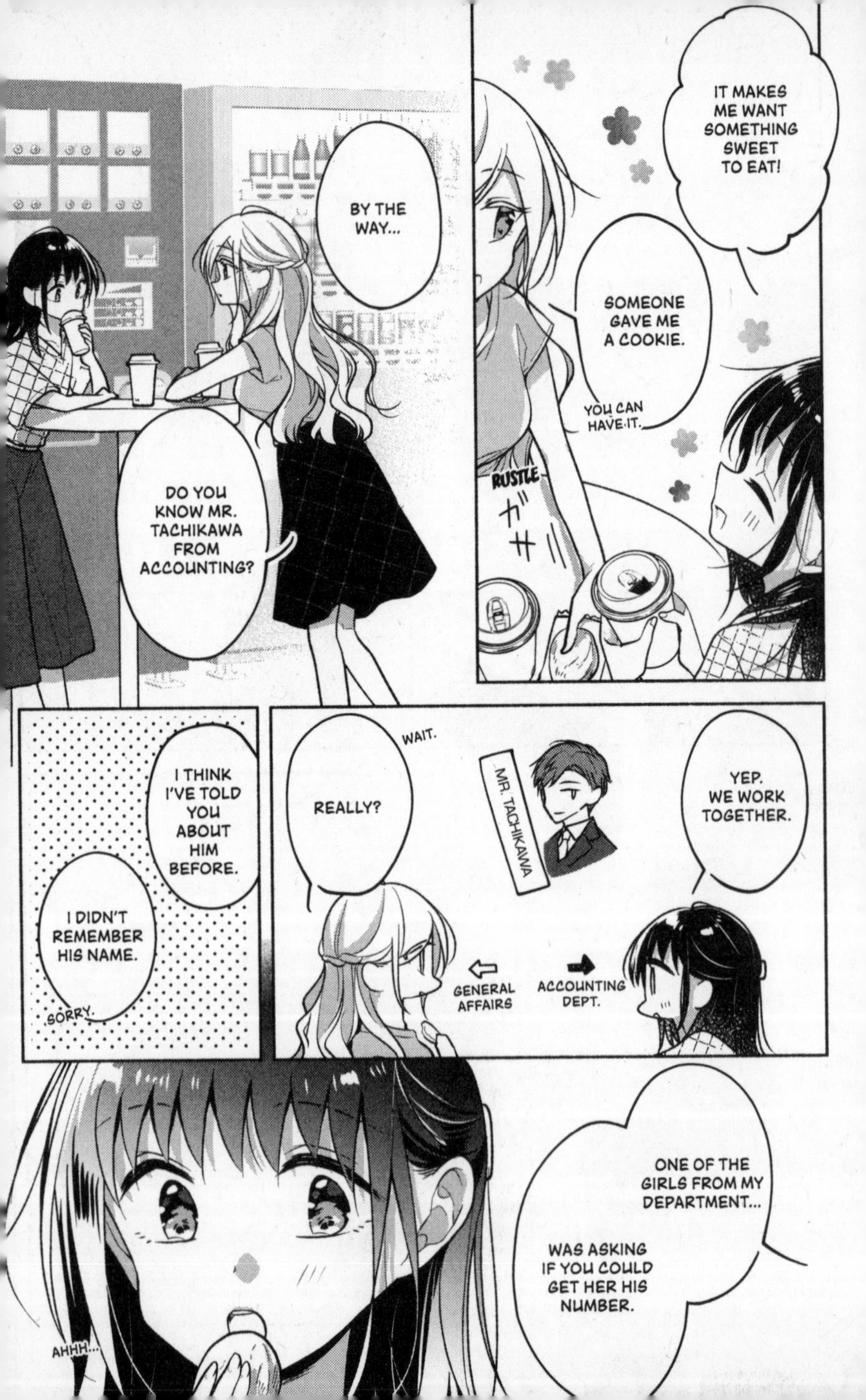
IT MAKES ME WANT SOMETHING SWEET TO EAT!
SOMEONE GAVE ME A COOKIE.
YOU CAN HAVE IT.
RUSTLE
ガサ
BY THE WAY...
DO YOU KNOW MR. TACHIKAWA FROM ACCOUNTING?
YEP. WE WORK TOGETHER.
MR. TACHIKAWA
WAIT.
REALLY?
ACCOUNTING DEPT.
GENERAL AFFAIRS
I THINK I'VE TOLD YOU ABOUT HIM BEFORE.
I DIDN'T REMEMBER HIS NAME.
SORRY.
ONE OF THE GIRLS FROM MY DEPARTMENT...
WAS ASKING IF YOU COULD GET HER HIS NUMBER.
AHHH...

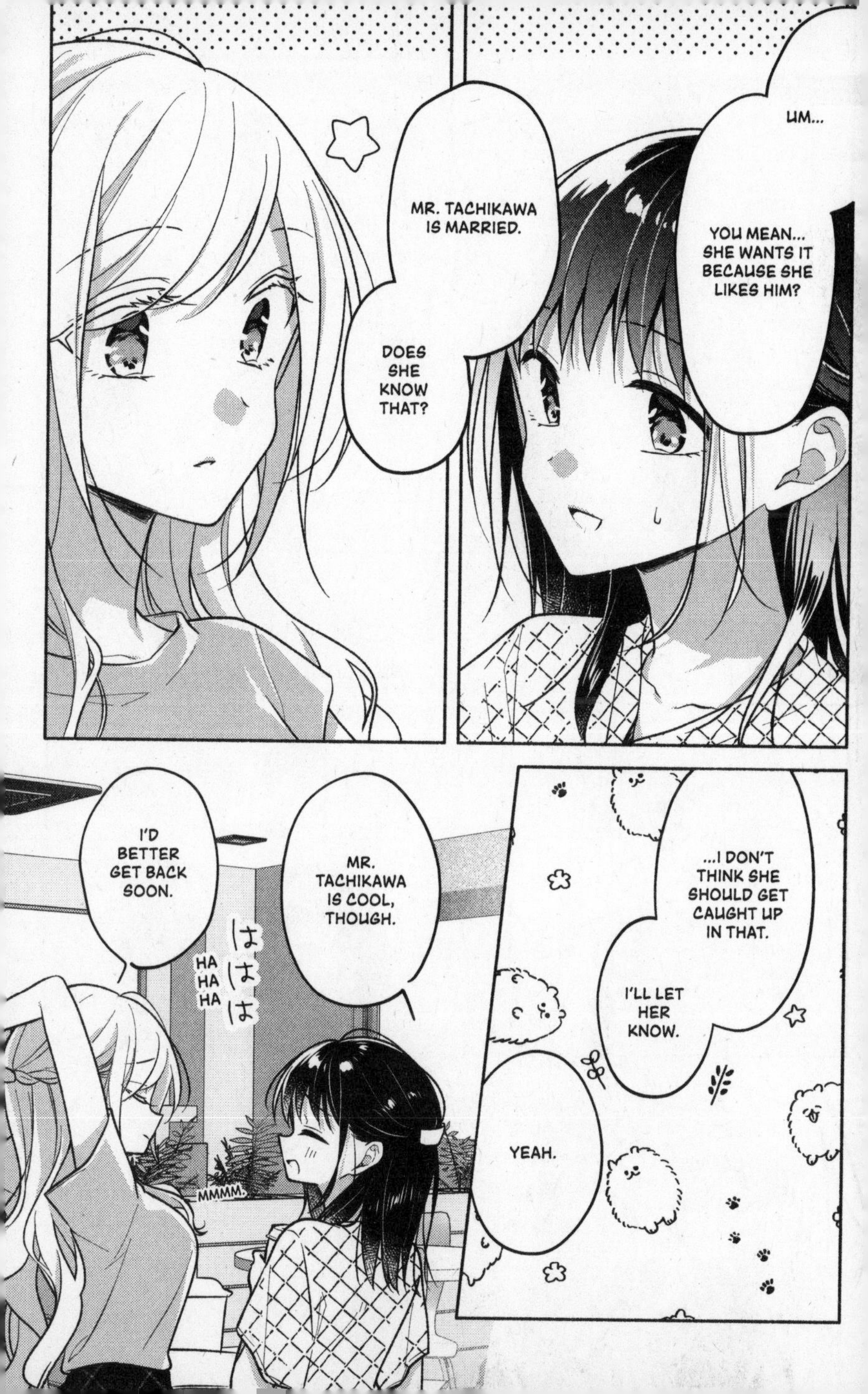
UM...
YOU MEAN... SHE WANTS IT BECAUSE SHE LIKES HIM?
MR. TACHIKAWA IS MARRIED.
DOES SHE KNOW THAT?
...I DON'T THINK SHE SHOULD GET CAUGHT UP IN THAT.
I'LL LET HER KNOW.
YEAH.
MR. TACHIKAWA IS COOL, THOUGH.
ははは
HA HA HA
I'D BETTER GET BACK SOON.
MMMM.

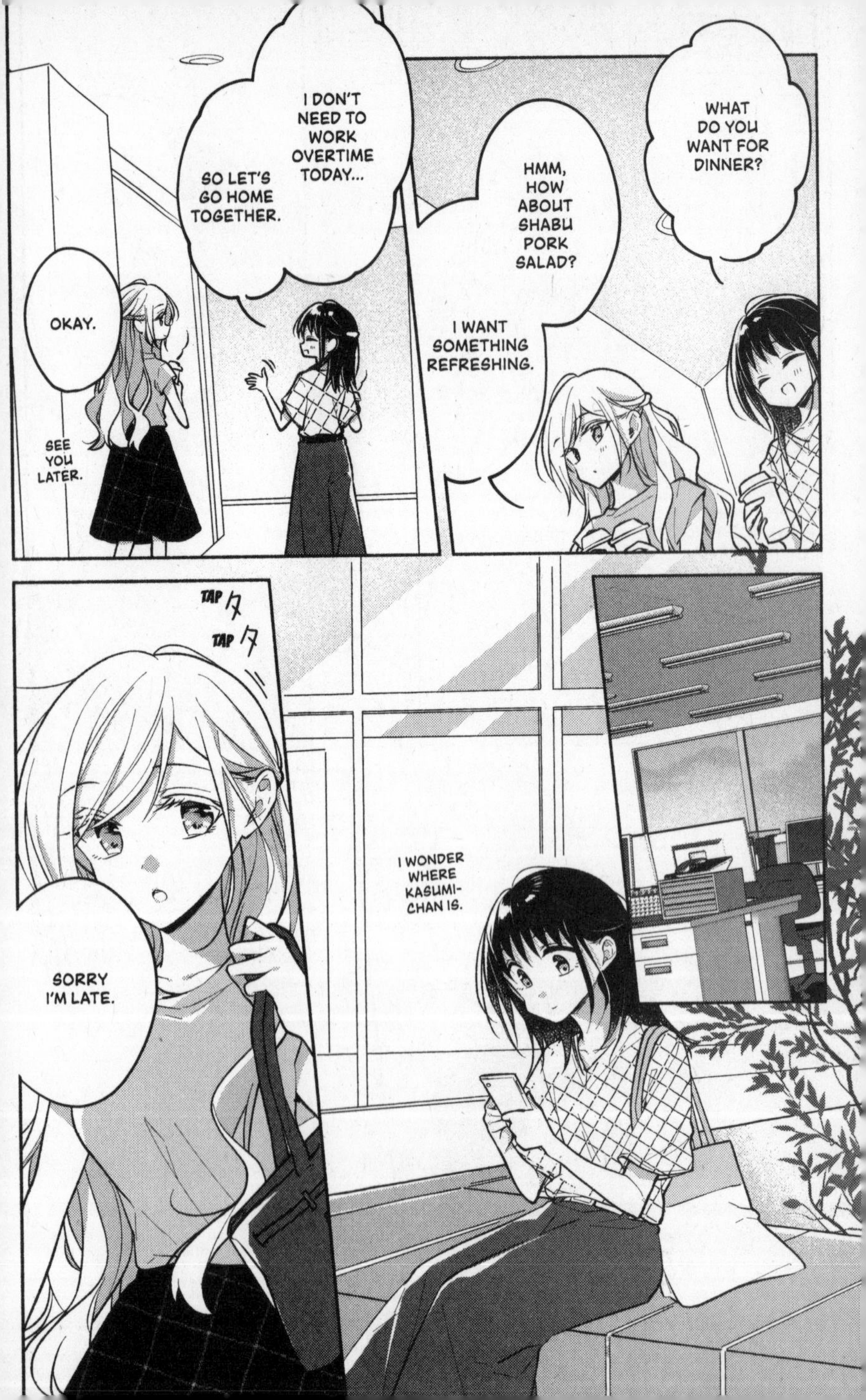
WHAT DO YOU WANT FOR DINNER?
HMM, HOW ABOUT SHABU PORK SALAD?
I WANT SOMETHING REFRESHING.
I DON'T NEED TO WORK OVERTIME TODAY...
SO LET'S GO HOME TOGETHER.
OKAY.
SEE YOU LATER.
I WONDER WHERE KASUMI-CHAN IS.
TAP
TAP
SORRY I'M LATE.

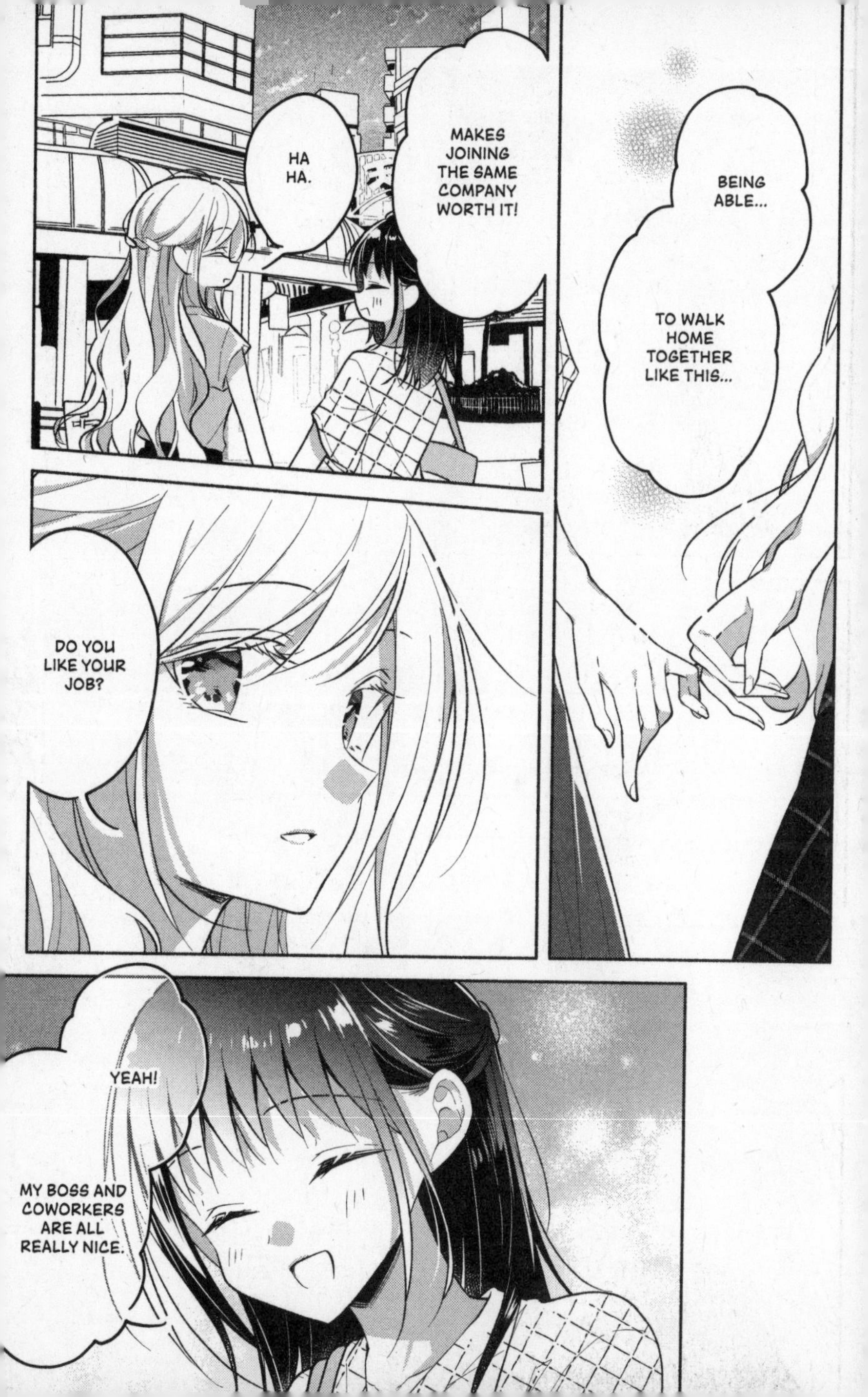
BEING ABLE...
TO WALK HOME TOGETHER LIKE THIS...
MAKES JOINING THE SAME COMPANY WORTH IT!
HA HA.
DO YOU LIKE YOUR JOB?
YEAH!
MY BOSS AND COWORKERS ARE ALL REALLY NICE.

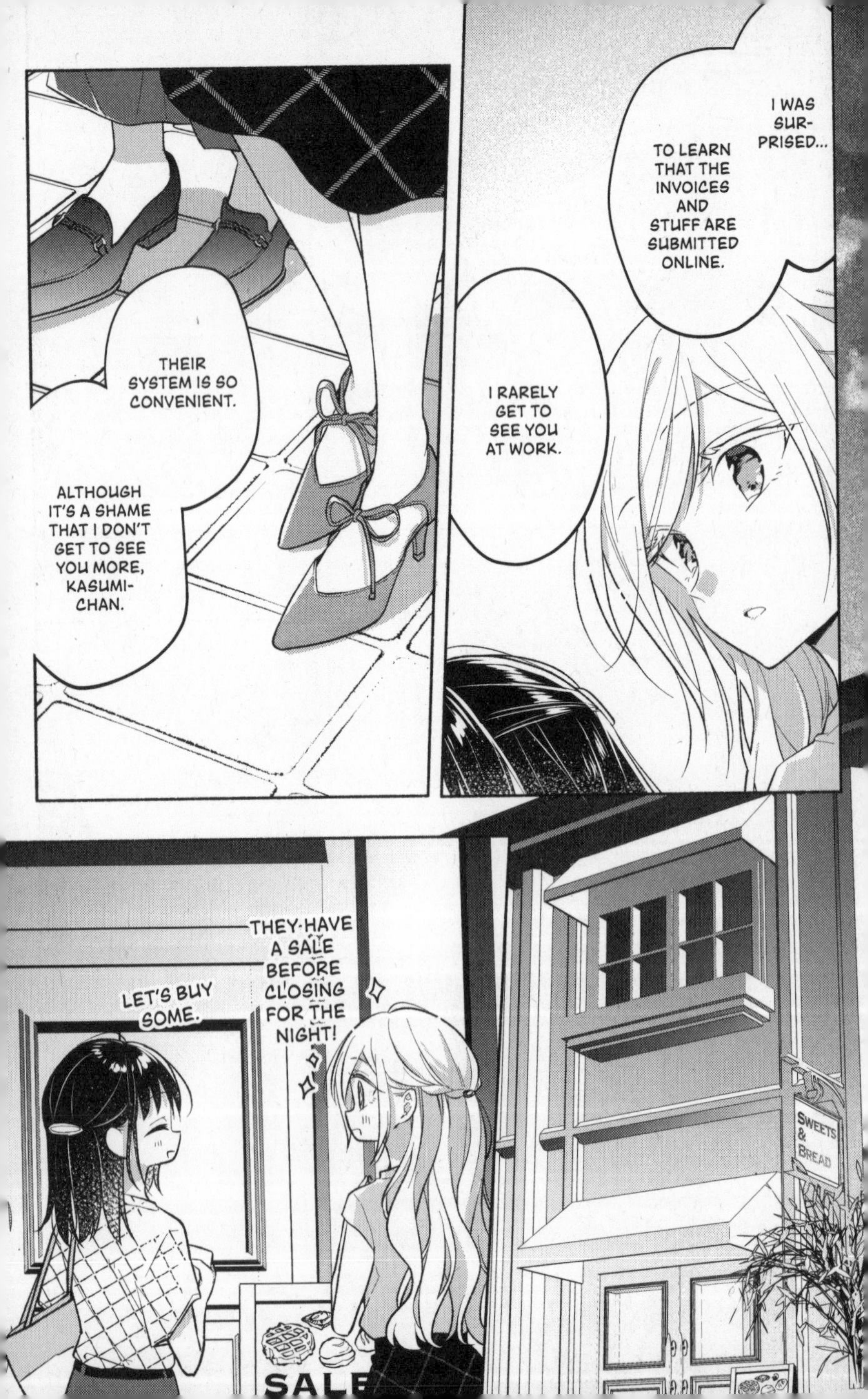
I WAS SURPRISED...
TO LEARN THAT THE INVOICES AND STUFF ARE SUBMITTED ONLINE.
I RARELY GET TO SEE YOU AT WORK.
THEIR SYSTEM IS SO CONVENIENT.
ALTHOUGH IT'S A SHAME THAT I DON'T GET TO SEE YOU MORE, KASUMI-CHAN.
THEY HAVE A SALE BEFORE CLOSING FOR THE NIGHT!
LET'S BUY SOME.
SWEETS & BREAD
SALE

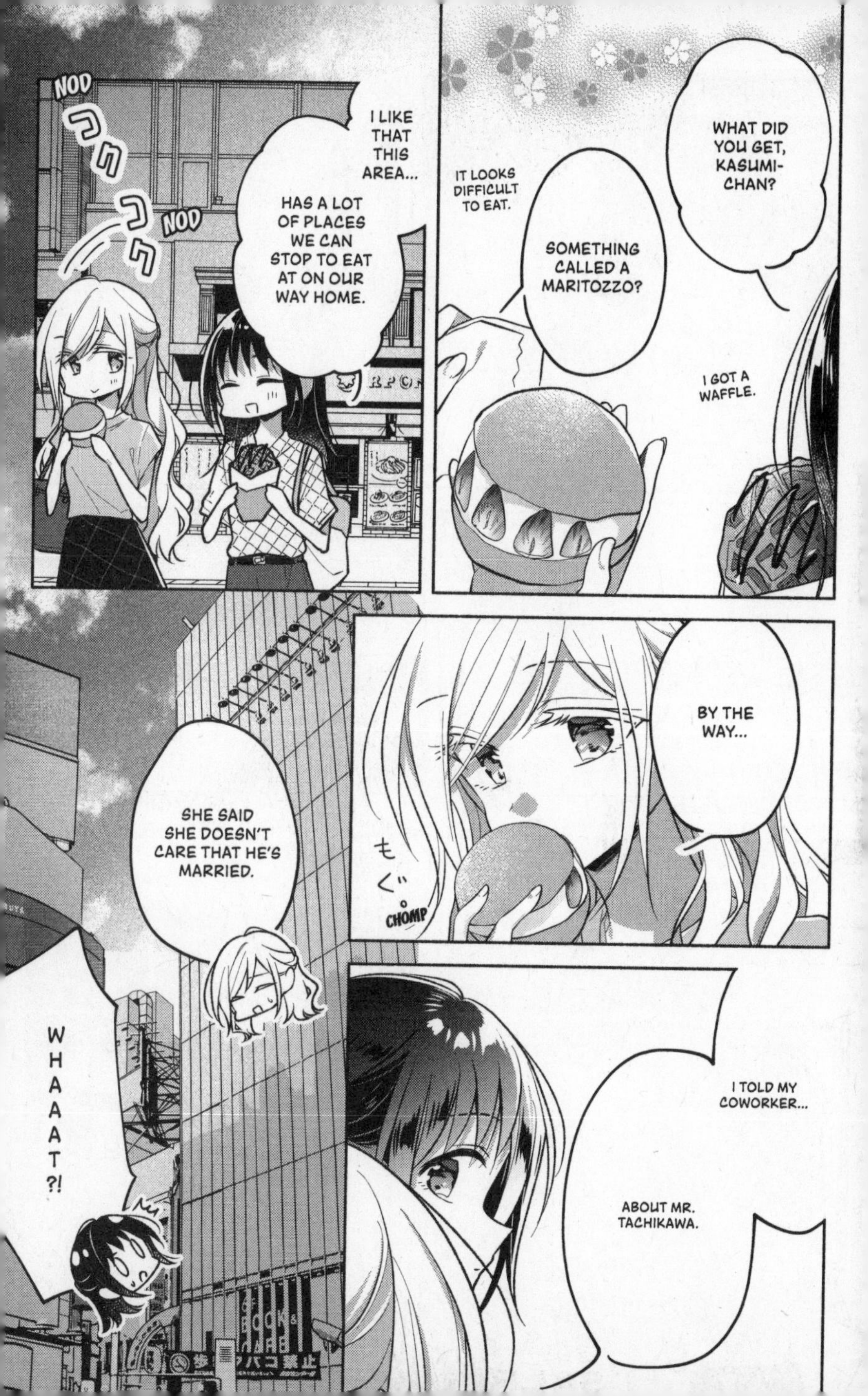
WHAT DID YOU GET, KASUMI-CHAN?
SOMETHING CALLED A MARITOZZO?
IT LOOKS DIFFICULT TO EAT.
I GOT A WAFFLE.
I LIKE THAT THIS AREA...
HAS A LOT OF PLACES WE CAN STOP TO EAT AT ON OUR WAY HOME.
NOD
コク
コク
NOD
BY THE WAY...
もぐ。
CHOMP
I TOLD MY COWORKER...
ABOUT MR. TACHIKAWA.
SHE SAID SHE DOESN'T CARE THAT HE'S MARRIED.
WHAAAAT?!

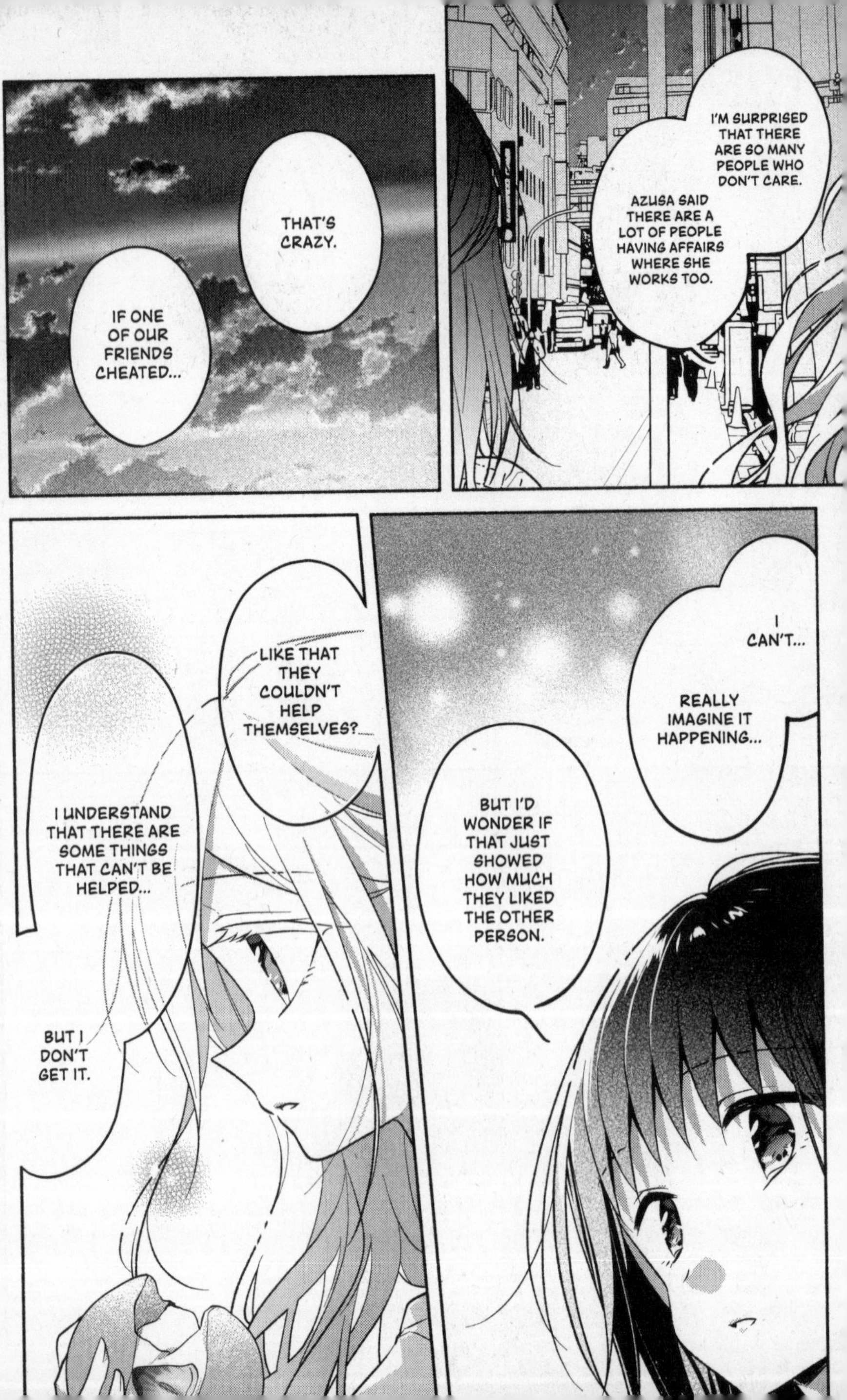
I'M SURPRISED THAT THERE ARE SO MANY PEOPLE WHO DON'T CARE.
AZUSA SAID THERE ARE A LOT OF PEOPLE HAVING AFFAIRS WHERE SHE WORKS TOO.
THAT'S CRAZY.
IF ONE OF OUR FRIENDS CHEATED...
I CAN'T...
REALLY IMAGINE IT HAPPENING...
BUT I'D WONDER IF THAT JUST SHOWED HOW MUCH THEY LIKED THE OTHER PERSON.
LIKE THAT THEY COULDN'T HELP THEMSELVES?
I UNDERSTAND THAT THERE ARE SOME THINGS THAT CAN'T BE HELPED...
BUT I DON'T GET IT.

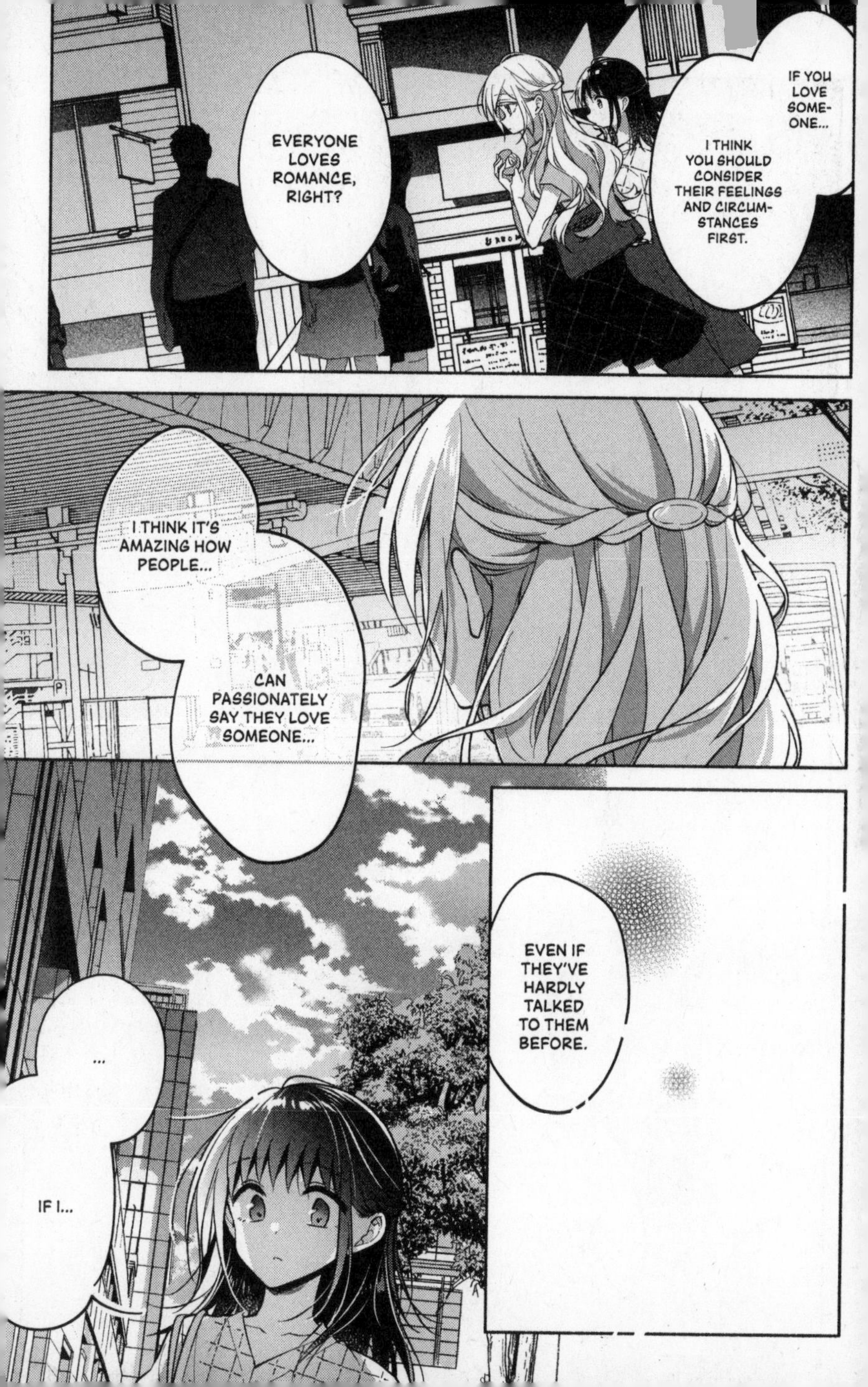
IF YOU LOVE SOMEONE... I THINK YOU SHOULD CONSIDER THEIR FEELINGS AND CIRCUMSTANCES FIRST.
EVERYONE LOVES ROMANCE, RIGHT?
I THINK IT'S AMAZING HOW PEOPLE... CAN PASSIONATELY SAY THEY LOVE SOMEONE...
EVEN IF THEY'VE HARDLY TALKED TO THEM BEFORE.
...
IF I...

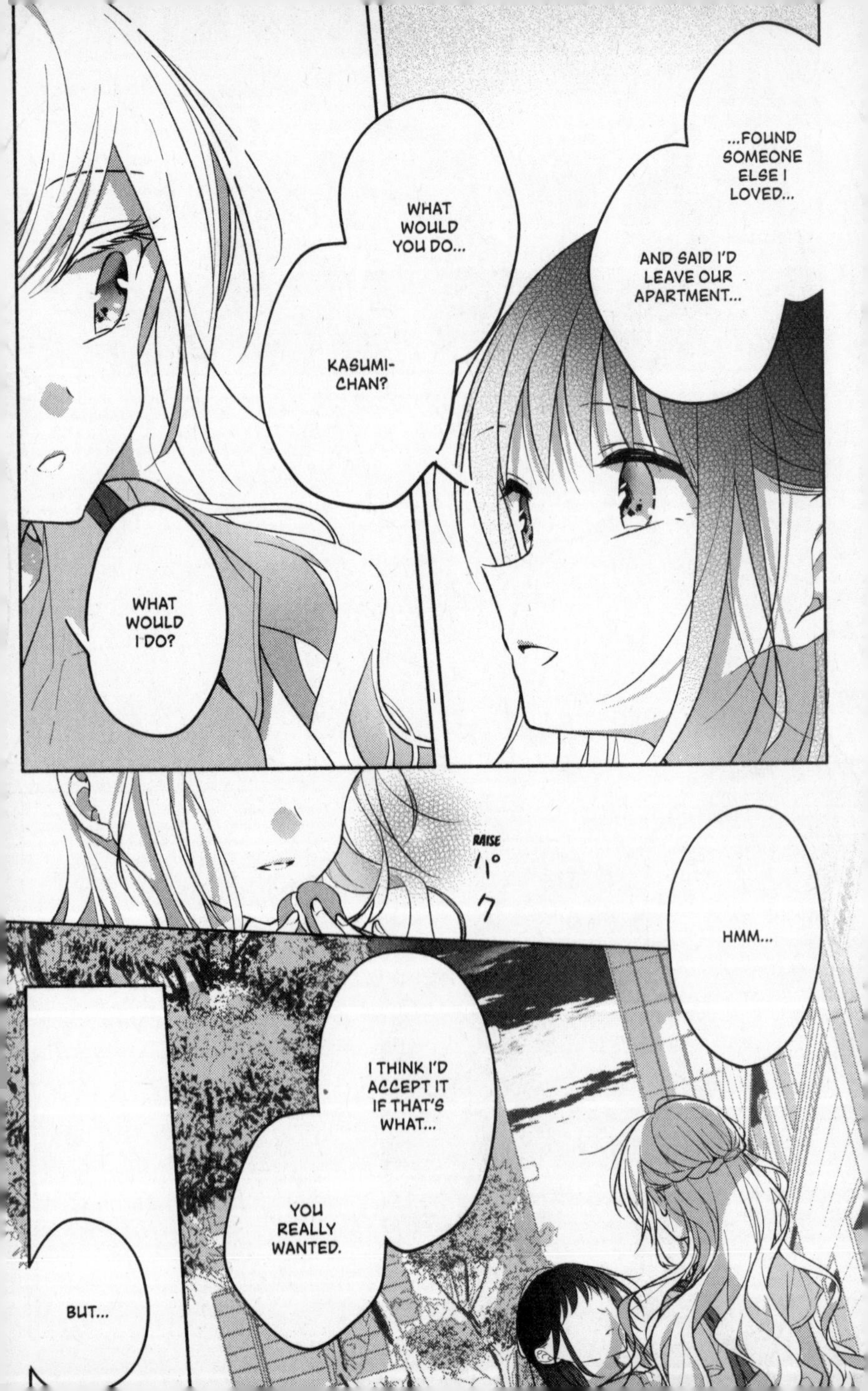
...FOUND SOMEONE ELSE I LOVED...
AND SAID I'D LEAVE OUR APARTMENT...
WHAT WOULD YOU DO...
KASUMI-CHAN?
WHAT WOULD I DO?
RAISE
パク
HMM...
I THINK I'D ACCEPT IT IF THAT'S WHAT...
YOU REALLY WANTED.
BUT...

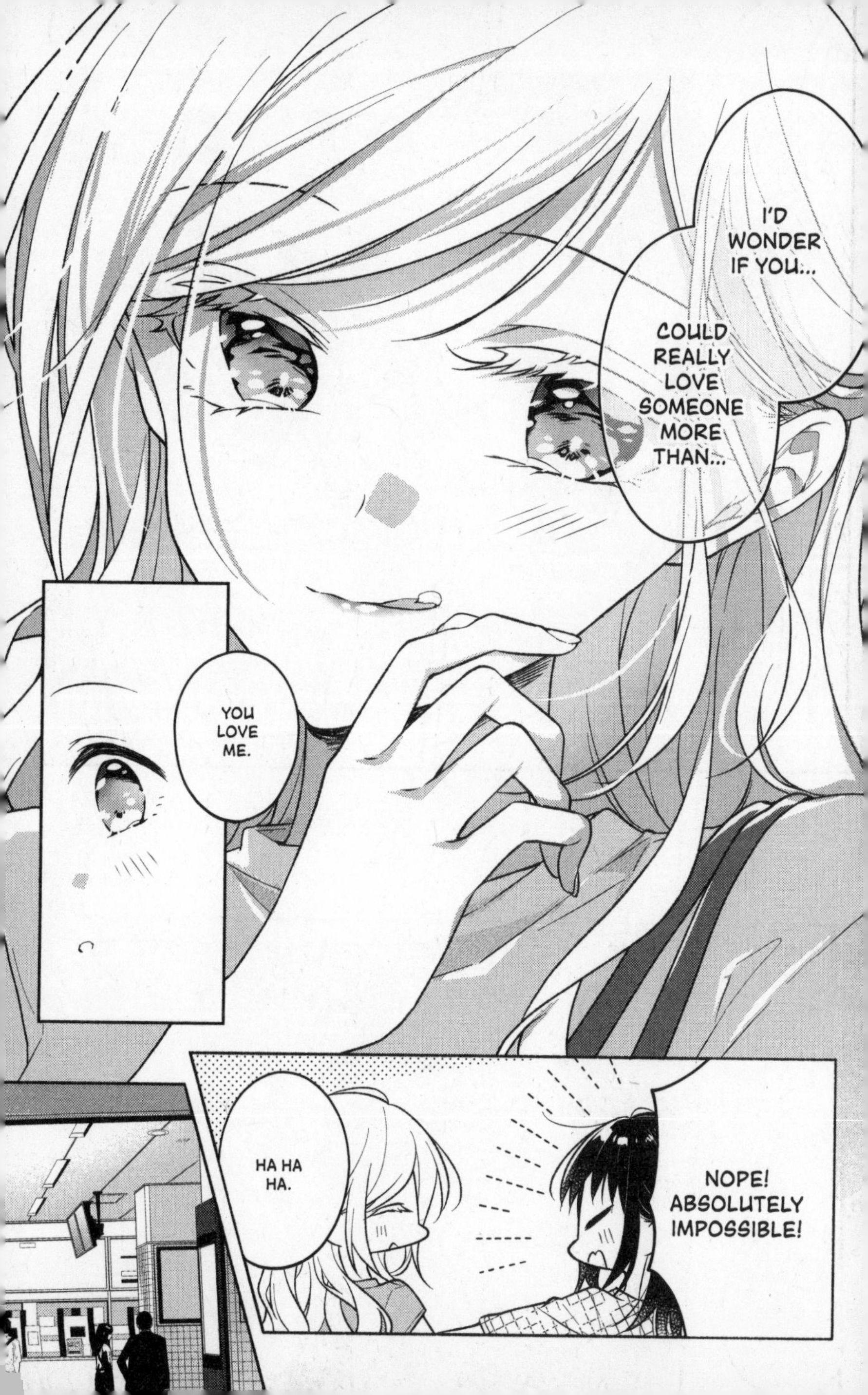
I'D WONDER IF YOU...
COULD REALLY LOVE SOMEONE MORE THAN...
YOU LOVE ME.
NOPE! ABSOLUTELY IMPOSSIBLE!
HA HA HA.

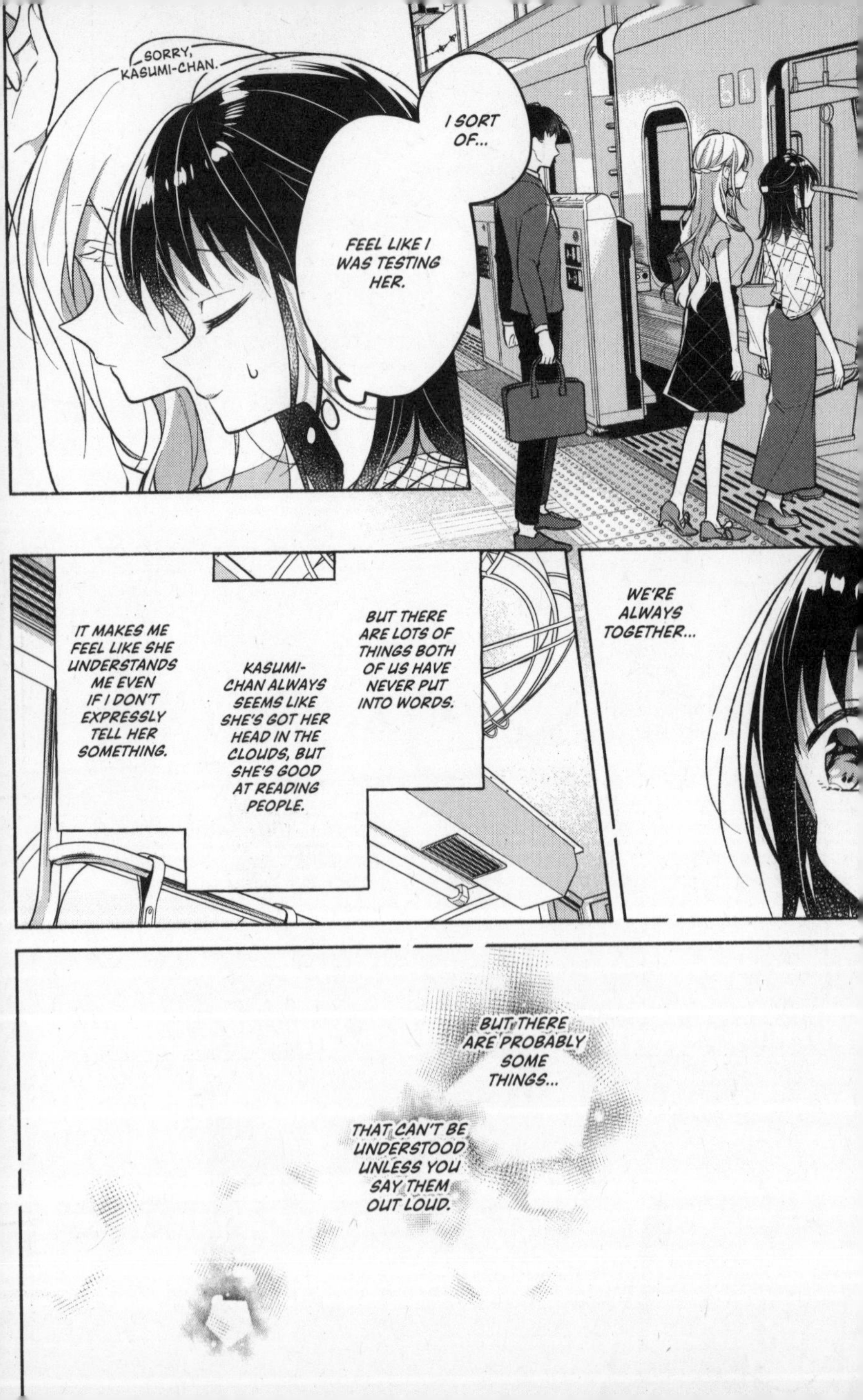
SORRY, KASUMI-CHAN.
I SORT OF... FEEL LIKE I WAS TESTING HER.
WE'RE ALWAYS TOGETHER...
BUT THERE ARE LOTS OF THINGS BOTH OF US HAVE NEVER PUT INTO WORDS.
KASUMI-CHAN ALWAYS SEEMS LIKE SHE'S GOT HER HEAD IN THE CLOUDS, BUT SHE'S GOOD AT READING PEOPLE.
IT MAKES ME FEEL LIKE SHE UNDERSTANDS ME EVEN IF I DON'T EXPRESSLY TELL HER SOMETHING.
BUT THERE ARE PROBABLY SOME THINGS...
THAT CAN'T BE UNDERSTOOD UNLESS YOU SAY THEM OUT LOUD.

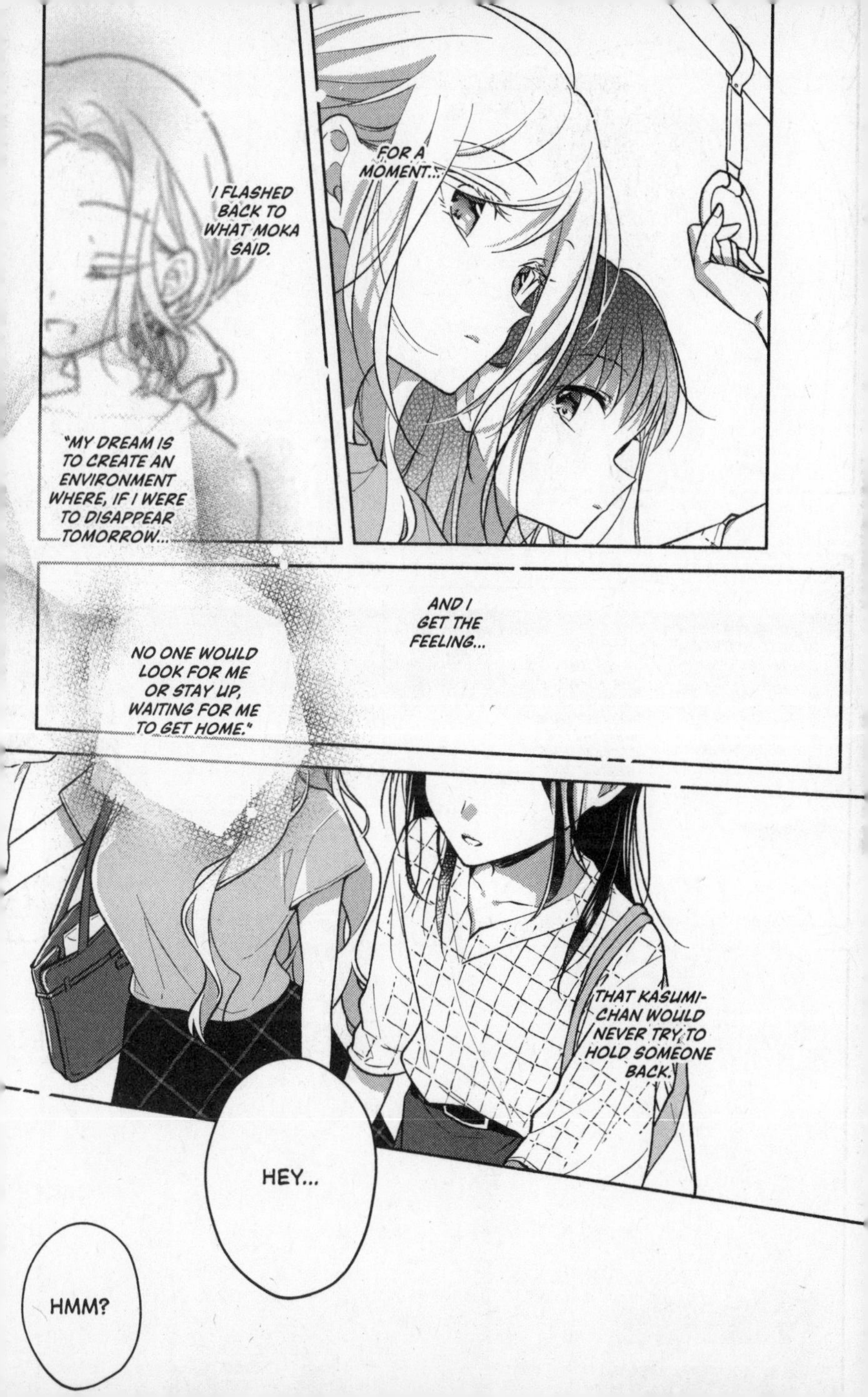
FOR A MOMENT...
I FLASHED BACK TO WHAT MOKA SAID.
"MY DREAM IS TO CREATE AN ENVIRONMENT WHERE, IF I WERE TO DISAPPEAR TOMORROW...
AND I GET THE FEELING...
NO ONE WOULD LOOK FOR ME OR STAY UP, WAITING FOR ME TO GET HOME."
THAT KASUMI-CHAN WOULD NEVER TRY TO HOLD SOMEONE BACK.
HEY...
HMM?

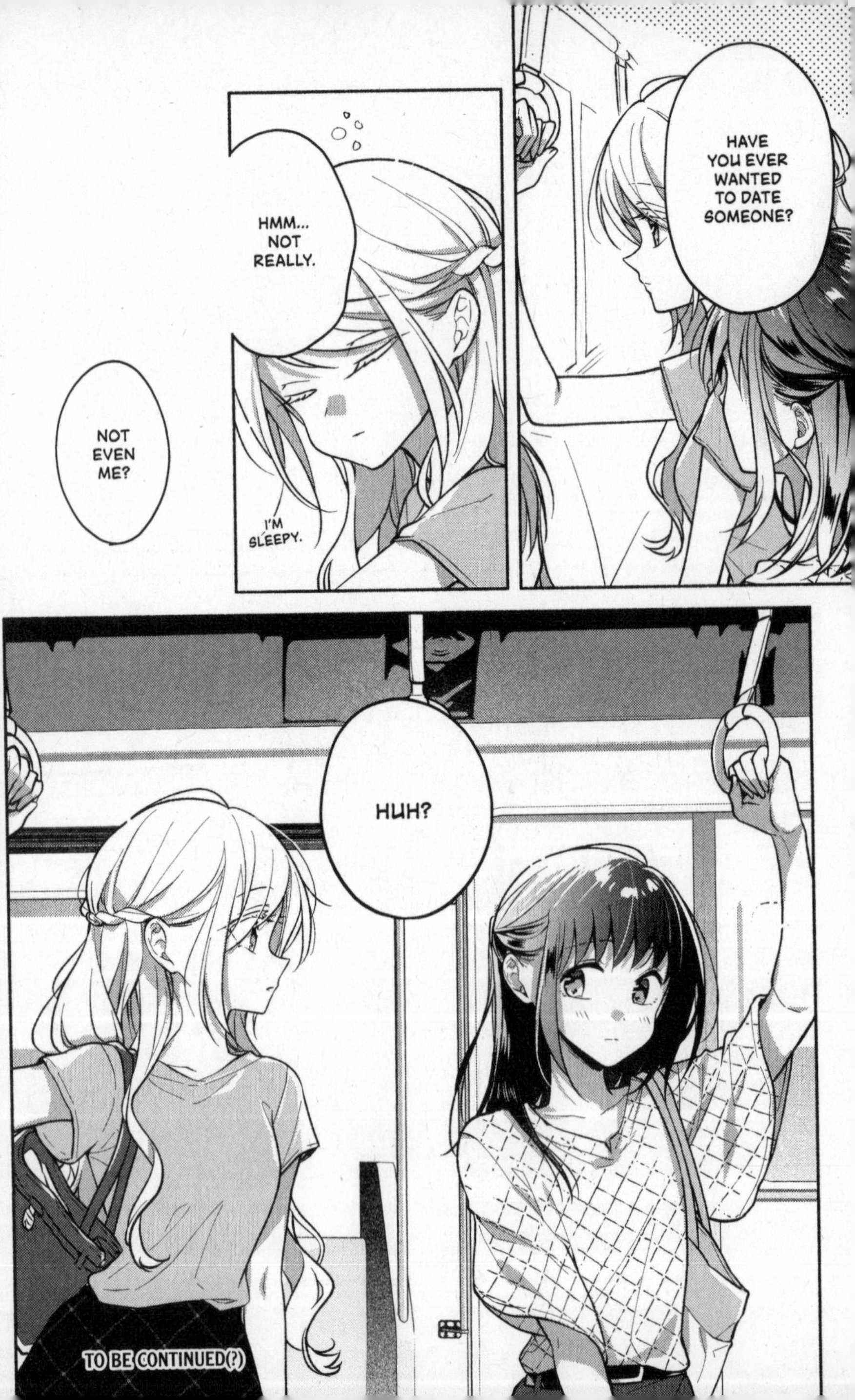
HAVE YOU EVER WANTED TO DATE SOMEONE?
HMM... NOT REALLY.
I'M SLEEPY.
NOT EVEN ME?
HUH?
TO BE CONTINUED(?)

Illustration gallery of Yukiko

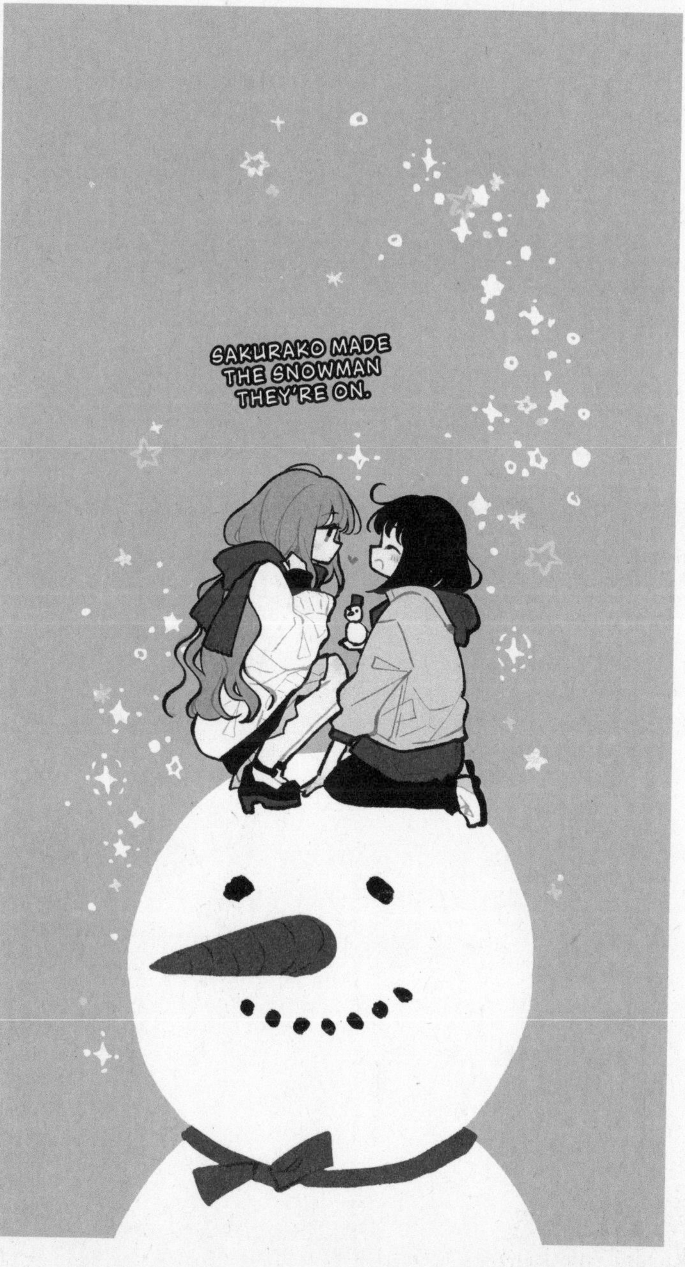
SAKURAKO MADE THE SNOWMAN THEY'RE ON.

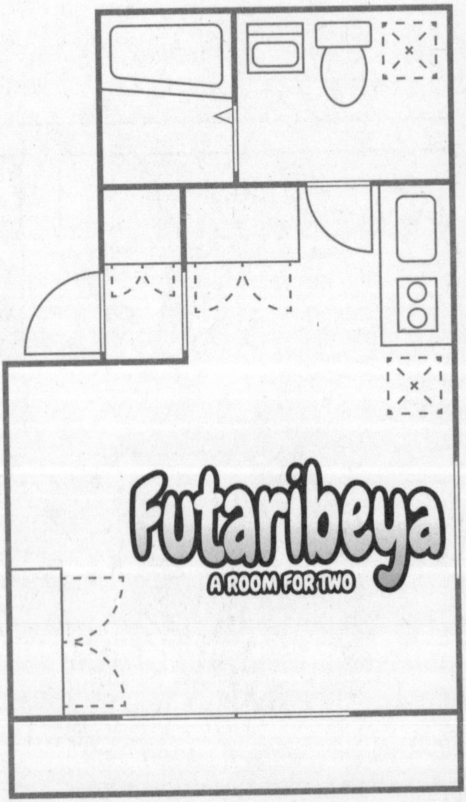
Futaribeya
A ROOM FOR TWO

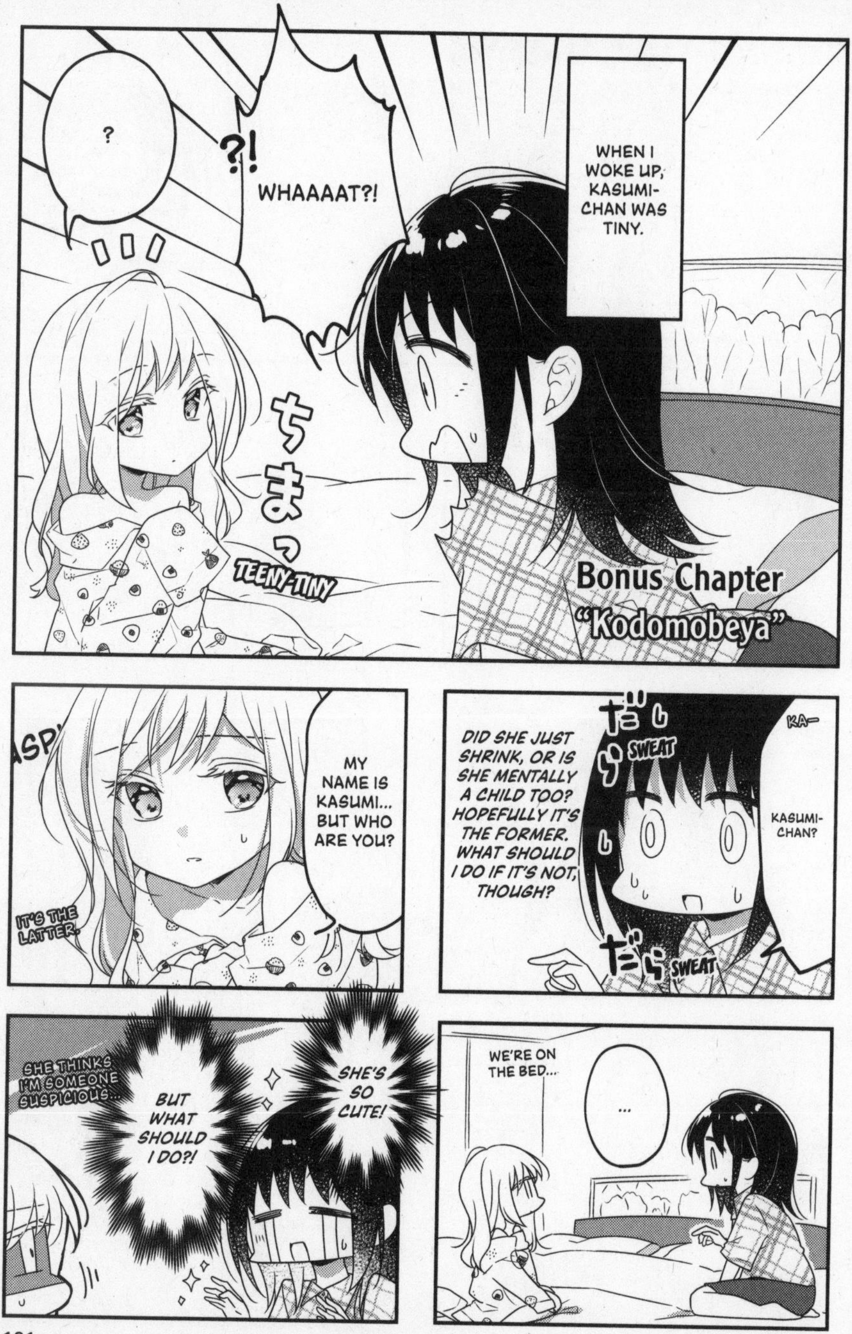

WHEN I WOKE UP, KASUMI-CHAN WAS TINY.
?!
WHAAAAT?!
?
ちまっ
TEENY-TINY
Bonus Chapter
"Kodomobeya"
KA—
KASUMI-CHAN?
DID SHE JUST SHRINK, OR IS SHE MENTALLY A CHILD TOO? HOPEFULLY IT'S THE FORMER. WHAT SHOULD I DO IF IT'S NOT, THOUGH?
だらだら
SWEAT
SWEAT
MY NAME IS KASUMI... BUT WHO ARE YOU?
IT'S THE LATTER.
WE'RE ON THE BED...
...
SHE'S SO CUTE!
BUT WHAT SHOULD I DO?!
SHE THINKS I'M SOMEONE SUSPICIOUS...

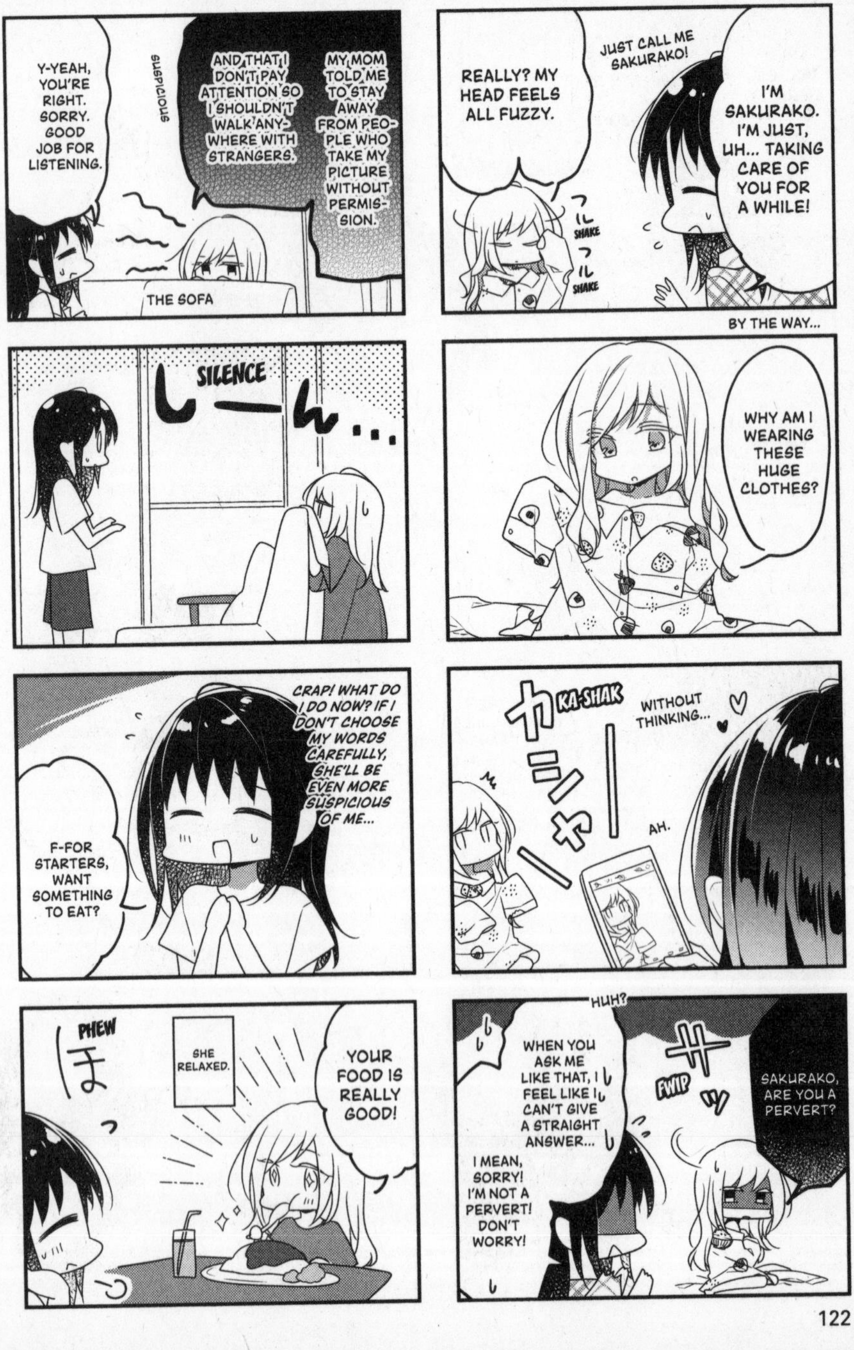
I'M SAKURAKO. I'M JUST, UH... TAKING CARE OF YOU FOR A WHILE!
JUST CALL ME SAKURAKO!
REALLY? MY HEAD FEELS ALL FUZZY.
フル SHAKE
フル SHAKE
BY THE WAY...
WHY AM I WEARING THESE HUGE CLOTHES?
カシャー KA-SHAK
WITHOUT THINKING...
AH.
HUH?
SAKURAKO, ARE YOU A PERVERT?
サッ FWIP
WHEN YOU ASK ME LIKE THAT, I FEEL LIKE I CAN'T GIVE A STRAIGHT ANSWER...
I MEAN, SORRY! I'M NOT A PERVERT! DON'T WORRY!
MY MOM TOLD ME TO STAY AWAY FROM PEOPLE WHO TAKE MY PICTURE WITHOUT PERMISSION.
AND THAT I DON'T PAY ATTENTION SO I SHOULDN'T WALK ANYWHERE WITH STRANGERS.
SUSPICIOUS
Y-YEAH, YOU'RE RIGHT. SORRY. GOOD JOB FOR LISTENING.
THE SOFA
しーん... SILENCE
CRAP! WHAT DO I DO NOW? IF I DON'T CHOOSE MY WORDS CAREFULLY, SHE'LL BE EVEN MORE SUSPICIOUS OF ME...
F-FOR STARTERS, WANT SOMETHING TO EAT?
YOUR FOOD IS REALLY GOOD!
SHE RELAXED.
ほっ PHEW

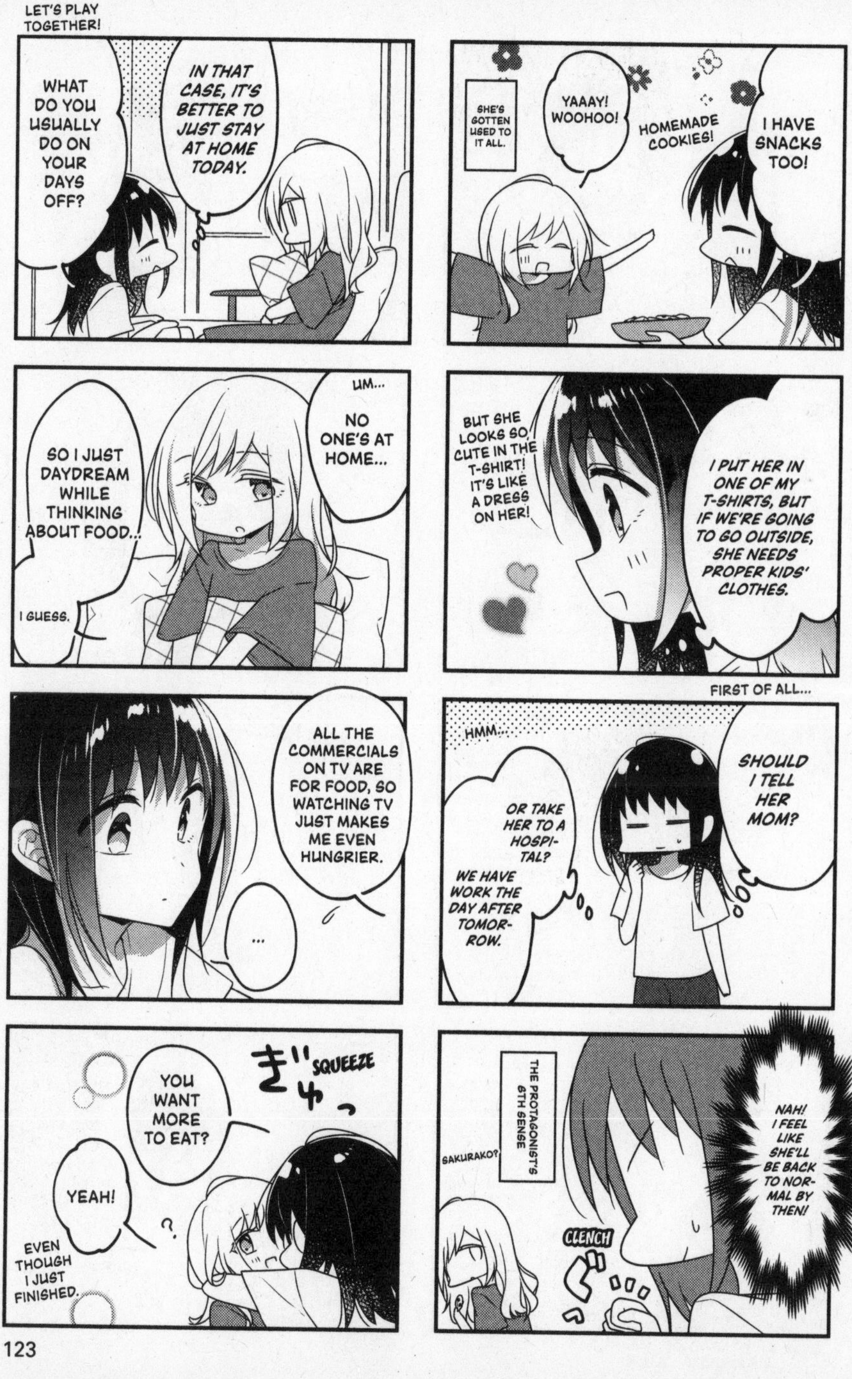
LET'S PLAY TOGETHER!
WHAT DO YOU USUALLY DO ON YOUR DAYS OFF?
IN THAT CASE, IT'S BETTER TO JUST STAY AT HOME TODAY.
UM... NO ONE'S AT HOME...
SO I JUST DAYDREAM WHILE THINKING ABOUT FOOD...
I GUESS.
ALL THE COMMERCIALS ON TV ARE FOR FOOD, SO WATCHING TV JUST MAKES ME EVEN HUNGRIER.
...
ぎゅっ SQUEEZE
YOU WANT MORE TO EAT?
YEAH!
EVEN THOUGH I JUST FINISHED.
I HAVE SNACKS TOO!
HOMEMADE COOKIES!
YAAAY! WOOHOO!
SHE'S GOTTEN USED TO IT ALL.
I PUT HER IN ONE OF MY T-SHIRTS, BUT IF WE'RE GOING TO GO OUTSIDE, SHE NEEDS PROPER KIDS' CLOTHES.
BUT SHE LOOKS SO CUTE IN THE T-SHIRT! IT'S LIKE A DRESS ON HER!
FIRST OF ALL...
SHOULD I TELL HER MOM?
OR TAKE HER TO A HOSPITAL?
WE HAVE WORK THE DAY AFTER TOMORROW.
HMM...
NAH! I FEEL LIKE SHE'LL BE BACK TO NORMAL BY THEN!
THE PROTAGONIST'S 6TH SENSE
SAKURAKO?
CLENCH

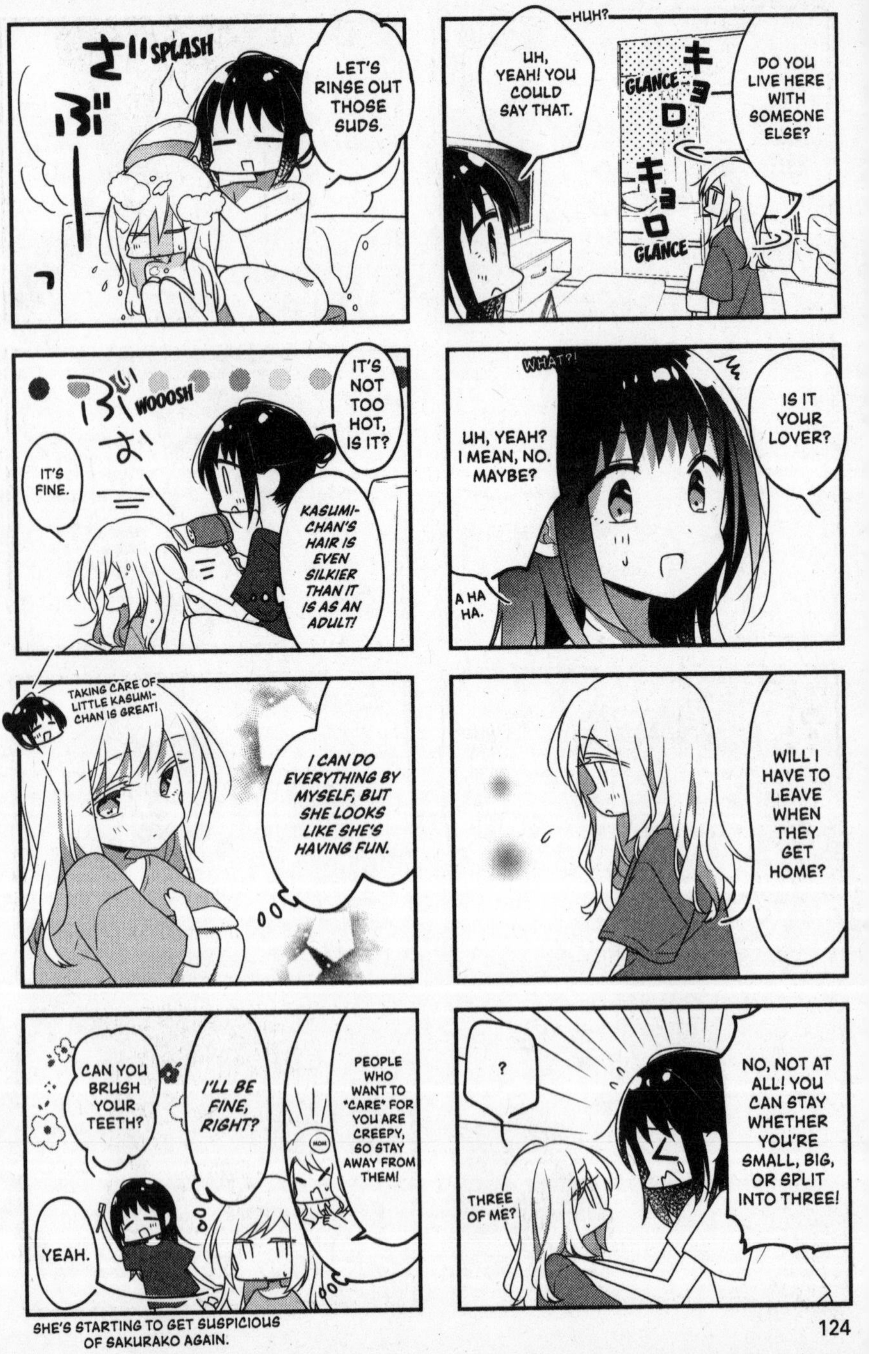
DO YOU LIVE HERE WITH SOMEONE ELSE?
キョロキョロ GLANCE GLANCE
HUH?
UH, YEAH! YOU COULD SAY THAT.
IS IT YOUR LOVER?
WHAT?!
UH, YEAH? I MEAN, NO. MAYBE?
A HA HA.
WILL I HAVE TO LEAVE WHEN THEY GET HOME?
NO, NOT AT ALL! YOU CAN STAY WHETHER YOU'RE SMALL, BIG, OR SPLIT INTO THREE!
?
THREE OF ME?
LET'S RINSE OUT THOSE SUDS.
さ SPLASH
ぶー
IT'S NOT TOO HOT, IS IT?
ぶぉ WOOOSH
IT'S FINE.
KASUMI-CHAN'S HAIR IS EVEN SILKIER THAN IT IS AS AN ADULT!
I CAN DO EVERYTHING BY MYSELF, BUT SHE LOOKS LIKE SHE'S HAVING FUN.
TAKING CARE OF LITTLE KASUMI-CHAN IS GREAT!
PEOPLE WHO WANT TO "CARE" FOR YOU ARE CREEPY, SO STAY AWAY FROM THEM!
MOM
I'LL BE FINE, RIGHT?
CAN YOU BRUSH YOUR TEETH?
YEAH.

SHE'S STARTING TO GET SUSPICIOUS OF SAKURAKO AGAIN.

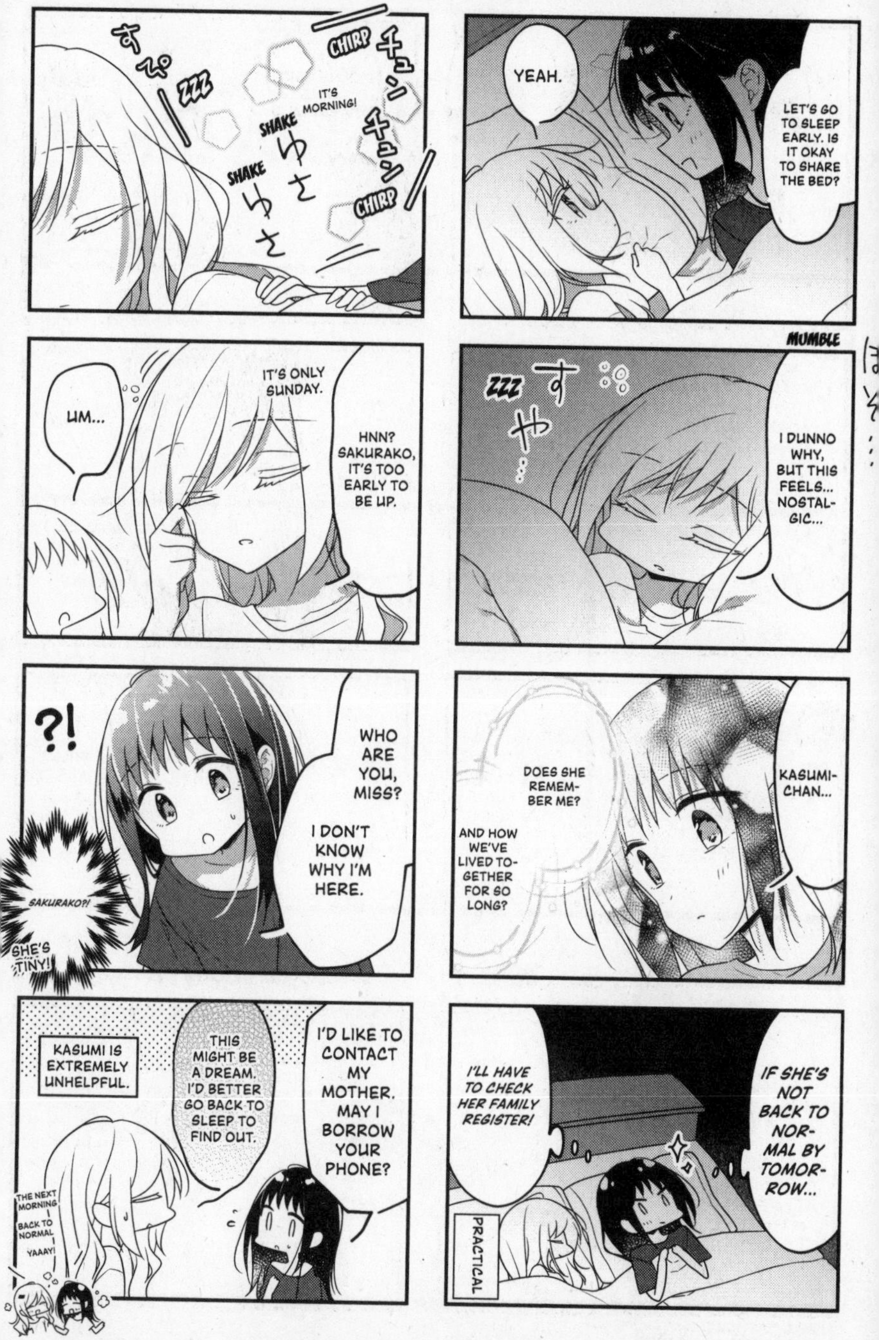
LET'S GO TO SLEEP EARLY. IS IT OKAY TO SHARE THE BED?
YEAH.
CHIRP チュン
チュン CHIRP
すぴ
ZZZ
IT'S MORNING!
SHAKE ゆさ
SHAKE ゆさ
MUMBLE ほそ…
I DUNNO WHY, BUT THIS FEELS... NOSTALGIC...
ZZZ すや…
HNN? SAKURAKO, IT'S TOO EARLY TO BE UP.
IT'S ONLY SUNDAY.
UM...
KASUMI-CHAN...
DOES SHE REMEMBER ME?
AND HOW WE'VE LIVED TOGETHER FOR SO LONG?
WHO ARE YOU, MISS?
I DON'T KNOW WHY I'M HERE.
?!
SAKURAKO?!
SHE'S TINY!
IF SHE'S NOT BACK TO NORMAL BY TOMORROW...
I'LL HAVE TO CHECK HER FAMILY REGISTER!
PRACTICAL
I'D LIKE TO CONTACT MY MOTHER. MAY I BORROW YOUR PHONE?
THIS MIGHT BE A DREAM. I'D BETTER GO BACK TO SLEEP TO FIND OUT.
KASUMI IS EXTREMELY UNHELPFUL.
THE NEXT MORNING
BACK TO NORMAL
YAAAY!

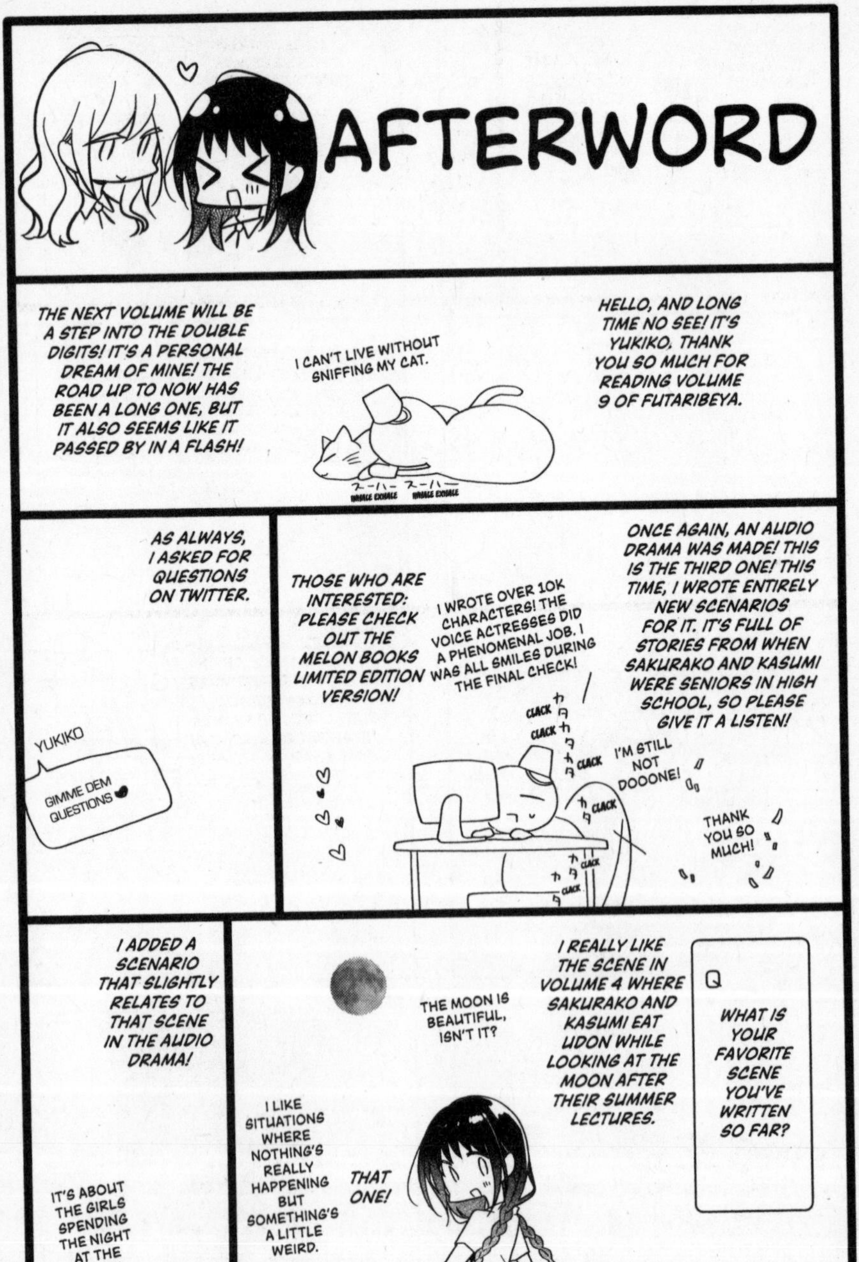
AFTERWORD
HELLO, AND LONG TIME NO SEE! IT'S YUKIKO. THANK YOU SO MUCH FOR READING VOLUME 9 OF FUTARIBEYA.
I CAN'T LIVE WITHOUT SNIFFING MY CAT.
スーハー スーハー
INHALE EXHALE INHALE EXHALE
THE NEXT VOLUME WILL BE A STEP INTO THE DOUBLE DIGITS! IT'S A PERSONAL DREAM OF MINE! THE ROAD UP TO NOW HAS BEEN A LONG ONE, BUT IT ALSO SEEMS LIKE IT PASSED BY IN A FLASH!
ONCE AGAIN, AN AUDIO DRAMA WAS MADE! THIS IS THE THIRD ONE! THIS TIME, I WROTE ENTIRELY NEW SCENARIOS FOR IT. IT'S FULL OF STORIES FROM WHEN SAKURAKO AND KASUMI WERE SENIORS IN HIGH SCHOOL, SO PLEASE GIVE IT A LISTEN!
I WROTE OVER 10K CHARACTERS! THE VOICE ACTRESSES DID A PHENOMENAL JOB. I WAS ALL SMILES DURING THE FINAL CHECK!
THOSE WHO ARE INTERESTED: PLEASE CHECK OUT THE MELON BOOKS LIMITED EDITION VERSION!
カタ CLACK カタ CLACK カタ CLACK
I'M STILL NOT DOOONE!
カタ CLACK
THANK YOU SO MUCH!
カタ CLACK カタ CLACK
AS ALWAYS, I ASKED FOR QUESTIONS ON TWITTER.
YUKIKO
GIMME DEM QUESTIONS
Q
WHAT IS YOUR FAVORITE SCENE YOU'VE WRITTEN SO FAR?
I REALLY LIKE THE SCENE IN VOLUME 4 WHERE SAKURAKO AND KASUMI EAT UDON WHILE LOOKING AT THE MOON AFTER THEIR SUMMER LECTURES.
THE MOON IS BEAUTIFUL, ISN'T IT?
THAT ONE!
I LIKE SITUATIONS WHERE NOTHING'S REALLY HAPPENING BUT SOMETHING'S A LITTLE WEIRD.
I ADDED A SCENARIO THAT SLIGHTLY RELATES TO THAT SCENE IN THE AUDIO DRAMA!
IT'S ABOUT THE GIRLS SPENDING THE NIGHT AT THE SCHOOL.

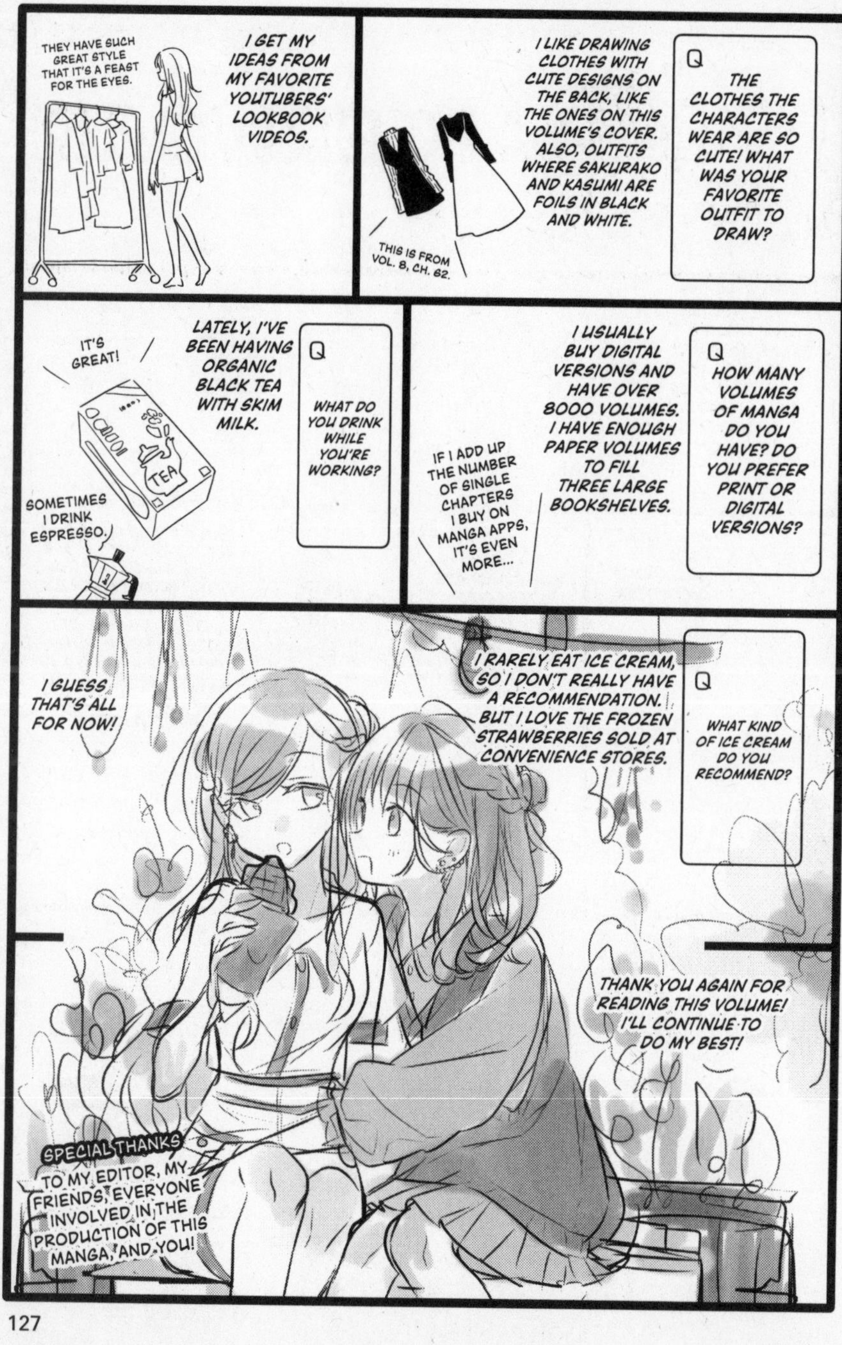
Q
THE CLOTHES THE CHARACTERS WEAR ARE SO CUTE! WHAT WAS YOUR FAVORITE OUTFIT TO DRAW?
I LIKE DRAWING CLOTHES WITH CUTE DESIGNS ON THE BACK, LIKE THE ONES ON THIS VOLUME'S COVER. ALSO, OUTFITS WHERE SAKURAKO AND KASUMI ARE FOILS IN BLACK AND WHITE.
THIS IS FROM VOL. 8, CH. 62.
I GET MY IDEAS FROM MY FAVORITE YOUTUBERS' LOOKBOOK VIDEOS.
THEY HAVE SUCH GREAT STYLE THAT IT'S A FEAST FOR THE EYES.
Q
HOW MANY VOLUMES OF MANGA DO YOU HAVE? DO YOU PREFER PRINT OR DIGITAL VERSIONS?
I USUALLY BUY DIGITAL VERSIONS AND HAVE OVER 8000 VOLUMES. I HAVE ENOUGH PAPER VOLUMES TO FILL THREE LARGE BOOKSHELVES.
IF I ADD UP THE NUMBER OF SINGLE CHAPTERS I BUY ON MANGA APPS, IT'S EVEN MORE...
Q
WHAT DO YOU DRINK WHILE YOU'RE WORKING?
LATELY, I'VE BEEN HAVING ORGANIC BLACK TEA WITH SKIM MILK.
IT'S GREAT!
TEA
SOMETIMES I DRINK ESPRESSO.
Q
WHAT KIND OF ICE CREAM DO YOU RECOMMEND?
I RARELY EAT ICE CREAM, SO I DON'T REALLY HAVE A RECOMMENDATION. BUT I LOVE THE FROZEN STRAWBERRIES SOLD AT CONVENIENCE STORES.
I GUESS THAT'S ALL FOR NOW!
THANK YOU AGAIN FOR READING THIS VOLUME! I'LL CONTINUE TO DO MY BEST!
SPECIAL THANKS
TO MY EDITOR, MY FRIENDS, EVERYONE INVOLVED IN THE PRODUCTION OF THIS MANGA, AND YOU!

LOVE x LOVE

TOKYOPOP believes all types of romances deserve to be celebrated. *LOVE x LOVE* was born from that idea and our commitment to representing a variety of stories and voices as diverse as our fans.

TOKYOPOP

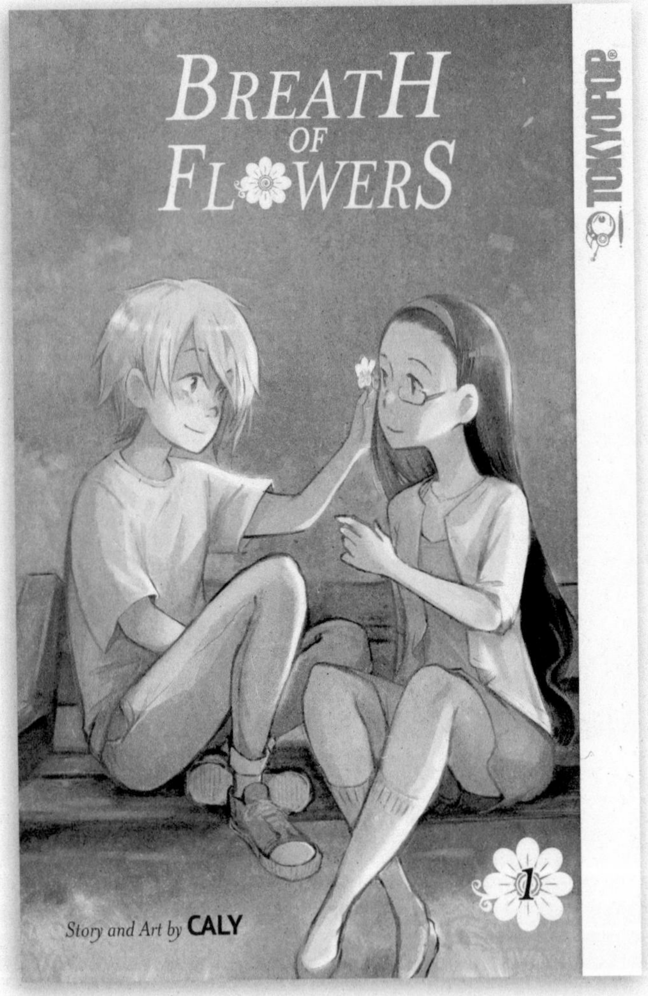
BREATH OF FLOWERS
TOKYOPOP
1
Story and Art by CALY

BREATH OF FLOWERS, VOLUME 1

Caly

♀LOVE-x-LOVE♀

Azami has always been attracted only to boys, especially the handsome Gwyn. Intelligent, sporty, attractive and just a little older than Azami, she's sure he would be an ideal boyfriend. Then, on the day Azami finally gets the courage to confess her feelings, everything she believes is suddenly called into question when she finds out that Gwyn is actually a girl! Despite her initial shock at learning Gwyn's secret, Azami quickly realizes that love transcends gender, putting her feelings for Gwyn before her previous prejudices. But it turns out Azami isn't the only girl who's got her eye on Gwyn!

TOKYOPOP

BREATH
OF
FL✿WERS

TOKYOPOP

Story and Art by **CALY**

2

♀LOVE-x-LOVE♀

TOKYOPOP

Azami always thought she was only attracted to boys, but after the unexpected revelation that her long-time crush Gwyn is actually a girl, she quickly learns that love doesn't have to be limited by gender. Now, the two of them are a happy couple, and lovestruck Azami couldn't be more excited to do all the cute relationship things she's read about in romantic manga! Unfortunately, their new relationship comes with new challenges as well. With Gwyn spending the summer at basketball camp and then transferring to a new school, Azami has to learn how to cope with her anxieties and jealousy in a healthy way. Meanwhile, Gwyn's dreams of playing basketball at her new school suffer an unexpected setback: someone on the team doesn't want her there, and is willing to expose her personal secrets to keep it that way.

ANA C. SÁNCHEZ

AlterEgo

TOKYOPOP

Ana C. Sánchez

ALTER EGO

?LOVE-x-LOVE?

Noel has always been in love with her best friend Elena, but she's never been able to find the courage to confess her feelings. Then, when her friend starts dating a boy, Noel's world collapses as she sees her chance at love slipping away.One night, in a moment of desperation, Noel ends up confessing her feelings for Elena to a complete stranger — but as fate would have it, this stranger turns out to be a girl named June, Elena's other best friend... and Noel's rival in love! Worst of all, now June knows Noel's secret. With everything suddenly going wrong, how can Noel ever win the girl of her dreams?

TOKYOPOP

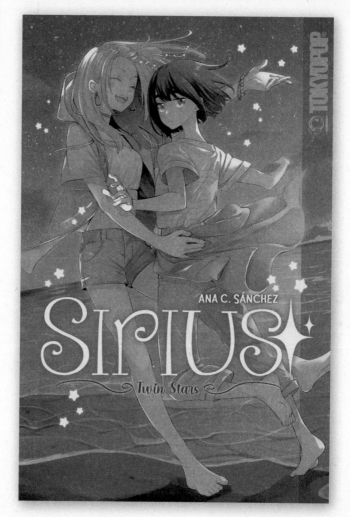

SIRIUS
Ana C. Sánchez

ANA C. SÁNCHEZ

Sirius
~ Twin Stars ~

TOKYOPOP

♀LOVE-x-LOVE♀

Dani's bright future as an elite tennis player comes to a sudden stop when, during a match, she has a heart attack. Her newly discovered condition affects not only her health, but also her relationship with her mother, and her career.   Wanting to get away from everything, she leaves the big city ⬚— and all her problems ⬚— behind, and goes with her cousin to a little coastal village. There she meets Blanca, a girl full of life and in love with astronomy. Bianca reminds Dani that life can be beautiful, and that she can shine again, like stars do.

YURI ESPOIR, VOLUME 1

Mai Naoi

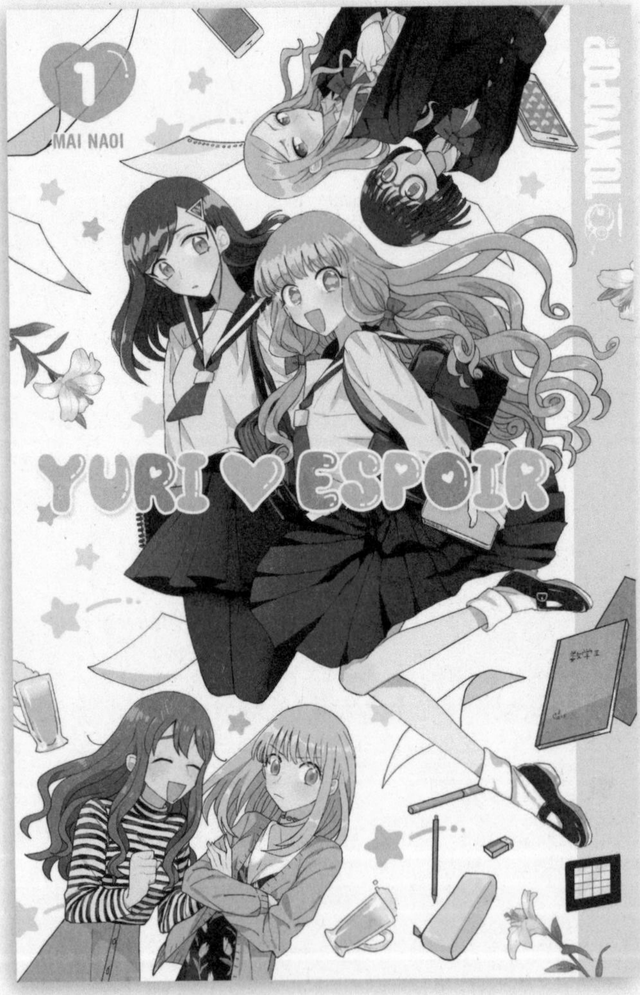
1
MAI NAOI
YURI ♥ ESPOIR
TOKYOPOP

♀LOVE-x-LOVE♀

After finding out she's to be forced into a marriage of convenience as soon as she graduates high school, Kokoro sees her life ending before her eyes at her father's wishes. And so, in her final year of high school, she decides to indulge in her love of other women — and create an incredible sketchbook of lesbian romance to leave behind as her legacy. As she observes the young women of her town, she learns more about their desires, their struggles, and the unpredictable whims of love.

TOKYOPOP

YURI ESPOIR, VOLUME 2

Mai Naoi

♀LOVE-×-LOVE♀

After finding out she is to be forced into an marriage of convenience as soon as she graduates high school, Kokoro sees her life ending before her eyes at her father's wishes. And so in her final year of high school, she decides to indulge in her love of other women, and create an incredible sketchbook of lesbian romance to leave behind as her legacy. As she observes the young women of her town, she learns more about their desires, their struggles, and the unpredictable whims of love.

STILL SICK, VOLUME 1

Akashi

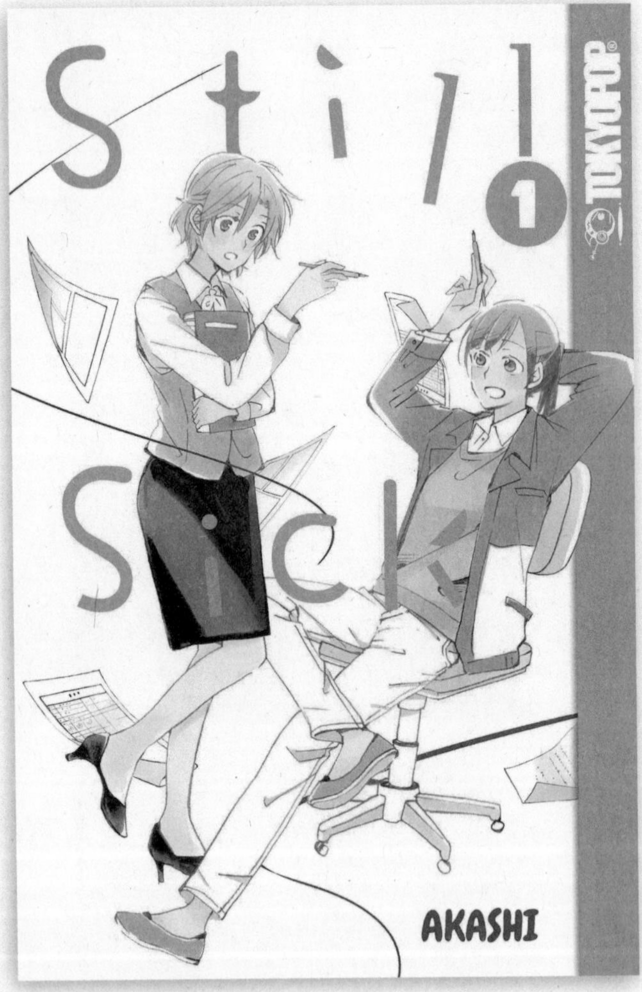

Still
Sick
1
TOKYOPOP
AKASHI

♀LOVE-x-LOVE♀

Makoto Shimizu is just an ordinary office worker, blending in seamlessly with her colleagues on the job... That is, until her coworker Akane Maekawa discovers her well-hidden secret: in her spare time, she draws and sells girls' love comics!Akane is the last person Makoto would think of as a nerd, but as the two grow closer, it starts to seem like Akane may have a secret of her own...

TOKYOPOP

STILL SICK, VOLUME 2

Akashi

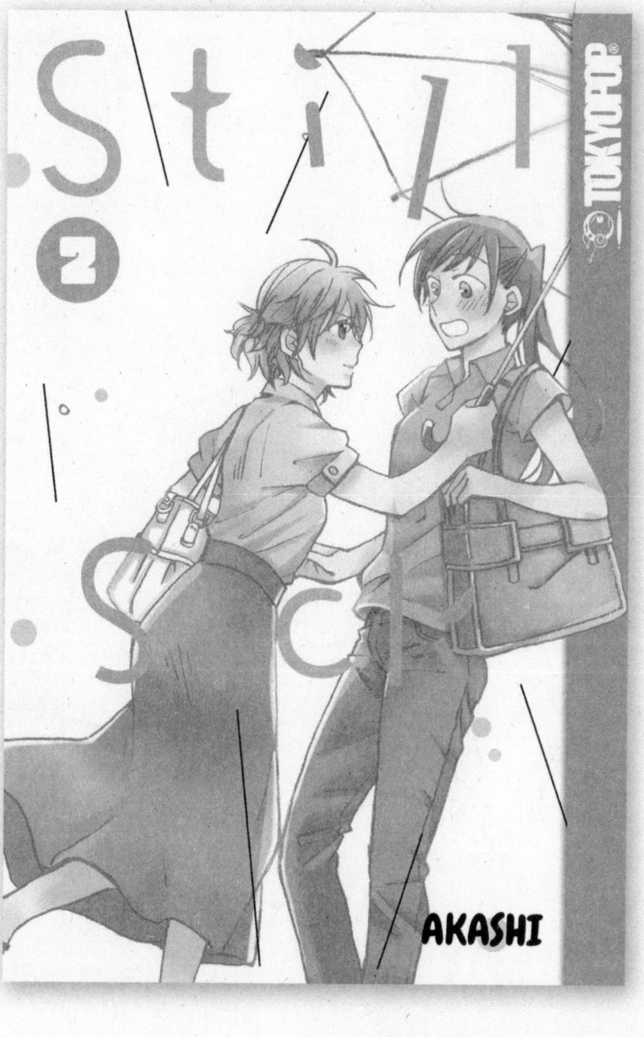

Still Sick
2
TOKYOPOP
AKASHI

♀LOVE-x-LOVE♀

TOKYOPOP

After finding out that her coworker Akane used to be a manga creator, Makoto encourages her new friend to recapture that dream. As an amateur comic artist herself, Makoto looks up to Akane and tries to help her overcome the difficulties that made her give up that profession in the past. Although Akane is often her own worst critic, Makoto inspires her to try reshaping her attitude toward her art.But matters become more complicated when Makoto realizes that, somewhere along the way, what started out as a professional friendship over a common interest has developed into... a serious crush!

Sakuya Amano

KONOHANA KITAN, VOL 1

FANTASY

Yuzu is a brand new employee at Konohanatei, the hot-springs inn that sits on the crossroads between worlds.
A simple, clumsy but charmingly earnest girl, Yuzu must now figure out her new life working alongside all the other fox-spirits who run the inn under one cardinal rule - at Konohanatei, every guest is a god!

KONOHANA KITAN, VOL 2
Sakuya Amano

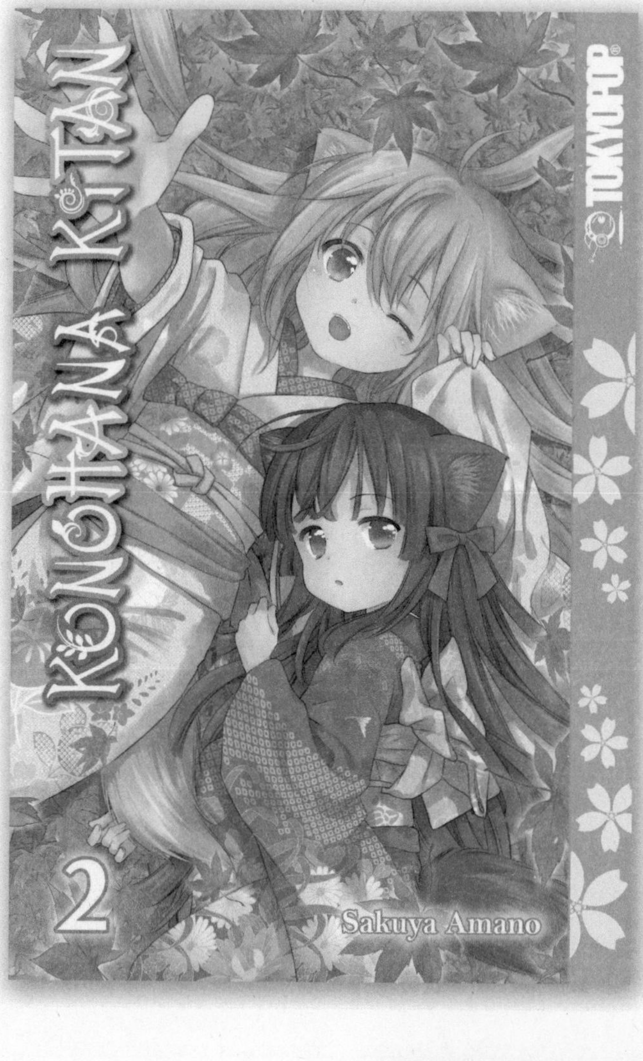
KONOHANA KITAN
2
Sakuya Amano
TOKYOPOP

FANTASY

At Konohanatei, every guest is considered a god — but when an actual deity, the Great Spirit of Bubbles, comes to the inn for a bath, Yuzu and her fox friends get (many) more of her than they bargained for!

Other guests stopping by the inn this time include a beautiful girl who weaves with the rain, a cursed Japanese doll, and... a mermaid?! Even Hiiragi, Satsuki's gorgeous older sister, drops in for a visit despite their rocky relationship. Perhaps the peaceful, otherworldly Konohanatei is just the right place to mend strained sibling bonds.

DEAR READERS,

Thank you for reading!

Have a question, suggestion, title recommendation, or just want to show some love? Visit us on social media, check out our website, or sign up to our newsletter for the latest release info and first dibs on exclusive sales and merchandise.

We appreciate your support, and can't wait to hear from you!

~ TOKYOPOP

@TOKYOPOP

We'd love to hear from you on our social media!

Scan code to visit
tokyopop.com/upcoming

THANK YOU

Futaribeya, Volume 9
Yukiko

Editor	-	Lena Atanassova
Translator	-	Katie Kimura
Copy Editor	-	Massiel Gutierrez
Quality Check	-	Daichi Nemoto
Graphic Designer	-	Sol DeLeo
Editorial Associate	-	Janae Young
Marketing Associate	-	Kae Winters
Digital Marketing Assistant	-	Kitt Burgess
Retouching and Lettering	-	Vibrraant Publishing Studio
Licensing Specialist	-	Arika Yanaka
Editor-in-Chief & Publisher	-	Stu Levy

A  Manga

TOKYOPOP and ⊙ are trademarks or registered trademarks of TOKYOPOP Inc.

TOKYOPOP Inc.
4136 Del Rey Ave., Suite 502
Marina del Rey, CA 90292-5604

E-mail: info@TOKYOPOP.com
Come visit us online at www.TOKYOPOP.com

f www.facebook.com/TOKYOPOP
🐦 www.twitter.com/TOKYOPOP
📷 www.instagram.com/TOKYOPOP

ISBN: 978-1-4278-6923-4
First TOKYOPOP Printing: August 2022
Printed in CANADA

STOP

THIS IS THE BACK OF THE BOOK!

How do you read manga-style? It's simple!
Let's practice — just start in the top right
panel and follow the numbers below!

READ
RIGHT
TO
LEFT